DUALITY OF THE MIND

A Bottom-Up Approach
Toward Cognition

DUALITY OF THE MIND

A Bottom-Up Approach
Toward Cognition

Ron Sun

University of Missouri
Columbia, Missouri

LEA
2002

LAWRENCE ERLBAUM ASSOCIATES, PUBLISHERS
Mahwah, New Jersey
London

Copyright © 2002 by Lawrence Erlbaum Associates, Inc.

Lawrence Erlbaum Associates, Inc., Publishers
10 Industrial Avenue
Mahwah, NJ 07430

Cover design by Kathryn Houghtaling Lacey

Library of Congress Cataloging-in-Publication Data

Sun, Ron, 1960–
Duality of the mind : a bottom-up approach toward cognition / Ron Sun.
      p.   cm.
   Includes bibliographical references and index.
ISBN 0-8058-3880-5 (hardcover : alk. paper)
1. Cognition. 2. Cognitive science. I. Title.
BF311 .S815   2001
153—dc21   2001025854
                                                                     CIP

Books published by Lawrence Erlbaum Associates are printed on acid-free paper, and their bindings are chosen for strength and durability.

Printed in the United States of America
10 9 8 7 6 5 4 3 2 1

Contents

Preface

This book is a condensation of a large body of work concerning human learning, carried out over a period of more than five years, by me and my collaborators.

Let me sketch out here what this work is all about and, more importantly, why I decided write a book about it. In a nutshell, this work is concerned with a broad framework for studying human cognition (beyond technical details of skill learning, which was the focal domain throughout this work), based on a new approach that is characterized by its focus on the dichotomy of, and the interaction between, explicit cognition and implicit cognition, and a computational model that implements this framework. I decided to write this book because I believe this work can be of some significant interest to a broad range of readers. For example, it can be of interest to lay readers who have interest in issues such as general principles of cognition, foundations of consciousness, or more specifically, the role of skill learning in cognitive processes, and so on. It can also be of interest to researchers and students of cognitive science, in that some general principles and frameworks, as well as their instantiations in computational models developed thereof, may have significant bearings on the understanding of cognition beyond specific skill learning domains that we focused on, and to those of artificial intelligence, in that many models developed here (and the fundamental principles embodied in them) may be of use beyond modeling cognitive processes in specific (skill learning) domains and they may be of significant use in understanding and developing intelligent systems in general.

In this work, a broad, generic computational model, that is, a cognitive architecture, was developed, that instantiates our framework and enables the testing of our theoretical approach in a variety of ways. As detailed in the book, there are different implementations, variations, and refinements of this model, the explanations of which constitute a major thread in this work.

With this model, we were able to produce results that compared model outputs with data of human cognition. We also carried out some formal—mathematical and computational—analyses to better understand the model and its numerous implementational details. Such comparisons and analyses serve to support the basic framework and the model developed herein.

Finally, it may be worthwhile to point out some theoretical underpinnings and implications of this approach. In this work, I partially embrace the perspective of situated cognition; that is, I emphasize the direct interaction between the agent and the world in the development of intelligence and cognition. But, on the other hand, I also emphasize the existence and the importance of explicit symbolic (internal) representations (although such representations have been downplayed by some advocates of situated cognition). However, I do stress the *primacy* of direct, unmediated interaction between agents and the world. Symbolic representations and concepts are mostly *derived* from such direct interaction, not prior to them.

In this book, I also discuss symbol grounding, intentionality, social cognition, consciousness, and other theoretical issues, in relation to our framework. The general framework and the model developed thereof generate interesting insights into these theoretical issues as well.

It certainly has been a rewarding experience for me to write this book. I will be even more satisfied if the reader also gains something from it. For more information about all the work related to this book, the reader is referred to the following Web page:

`http://www.cecs.missouri.edu/~rsun`

Acknowledgments

I wish to acknowledge the following individuals for their help with this work. Ed Merrill and I were co-authors of a number of previous papers related to this work. He and his students were responsible for the human experiments cited here. The experiments were carried out by Walter Carr, Toma Ozari, and Sandra Willis. Todd Peterson, Chad Sessions, Paul Slusarz, Chris Terry, Dehu Qi, and Xi Zhang carried out implementations of many different versions of computational models. They were co-authors with me on various papers.

Jeff Shrager, Jack Gelfand, Dave Waltz, and Jennifer Bonilla commented on my work during the early days of this project, thus helping to shape the project.

I have also benefitted from interactions with Robert Mathews, George Graham, William Bechtel, Max Hocutt, Mark Bickhard, Lee Giles, Axel Cleeremans, Jim Hendler, Michael Dyer, Carl Looney, David Roskos-Ewoldsen, Beverly Roskos-Ewoldsen, Charles Ling, Kevin Reilly, Frank Amthor, Nik Kasabov, Antony Satyadas, Bernard Baars, and Vasant Honavar.

Diana Gordon, Alan Schultz, and Jim Ballas provided the navigation simulator used in various experiments related to this work. We also had some useful discussions related to navigation tasks.

Bill Clancey provided critical reviews of the earlier drafts of this work. His insight was much appreciated.

I owe especially a great deal of intellectual debts to a number of afore-mentioned collaborators. Over the past five years, Ed Merrill and I have had some long discussions over a wide range of topics, especially on designing human experiments. Todd Peterson carried out computational implementation of many learning models, some of which are discussed in this book. His implementation and testing led to further refinements of these models. Several other graduate students contributed in this way also.

This work was supported in large part by Office of Naval Research grant N00014-95-1-0440 in 1995 and by a supplemental grant in 1997. Support was also provided by NEC Research Institute, University of Missouri-Columbia, and University of Alabama. Army Research Institute is currently providing support for continuing research.

I wish to thank Helen Gigley and Susan Chipman of ONR for the grant in support of this research.

I wish to thank David Waltz, president of NEC Research Institute, for providing financial support, and advice, during my sabbatical leave of the 1998-1999 academic year, so that I could complete this work as well as carry out other research.

I also wish to express my gratitude to Raymond Flumerfelt, Dean of Engineering (1995-1998) of University of Alabama, who provided lowered teaching load so that this work could be successfully carried out.

Ron Sun

Chapter 1

The Essentials of Human Activities

But it could be that we ...... will forever be unable to understand, that is, to think and speak about, the things which we are able to do.
— Hannah Arendt: *"The Human Condition"*

In order to understand cognition, there are some fundamental questions that need to be asked:

- What are the activities most essential to human existence and thus to human cognition?
- How does cognition emerge in such activities?
- What are the essential features and aspects of cognition within this context?
- How do we capture, in computational terms, these essential features and aspects?

It is the view of many that cognition needs to be studied on the basis of essential existential context—everyday activities of human beings in their everyday world, because cognition has been evolved to deal with exactly such activities in everyday life, and conversely, everyday activities have been structured, culturally and historically, to enable, involve, and facilitate cognition. Thus, it is not too farfetched to suggest that cognition cannot be understood without a proper focus on its *natural context*—the essential existential context in the everyday world.

Let us make an attempt to identify the essential characteristics of cognition in such activities.

1.1 Characteristics of Human Activities

A careful examination of existing literatures, not only in psychology and cognitive science, but also in philosophy, sociology, anthropology, and computer science, led to the identification of some major characteristics of cognition in human everyday activities. First of all, there are a few *behavioral* characteristics commonly exhibited in human everyday activities:

- Reactivity. In most human activities, behavioral responses are generated without involving elaborate computation, such as the elaborate computation of comparing all possible alternatives at length. Reactivity of human behavior also entails relatively fixed responses, so that an individual does not have to recompute responses every time a response is needed. Such reactivity is also direct and immediate; that is, it is "non-representational" (without involving complex mediating conceptual representations). See, for example, Agre and Chapman (1987), Agre (1988), and Clark (1997) for detailed characterization of this aspect of human behavior.

- Sequentiality. Human activities are mostly sequential: They are carried out one step at a time, stretched out temporally. Temporal dependencies and structures are essential to such activities and are the basis for behavioral responses (see Willingham et al. 1989, Stanley et al. 1989, Sun 2000). Heidegger (1927a) provided a philosophical treatment of the temporal nature of human activities.

- Routineness. Human activities are very much routinized and thus largely made of routines, or habitual sequences of behavioral responses. We may view different routines as different sets of skills for coping with the everyday world that humans find themselves in. If we believe in (1) sequentiality and (2) relatively fixed (or habitualized) reactivity, then we have to believe in also the routineness of human activities. However, we also need to take notice of gradual adaptation, or learning, of these routines—Generally, they are formed gradually and subject to constant changes and modifications. Therefore, overall, we may view human activities as consisting of forming, changing, and following routines. See, for example, Heidegger (1927a), Agre and Chapman (1987), and Yu (1991) for various discussions of routines.

- Trial-and-error adaptation. The learning of reactive routines is mostly, and essentially, a trial-and-error adaptation process. Various manifestations of such adaptation have been studied under the rubric of law of effect (Thorndike 1911), classical and instrumental conditioning (Rescorla and Wagner 1972, Sutton and Barto 1981, Shanks 1993), and probability learning (Wasserman et al. 1993, Reber and Millward 1971). We have reason to believe that this type of learning is the most essential to human activities. I will further justify and elaborate on this point in later chapters in relation to the idea of "bottom-up" learning (Sun 1997, 1999, 2000).

Now, let us turn to the *cognitive* characteristics of human everyday activities. That is, we want to look into the characteristics of the inner working of human cognitive processes, along the line of contemporary cognitive science, under some most basic and most common assumptions of cognitive science, such as physical nature of cognition (Fodor 1975, Churchland 1986, Von Eckardt 1992), universality of cognitive architecture (Newell 1990, Anderson 1993), and modularity of the mind (Fodor 1983).

Here is a list of some essential cognitive characteristics that I consider to be the most important, which I will further justify in chapter 2:

- Dichotomy of the implicit and the explicit. Generally speaking, implicit processes are inaccessible, "holistic", and imprecise, while explicit processes are accessible and precise (Sun 1994, 1997, 2000, Dreyfus and Dreyfus 1987, Smolensky 1988, Reber 1989). This dichotomy is closely related to some other well-known dichotomies: the dichotomy of symbolic versus subsymbolic processing (Rumelhart et al. 1986), the dichotomy of conceptual versus subconceptual processing (Smolensky 1988), and the dichotomy of the conscious versus the unconscious (Jacoby et al. 1994, Sun 1999). It can also be justified psychologically, by the voluminous empirical studies of implicit and explicit learning, implicit and explicit memory, implicit and explicit perception, and so on. Denoting more or less the same thing, these dichotomies are justifications for the general distinction between the implicit and explicit cognition.

- Bottom-up learning. The interaction between the two sides of the dichotomy with regard to learning includes top-down (explicit learning first and implicit later), bottom-up (implicit learning first and explicit later), and parallel learning (simultaneous implicit and explicit learning). However, there are reasons to believe that the most important and the most essential to human everyday activities is bottom-up learning. There are various indications of this; among them are (1) philosophical arguments, such as Heidegger (1927a), Dewey (1958), and Merleau-Ponty (1963), in which the primacy of direct interaction with the world (in an implicit way) is emphasized; (2) psychological evidence of the acquisition and the delayed explication of implicit knowledge (e.g., Karmiloff-Smith 1986, Stanley et al. 1989, Bowers et al. 1990, Mandler 1992, Siegler and Stern 1998). More discussions of this point will follow in subsequent chapters.

- Synergistic interaction. There have been recently some emerging indications of synergy between implicit and explicit cognition. I hypothesized (see Sun 1997, 1999) that the reason for having the two separate components, the implicit and the explicit, or any other similar combination of components, was that these different systems could (potentially) work together synergistically, supplementing and complementing each other in a variety of different ways. This is because these two components have qualitatively different characteristics, thus generating better overall results when they are combined (Breiman 1996). See, for example, Dreyfus and Dreyfus (1987), Mathews et al. (1989), Sun (1997, 1999), and Sun et al. (2001) for more discussions, demonstrations and arguments related to synergy.

- Modularity. Some cognitive faculties are separate and specialized, either because they are functionally encapsulated (i.e., their knowledge and processes do not transfer into other domains) or because they are physically (neurophysiologically) encapsulated. It is relatively easy to justify modularity teleologically, which is one of the ways for containing the growth of complexity. Modular structures can be formed evolutionarily so as to simplify learning ontogenetically (or to bypass learning altogether in some cases). Modular structures can be used to guarantee efficiency for important or critical behaviors and routines (whether they are a priori or learned). See, for example, Fodor (1983), Timberlake and Lucas (1993), Cosmides and Tooby (1994), and Pinker (1994) for various notions and justifications of modularity.

1.2   Past Work on Human Activities

Before proceeding to develop a comprehensive new theory, at this point, I would like to take a (very brief) tour of past work on human everyday activities that may have bearing on a general theory of cognition. This examination can identify gaps to be filled and issues to be explored, and thus motivate a new theory.

In *philosophy of everyday activities*, there is one important set of ideas concerning *existential context* in cognition, which emanates from the work of phenomenological philosophers such as Martin Heidegger and Maurice Merleau-Ponty. What is particularly relevant is the notion of *being-in-the-world* (Heidegger 1927a), which entails that existence in the world is fundamental to human cognition. *Being-in-the-world* also entails that humans constantly interact with the world, in an essentially direct, immediate, non-deliberative, and non-reflective way. Such "mindless" everyday interaction, activities, or coping with the world, on top of biological pre-endowment, is the basis of human cognition. Explicit and deliberative thinking occurs in more limited circumstances, and is secondary (or derived).

According to Heidegger, everyday reactive coping with the world, as well as explicit deliberative thinking (when such thinking occurs), presupposes a background of common everyday practices (Dreyfus 1992). The "background of practices" is not represented, in an explicit and elaborate fashion, but implied in primordial *comportment* toward the world. In other words, the most fundamental part of the human mind is implicitly *embodied*, not explicitly represented, and thus it is not directly and explicitly accessible to reflection. However, this is not to deny the existence of explicit representations and explicit processes in the mind (which has been studied extensively previously in cognitive science and artificial intelligence). High-level explicit thinking (involving explicitly accessible representations) does occur, but it is not as basic and as prevalent as many in cognitive science have believed. Moreover, explicit processes occur only on the basis of direct, primordial comportment toward the world.

Maurice Merleau-Ponty (1963) extended Heidegger's thoughts in further investigating behavioral structures involving both the cognitive agent and its world. Combining views from Gestalt psychology and behavioral psychology, he emphasized the role of the structural whole:

Situations and reactions are linked on the basis of their shared participation in structures that are comprised of agents and the world. It is not just external situations and internal reactions, but the structural connection that links the two that matters. Temporal and spatial patterns are formed in behavior to link various external situations to reactions and vice versa. Such patterns, or structures, form the basis of cognitive agents and determine their essential characteristics. This notion of structures further substantiated the Heideggerian notion of primordial "comportment" toward the world.

L. S. Vygotsky (1962, 1986) followed a similar line in characterizing human cognition, but with a different slant. He viewed the development of thinking as gradual assimilation of, and adaptation to, external activities, signs, symbols, and speech, the process of which was termed *internalization* (of external environments). Consequently, thinking was believed to be largely determined by these activities. A related notion of Vygotsky's (see especially Vygotsky 1986) is *mediation*: Every culture develops signs, tools, and other cultural artifacts, which have overwhelmingly important impact upon an individual's thinking. They mediate one's perception and action, in the sense of enabling one to single out a particular aspect of a situation, to group and unite various experiences in a particular way, and to plan action with a specific outlook in mind, and so on. A system of signs (and other cultural artifacts) enables an individual to see and act on things in some specific ways, but at the same time prevents the individual from seeing and acting on things in some other ways. Because signs, tools, and other artifacts can only be created and employed in a cultural context, mediation is socially and culturally determined in a way (Vygotsky and Luria 1993, Rieber and Carton 1987). All of these factors are part of the existential context of an agent as mentioned earlier (Heidegger 1927a).

Let us turn to empirical work. In *psychology of skill learning*, there have been some approaches, methods, and theories that are highly relevant to the study of human activities, emphasizing the behavioral and cognitive characteristics that we identified earlier. For example, Berry and Broadbent (1984), Lewicki et al. (1987), and Logan (1988) belong to this category. Such empirical studies call for more general theoretical treatments and more principled mechanistic (computational) accounts, so as to demonstrate how *processes* of situated cognition and learning are possible, in a generalized way.

Among such work, *cognitive skill acquisition*, such as studied by Anderson (1983, 1993), Rosenbloom et al. (1993), Epstein (1994), and Siegler and Stern (1998), is relevant, even though its focus was not on everyday activities. These studies are relevant because they captured, each in its own ways, some elements of everyday activities. For example, Anderson's models and empirical studies captured well the kind of learning activities when individuals were given a priori instructions of how to perform a task. Epstein (1994) studied in detail how learning occurred (in playing complex games) when people had sufficient knowledge about the task to begin with. Such learning supplements what we perceive to be the more essential mode of learning—autonomous (reactive and trial-and-error) learning processes. However, what is needed in these studies is an account of how domain knowledge comes about in the first place and how individuals *learn* domain knowledge. We would also like to understand the interaction between autonomous learning and instructed learning.

The work on *implicit learning*, such as reviewed by Reber (1989) and Seger (1994), is particularly relevant. They captured the kind of learning that started without, or with little, a priori knowledge and operated in a (mostly) autonomous and on-going way. Typically, learning in these studies were trial-and-error processes that were implicit and inaccessible. Such learning typically does not require much, or any, a priori knowledge, in contrast to the afore-reviewed work on cognitive skill acquisition. However, a shortcoming of this line of work is that there have been few studies that combine implicit and explicit learning, which nevertheless seems necessary for human everyday activities and an essential characteristic of human cognition (Sun 1997, 1999).

In addition, in other areas of cognitive science, Lakoff and Johnson (1980), Karmiloff-Smith (1992), Norman (1993a, 1993b), Pinker (1994), and Bruner (1995) touched upon at least some of the essential characteristics of human activities. For example, Lakoff and Johnson (1980) described how basic sensory-motor activities of the body were utilized in perceiving and in conceptualizing high-level cognitive and social activities. Pinker (1994) described how the human language faculty evolved in the course of coping with the world as an encapsulated "instinct". Karmiloff-Smith (1992) described how, during development, low-level implicit representations were first formed and used by children and then explicit representations were created that made knowledge more explicit. With respect to these theories and conjectures, we would like to see detailed computational models that can shed light on how such processes are possible mechanistically (computationally), thus justifying and substantiating these theories.

To address computational processes underlying the afore-identified theoretical constructs (especially Heidegger 1927a) and empirical results (especially Reber 1989), which are needed to clarify existing data and frameworks, we have undertaken substantial work on computational cognitive model development, which has been reported in various previously published articles such as Sun (1994, 1995, 1997, 1999), Sun et al. (1998, 2001), Sun and Peterson (1998a, 1998b, 1999), Sun and Sessions (1999a, 1999b), and Sun and Qi (2000). The goal of the present book is to present a comprehensive theory on the basis of these results as building blocks.

Below, let us look into some basic methodological issues in developing computational accounts of cognition.

1.3   Pitfalls of Representation

A fundamental theme in classic cognitivism is *representation*: That is, an agent has an internal copy, an explicit model, of the world; internal states in an agent encode the external states in the world (Fodor and Pylyshyn 1988). Cognition therefore consists of developing, maintaining, and modifying these internal states (i.e., representations). This representational stance has, unfortunately, been pervasive and deeply entrenched in cognitive science (Bickhard 1993).

Two popular representational media in cognitive science have been symbolic representations and connectionist representations. For either of these two types of representations, the same problem, the problem of "intentionality", persists: How do they come to represent what they purport to represent? In virtue of what do representations have their meanings or signification? We know by now that arbitrarily constructed representations cannot suffice by themselves to account for human cognition, precisely because they are arbitrarily interpretable. No argument more clearly demonstrates the limitations of arbitrarily constructed representations than Searle's Chinese Room argument (Searle

1980). It shows, unambiguously, that arbitrary denotation *cannot* be the basis of cognition. The question is: How is it possible to move away from this traditional, untenable notion of meaning as the relationship between arbitrary representations to a notion of "intrinsic" meaning? That is, how do we relate representations to whatever is out there, in the world, in an intrinsic way?

The approaches that focus exclusively on representation have also met other serious criticisms over the year, for example, by Dreyfus (1972), Dreyfus and Dreyfus (1987), Winograd and Flores (1987), Bickhard (1993), Sun (1994), and Clark (1997). It has been strongly felt that it may be more important to understand how representations come about and how they function in interacting with the world than to focus only on the properties of a representational medium in isolation.

In a somewhat related vein, there have been, are still lingering, some debates between the two main camps of representationalists, symbolicists and connectionists, regarding what a proper representational medium should be like. Their debates centered around issues such as which paradigm produces a slightly more accurate match with a particular cognitive data set (for example, among data sets in skill learning, psycholinguistics, or neuropsychology), whether connectionist models can have sufficient symbol manipulation capabilities, whether symbolic models can incorporate gradedness, and so on. Such debates are actually much less relevant than one might think, because these questions have really no direct bearing on what intelligence is, or how cognition functions, in the natural context of human activities. We would be better off in the quest for the essence of cognition if we leave alone such questions concerning the ultimate capabilities, or the lack of them, of any particular representational paradigm and try to use whatever technical tools we might have at our disposal. Whether the mind is a connectionist network with symbolic processing capabilities or a symbolic model with graded representations, connectivity, and massive parallelism is ultimately irrelevant.

The emergence of hybrid models in studying cognition (see, e.g., Sun and Bookman 1994, Sun and Alexandre 1997, Wermter and Sun 2000) is, in a way, a refutation of such debates on representational media. Hybrid models point to the fact that any reasonable representational media can and should find their proper use in understanding cognition, and the use of one medium does not exclude the use of others. Moreover, there may be ways of structuring different representations, in a principled way, to best utilize different representations and their possible interactions. For example, the hybrid model work reported in Sun (1995) and in Sun (1997) combined multiple representations and utilized their synergistic interactions.

We need to re-affirm the following point: It is not representations, connectionist or symbolic, that are important but the capturing of essential characteristics of human cognition, in whatever representational media available. Below, I further argue that, in order to capture these essential characteristics, the acquisition of skills, knowledge, and representations should instead be focused on.

1.4   Importance of Learning

As analyzed earlier, everyday activities are made up of habitual routines. Thus the everyday world may be characterized as an interwoven set of habitual domains (Yu 1991): Learned skills, routines, or habits are used in their respective domains, that is, in those situations for which skills, routines, or habits were developed and in other situations that are similar in some ways to those situations. In these domains, habitual routines help individuals to cope in a reactive, nondeliberative way, thus reducing the level of effort needed.[1]

However, as characterized earlier, everyday activities involve continuous processes of forming and changing (as well as following) habitual routines, and they may be thought of as *skill learning* in the everyday world. Skills, routines, and habits are adapted in the context of individual existence, with respect to the goals and needs (explicit or implicit) of cognitive agents.

We need to go back to the genesis of cognition—the acquisition of the capacities to react, think, and take on everyday routines, because this process is a key factor of everyday activities, a key to avoid the

---

[1] My view coincides with situated cognition to some extent (Suchman 1987, Brooks 1991, Clancey 1997). However, the pitfall of some existing situated cognition views is the lack of an account of the role and the function of explicit representations and explicit processes. What I am aiming for is a principled reconciliation of the representationalist view and the situated view, on the basis of the process of "bottom-up" learning (more details later in chapter 2).

representationalist impasse, and a key to a possible reconciliation of the representationalist view and the situated view. If we want to get to the bottom of human cognition, we cannot ignore the study of adaptivity of cognitive processes and capacities, which is believed to be ever-present. The adaptive process should include both (collective) evolution, which is on a longer time scale, and (individual and collective) learning, which is on a shorter time scale.

Some recently emerged paradigms of learning provide hope for better computational modeling of learning and evolution in cognition and thus better understanding of cognition. These new paradigms include reinforcement learning, evolutionary computation, game theoretic learning, and symbolic rule learning. For example, in reinforcement learning, proper (or optimal) responses to situations are learned through observing the consequences of sequences of actions. Typically, gradual adjustments are made on the basis of observations, to form a value function that indicates "values" of different actions in different situations. Action responses can then be selected on the basis of the value function. Reinforcement learning may be suitable for capturing the learning of reactive, habitual routines in the everyday world (i.e., capturing routinization). On the other hand, rule learning generates symbolic rules and other symbolic representations (such as trees) from a set of exemplars, positive or negative, that are provided to a learning agent. Such learning algorithms may be adapted for on-going, "bottom-up" learning of explicit representations (by utilizing information from learned reactive routines, which can provide the requisite "exemplars", thus leading to an extraction, or explication, process, i.e., bottom-up learning). Game theoretic learning may be used to capture collective learning, especially co-learning (learning to coordinate actions among a group of agents) in a social (interactive) setting. Evolutionary computation may be coupled with individual and collective learning, and provide a basis for capturing larger-scale evolution of cognition.

1.5 A Broad Theory

A broad theory of human learning in everyday activities will be developed in detail in this book, along the line outlined above. Here, I would like to draw a quick sketch of the overall framework, before moving on to develop various details of it (which will be carried out in subsequent chapters).

Minimum initial structures (that is, genetic and biological pre-endowment) will be assumed in a cognitive agent (cf. Pinker 1994, Cosmides and Tooby 1994, Shepard 2001).[2] Most of the structures in cognition will have to be developed in an on-going, gradual fashion, during the course of individual ontogenesis. The development of behavioral structures hinges on interactions with the world, which includes both the physical world and the sociocultural world. The interaction prompts the formation of reactive habitual routines (skills) for interacting with the world in a direct and nondeliberative way, which in turn lead to the emergence of high-level explicit representations and explicit thought processes for the sake of further enhancing cognitive capabilities.

In this framework, ontogenesis is determined by (at least) two important factors: (1) innate "biases", or built-in constraints, predispositions, and tendencies, and (2) structures in the external (physical and sociocultural) world (as perceived by the agent interacting with it). Such perceived external structures are dependent on the current behavioral structures in the agent (that have been developed thus far) and therefore on the (onto-genetic and phylogenetic) history of the interaction between agents and the world. The generation of high-level, explicit, and symbolic representations is, to a significant extent, determined by low-level (implicit, reactive, and habitual) processes. Culture has the role of structuring the interaction of an individual agent with the world (through mediating tools, signs, and other cultural artifacts), and thus it affects both high-level and low-level processes.[3]

On this view, high-level explicit symbolic representations are rooted in low-level processes. This is because of the way in which most high-level representations are produced. They are, in the main, extracted out of low-level processes.

Connectionist models (and associated learning algorithms) will be utilized as the unifying medium in computational implementation. Distributed connectionist networks will be used to represent implicit knowledge. Localist connectionist networks will be used to represent

---

[2] Some of these initial structures have to do with "pre-wired" reflexes, or predisposition for developing such reflexes. Some others have to do with learning capabilities.

[3] In contrast to Vygotsky, however, in this book, I will not emphasize exclusively externally provided signs and symbols, but also equally emphasize internally generated signs and symbols.

explicit symbolic knowledge. Reinforcement learning (in distributed connectionist networks) will be used for capturing the learning of implicit knowledge. Symbolic hypothesis testing learning will be used as the main means for capturing the learning of explicit knowledge.

It should be clear that this approach rests upon two foundations: (1) observations of the characteristics of human cognition in the everyday context, such as the roles of reactivity, habituality, and skills, and (2) theoretical considerations such as the dichotomy of the implicit and the explicit.

The approach has been tested against a wide range of human learning data. The work described in subsequent chapters demonstrates cognitive validity and power of the approach, by way of capturing a wide range of human learning phenomena. Computational properties of the model has also been explored through experiments that manipulate implicit and explicit processes to optimize performance.

1.6 My Plan

The plan for the remainder of the book is as follows:

- Chapter 2 motivates and develops an abstract theory, based on which a detailed computational model is later specified.
- Chapter 3 develops the details of the computational implementation of the theoretical model.
- Chapter 4 describes the qualitative match between the model and known human data.
- Chapter 5 describes the quantitative match between the model and human data.
- Chapter 6 explores, in-depth, the issues of situated cognition and symbol grounding, in the context of the model.
- Chapter 7 explores various issues related to consciousness, in relation to the model.
- Chapter 8 extends the discussion to issues related to sociocultural factors in cognition.
- Chapter 9 presents a detailed, and occasionally very technical, comparison of the model with various existing theories, approaches, architectures, and computational models.

- Chapter 10 then concludes the book by emphasizing four major theses of the book.

A methodological note is in order. It is believed by some that philosophical ideas are beyond empirical testing and thus meaningless, and they should not even be mentioned in scientific work. Contrary to such a view, I try to examine empirical work in the light of philosophical theories and conjectures, and thus unify, to some extent, computational, psychological, and philosophical accounts. Philosophical conjectures have always been a great motivating force behind scientific progress. It is up to the scientific community to validate or invalidate plausible philosophical conjectures. And as science progresses, seemingly elusive ideas may become testable. In this regard, an open-minded approach is preferable.

1.7 Summary

In this chapter, we motivated the development of a cognitive theory from the point of view of capturing cognition in its natural context of everyday activities. We first characterized the essential features of human everyday activities, and those of cognition in that context. We then moved on to consider existing approaches to studying cognition and the methodological issues in this endeavor (such as the focuses on representation or learning), which led to the sketch of a broad theory. The remainder of this book will be devoted to explicate and develop this theory.

Chapter 2

A Theoretical Model

> *Concept without intuition is empty. Intuition without concept is blind.*
> — E. Kant: *"A Critique of Pure Reason"*

Against this complex background of ideas sketched earlier, in this chapter, I undertake a more careful development of a theoretical model that embodies these previously identified ideas, through examining a variety of evidence from psychological and philosophical literatures. The plan is as follows: I first explore a few important desiderata of model development in section 2. Then, in section 3, based on these desiderata, a theoretical model is proposed and discussed. The details of implementation of this model are tackled later in chapter 3.

2.1 Desiderata

One of the necessary considerations in developing cognitive models, in the context of human everyday activities, is a due emphasis on low-level, reactive, skilled (habitualized) activities, as argued in chapter 1. The acquisition and use of skills constitute a major portion of human activities. Naturally, the study of skill learning is a major focus in cognitive science.[1] However, skills vary in complexity and degree of

[1] The most widely studied in cognitive science is cognitive skill acquisition (see, e.g., VanLehn 1995), which refers to learning to solve problems in intellectually oriented tasks such as arithmetic, puzzle solving, elementary geometry, and LISP programming (Anderson 1983, 1993, Rosenbloom et al. 1993).

cognitive involvement. They range from simple motor patterns to high-level intellectual skills. Besides studying highly intellectual tasks, it is more important to study "lower"-level skills (habitualized reactive routines), which are of fundamental importance to cognition but have not received sufficient attention.

Another important consideration in developing theoretical models is to deal with learning that is, more or less, autonomous and thus does not require a large amount of a priori knowledge (e.g., in the form of instructions or examples). Most existing studies are more concerned with "top-down" learning: They generally assume that individuals learn generic, verbal, declarative knowledge first and then, through practice, turn such knowledge into specific procedural skills. However, when individuals are not provided a sufficient amount of a priori knowledge, learning may proceed differently. In the everyday world, it is more likely that many skills develop prior to the learning of explicit knowledge, with explicit knowledge being constructed only after skills (habitualized routines) are at least partially developed. We need to capture this type of "bottom-up" learning.

To further motivate the development of a model, in the following subsections, I discuss in turn (1) the distinction between implicit and explicit knowledge, (2) the interaction between the two types of knowledge during learning, especially bottom-up learning that proceeds from implicit to explicit knowledge, and (3) the on-line nature of learning.

2.1.1   Implicit versus Explicit Knowledge

The distinction between implicit knowledge and explicit knowledge, which is central to this work, has been made in many theories of learning and cognition, for example, in Anderson (1983, 1985, 1993), Keil (1989), Damasio (1994), and Sun (1994, 1995, 1997). It is believed that both types of knowledge are essential to cognitive agents.

Anderson (1983) proposed the distinction between declarative and procedural knowledge, to account for changes in performance resulting from extensive practice, based on data from a variety of skill learning studies ranging from arithmetic to geometric theorem proving. For Anderson, the initial stage of skill development is characterized by the acquisition of declarative knowledge (explicit knowledge concerning a task). During this stage, the learner must attend to this knowledge in order to successfully perform the task. Through practice, a set of specific procedures develop that allow aspects of the task to be performed without using declarative knowledge. When the skill is proceduralized, it can be performed with almost no access to explicit declarative knowledge and often even without concurrent conscious awareness of specific details involved. Similar distinctions have been made by other researchers based on different sets of data, in the areas of skill learning, concept formation, and verbal informal reasoning (e.g., Fitts and Posner 1967, Keil 1989, Sun 1994).

Several other distinctions made by other researchers capture a similar difference between different types of processing. For example, Smolensky (1988) proposed a distinction between conceptual (publicly accessible) and subconceptual (inaccessible) processing. According to this framework, explicit knowledge is based on conceptual processing (and thus accessibly) and implicit knowledge is based on subconceptual processing (and thus inaccessible). Dreyfus and Dreyfus (1987) proposed the distinction of analytical and intuitive thinking, and believed that the transition from the former to the latter was essential to the development of complex cognitive skills (on the basis of phenomenological analyses of chess playing at different stages of learning chess). This transition is very similar to the declarative-to-procedural transition as advocated by Anderson (1983, 1993), although they are not exactly identical. In addition, the distinction between conscious and unconscious processing (cf. Reber 1989, Lewicki et al. 1992) fits this framework, in that explicit knowledge is potentially accessible to consciousness whereas implicit knowledge is not. Taken together, the distinction between explicit knowledge and implicit knowledge is well supported in many ways.

The distinction of implicit and explicit knowledge has been empirically demonstrated in the implicit learning literature. Let us briefly review three common tasks of implicit learning. The *serial reaction time* tasks (Nissen and Bullemer 1987 and Willingham, Nissen, and Bullemer 1989) tap subjects' ability to learn a repeating sequence. On each trial, one of the four lights on a display screen was illuminated. Subjects were to press the button corresponding to the illuminated light. In one condition, the lights were illuminated in a repeating 10-trial sequence. It was found that there was a rapid and significant reduction in response time to repeating sequences relative to random sequences. The reduction in response time was attributed to the learning of the sequence. However, subjects might not be able to explicitly report the repeating sequence, and were sometimes unaware that a repeating sequence was involved. Amnesic patients with Korsakoff's syndrome were also tested, and similar learning occurred. In another condition, much more complex sequences were also tested (see, e.g., Lewicki et al. 1987), and similar learning occurred, albeit over a much longer period of time.

On the other hand, the *process control* tasks (Berry and Broadbent 1988) examine subjects' ability to learn a static relation between the input and output variables of a controllable system, through interacting with the system dynamically. Subjects were required to control an output variable by manipulating an input variable. In one instance of the task, subjects were to manage a (simulated) sugar production factory and the goal was to reach and maintain a particular production level, by means of manipulating the size of the workforce. In another instance of the task, subjects were to interact with a computer simulated "person" whose behavior ranged from "very rude" to "loving" and the task was to maintain the behavior at "very friendly", by controlling his/her own behavior (which could also range from "very rude" to "loving"). In both instances, the input and output variables in the to-be-controlled systems could follow the same mathematical relation. Although they often did not recognize the underlying relations explicitly, subjects reached a high level of performance in these tasks.

Similarly, in the *artificial grammar learning* tasks (Reber 1989), subjects were presented strings of letters that were generated in accordance with a finite state grammar. After memorization, subjects showed an ability to distinguish new strings that conformed to the artificial grammar used to generate the initial strings from those that did not. Although subjects might not be explicitly aware of the underlying grammars (barring some fragmentary knowledge), when they were asked to judge the grammaticality ("well-formedness") of novel strings, they performed significantly beyond the chance level. In all, these tasks share the characteristic of involving a great deal of implicit processes.[2] There are many other tasks that are similar in this regard, such as various concept

---

[2] Some have disputed the existence of implicit processes, based on the imperfection and incompleteness of tests for explicit knowledge (e.g., Shanks and St.John 1994). The reader is referred to Sun et al. (2001) for arguments concerning the overwhelming amount of evidence in support of the distinction between implicit and explicit processes.

learning, automatization, and instrumental conditioning tasks.

2.1.2   Interaction of Implicit and Explicit Knowledge

Although implicit learning and implicit knowledge have been actively investigated,[3] the complex and multifaceted interaction between the implicit and the explicit and the importance of this interaction have not been universally recognized. To a large extent, such interaction has been downplayed or ignored, with only a few notable exceptions (e.g., Mathews et al. 1989; Sun 1997). In the implicit learning literature, for example, research has been focused on showing the *lack* of explicit learning in various learning settings (see especially Lewicki et al. 1987) and on controversies stemming from such claims. Similar oversight is also evident in computational simulation models of implicit learning. For example, Cleeremans and McClelland (1991) simulated implicit learning of sequences based on stochastic grammars, using a recurrent neural network, in which there was no provision for the role of explicit processes. Likewise, Dienes (1992) simulated implicit learning of artificial grammars, using a variety of connectionist models, without ever considering explicit processes that might be involved in it.

Despite the lack of study of interaction, it has been gaining recognition recently that it is difficult, if not impossible, to find a situation in which only one type of learning is engaged (Reber 1989, Seger 1994). A review of existing data has indicated that, while one can manipulate conditions to emphasize one or the other type, in most situations, both types of learning are involved, with a varying amount of contribution from each (see, e.g., Sun et al. 2001, Stanley et al. 1989, Willingham et al. 1989).

Likewise, in the development of cognitive architectures, the distinction between procedural and declarative knowledge has been around for a long time (see especially Anderson 1983, 1993). However, focus has been almost exclusively on "top-down" models, the bottom-up direction has been largely ignored, paralleling and reflecting the related neglect of the complex interaction of explicit and implicit processes in the implicit learning

---

[3] The role of implicit learning in human cognition (especially in skill learning) and the distinction between implicit and explicit learning have been recognized in recent years. See,, for example, Reber (1989), Stanley et al. (1989), Willingham et al. (1989), Proctor and Dutta (1995), Anderson (1993), and Sun (1999).

literature. Nevertheless, there have been a few studies that demonstrated the parallel development of the two types of knowledge or the extraction of explicit knowledge from implicit knowledge (e.g., Owen and Sweller 1985, Willingham et al. 1989, Stanley et al. 1989, Rabinowitz and Goldberg 1995, and Sun et al. 2002), contrary to usual top-down approaches in developing cognitive architectures.

Empirical research has shown that human learning depends on the interaction of two types of processes. Mathews et al. (1989) proposed that "subjects draw on two different knowledge sources to guide their behavior in complex cognitive tasks"; "one source is based on their explicit conceptual representation"; "the second, independent source of information is derived from memory-based processing, which automatically abstracts patterns of family resemblance through individual experiences". Likewise, Sun (1994) pointed out that "cognitive processes are carried out in two distinct levels with qualitatively different mechanisms", although "the two sets of knowledge may overlap substantially". Reber (1989) pointed out that nearly all complex skills in the real world (as opposed to small, controlled laboratory settings) involved a mixture of explicit and implicit processes interacting in some way, and the relationship between the two might be complex.

Various demonstrations of interaction exist using artificial grammar learning, process control, and other tasks. For instance, Stanley et al. (1989) and Berry (1983) found that under some circumstances concurrent verbalization (which generated explicit knowledge) could help to improve subjects' performance in a process control task. Reber and Allen (1978) similarly showed in artificial grammar learning that verbalization could help performance (i.e., the synergy effect; Sun et al. 2001). In the same vein, although no verbalization was used, Willingham et al. (1989) showed that those subjects who demonstrated more explicit awareness of the regularities in the stimuli (i.e., those who had more explicit knowledge) performed better in a serial reaction time task, which likewise pointed to the helpful effect of explicit knowledge. Ahlum-Heath and DiVesta (1986) also found that verbalization led to better performance in learning Tower of Hanoi.

However, as Reber (1976, 1989) pointed out, verbalization and the resulting explicit knowledge might also hamper (implicit) learning, under some circumstances, especially when too much verbalization induced an overly explicit learning mode in subjects performing a task that was not suitable for learning in an explicit way, for example, when learning a rather complex artificial grammar. Similarly, in a minefield navigation task, Sun et al. (2001) reported that too much verbalization induced overly explicit learning that was detrimental to performance.

As variously demonstrated by Berry and Broadbent (1984, 1988), Stanley et al. (1989), and Reber et al. (1980), verbal instructions (given prior to learning) can facilitate or hamper task performance too. One type of instruction was to encourage explicit search for regularities that might aid in task performance. Reber et al. (1980) found that, depending on the ways stimuli were presented, explicit search might help or hamper performance. Owen and Sweller (1985) and Schooler et al. (1993) found that explicit search hindered learning. Another type of instruction was explicit how-to instruction that told subjects specifically how a task should be performed, including providing detailed information concerning regularities in stimuli. Stanley et al. (1989) found that such instructions helped to improve performance significantly, although the findings in Berry and Broadbent (1988) were more ambivalent. However, Dulaney et al. (1984) showed that correct and potentially useful explicit knowledge, when given at an inappropriate time, could hamper learning.

There is evidence that implicit and explicit knowledge may develop independently under some circumstances. Willingham et al. (1989), for example, reported data in a serial reaction time task that were consistent with the parallel development of implicit and explicit knowledge. By using two different measures (with varying criterion levels) for assessing two types of knowledge respectively, they compared the time course of implicit and explicit learning. It was shown that implicit knowledge might be acquired in the absence of explicit knowledge and vice versa. The data ruled out the possibility that one type of knowledge was *always* preceded by the other type. Rabinowitz and Goldberg (1995) similarly demonstrated parallel development of procedural and declarative knowledge in an alphabetic arithmetic task.

However, in many skill learning tasks, a subject's performance typically improves earlier than explicit knowledge can be verbalized by subjects (Stanley et al. 1989). For instance, in the experiments of Stanley et al. (1989) using process control tasks, although the performance of the subjects quickly rose to a high level, their verbal knowledge improved far slower. The subjects could not provide usable verbal knowledge (for novice subjects to use) until near the end of their training. It appears that in these tasks, it is much easier to acquire implicit skills than to acquire explicit, veridical knowledge, and hence there is the delay in the development of explicit knowledge. Bowers et al. (1990) also showed delayed learning of explicit knowledge. When subjects were given patterns to complete, they first showed implicit recognition of proper completion (although they did not have explicit recognition). Their implicit recognition improved over time until eventually an explicit recognition was achieved. This phenomenon was also demonstrated by Reber and Lewis (1977) in artificial grammar learning. In all of these cases, as suggested by Stanley et al. (1989) and Seger (1994), due to the fact that explicit knowledge lags behind but improves along with implicit knowledge, explicit knowledge is in a way "extracted" from implicit knowledge. That is, learning of explicit knowledge is through the (delayed) *explicitation* of implicit knowledge (i.e., through bottom-up learning).

2.1.3 Bottom-Up Learning

Let me further justify the idea of bottom-up learning.

As mentioned earlier, most of the work that makes the distinction between two types of knowledge assumes a top-down approach; "proceduralization" leads to skilled performance. In Anderson (1983), proceduralization is accomplished by converting explicit declarative knowledge into implicit production rules, which are subsequently refined through practice. In Anderson (1993), this is accomplished by maintaining explicit memory of instances, which are utilized in performance through analogical processes, and by creating production rules from these instances after repeated use. In Rosenbloom et al. (1993), the equivalent of proceduralization is accomplished through "chunking" (i.e., combining production rules). In Jones and VanLehn (1994), procedural skills are developed through modifying conditions of rules based on statistical information generated during practice. These models have been applied to a range of domains, for example, in the learning of theorem proving, text editing, LISP programming, arithmetic, and many other tasks. However, these models were not developed to account for learning in the absence of, or independent from, preexisting explicit domain knowledge.

Several lines of research demonstrate that agents may learn skills (or habitual routines) without first obtaining a large amount of explicit knowledge. In research on implicit learning, Berry and Broadbent (1988), Willingham et al. (1989), and Reber (1989) expressly demonstrated a *dissociation* between explicit knowledge and skilled performance, in a variety of tasks including process control tasks, artificial grammar learning tasks, and serial reaction time tasks. Berry and Broadbent (1984) argued that the human data in process control tasks were not consistent with exclusively top-down learning models, because subjects could learn to perform a task without being provided a priori explicit knowledge and without being able to verbalize the rules they used to perform the task. This indicates that skills are not necessarily accompanied by explicit knowledge, which would not be the case if top-down learning is the only way to acquire skills. Nissen and Bullemer (1987) and Willingham et al. (1989) similarly demonstrated that implicit knowledge was not *always* preceded by explicit knowledge in human learning, and that implicit and explicit learning were not necessarily correlated. As reviewed earlier, there are even indications that explicit knowledge may arise from implicit skills in many circumstances (Stanley et al. 1989). Using a process control task, Stanley et al. (1989) found that the development of explicit knowledge paralleled but lagged behind the development of implicit knowledge.   Reber and Lewis (1977) made a similar observation. Even in high-level cognitive skill acquisition (VanLehn 1995), Schraagen (1993) reported that learning in the domain of designing psychological experiments often involved generalizing specific knowledge to form generic schemas/rules (which was, in a sense, bottom-up) in addition to specializing general knowledge to form specific knowledge. Rabinowitz and Goldberg (1995) showed that there could be parallel learning separately.

Similar claims concerning the development of implicit knowledge prior to the development of explicit knowledge have been made in areas outside the skill learning literature and provide additional support for the bottom-up approach.   The implicit memory research (e.g., Schacter 1987) demonstrates a dissociation between explicit and implicit knowledge/memory in that an individual's performance can improve by virtue of implicit "retrieval" from memory and the individual can be unaware of the process. This is not amenable to the exclusively top-down approach. Instrumental conditioning also reflects a learning process that is not entirely consistent with the top-down approach, because the process can be non-verbal and non-explicit (without conscious awareness; see, e.g., William 1977) and lead to forming action sequences without a priori explicit knowledge. Such conditioning is applicable to both simple organisms as well as humans (Thorndike 1927, Wasserman et al. 1993, Gluck and Bower 1988). In developmental psychology, Karmiloff-Smith (1986) proposed the idea of "representational redescription". During development, low-level implicit representations are transformed into more abstract and explicit representations and thereby made more accessible. This process is not top-down either, but in the exactly opposite direction.[4]

In summary, there are data and theories available that indicate that learning can proceed from implicit to explicit knowledge (as well as the reverse). Thus, bottom-up learning can be justified on both empirical and theoretical grounds.

2.1.4   Benefits of Interaction

Acquiring explicit knowledge, in addition to acquiring implicit knowledge, has some practical advantages, which make it indispensable to a learning agent, despite the fact that implicit skills may be more efficient or easier to learn. These advantages are:

- It helps to guide the exploration of new situations, and reduces the time spent on developing skills in new situations. In other words, it helps the transfer of knowledge (e.g., as shown by Willingham et al. 1989).

- Explicit knowledge can help to speed up learning. If properly used, explicit knowledge that is extracted on-line during skill learning can help to facilitate the learning process itself (Willingham et al. 1989, Stanley et al. 1989, Sun et al. 2001).

- Explicit knowledge can also help in communicating learned knowledge and skills to other agents (Sun and Peterson 1998a).

[4] This idea can be traced back to Piaget's idea of *restructuring*, and has also been proposed in various forms by other developmental psychologists (e.g. Vygotsky 1986, Keil 1989, and Mandler 1992).

We may attribute such benefits to the *synergy* of these two types of knowledge.

2.1.5 On-Line Learning

As empirically demonstrated by, for example, Dominowski (1972), Medin et al. (1987), Nosofsky et al. (1994) and many others in psychological experiments, human learning is often gradual, on-going, and concurrent with task performance. Although their data and theories are mostly concerned with concept learning, the point applies equally well to other types of learning, especially skill learning, as we hypothesized earlier. This view has been implemented in existing top-down learning models such as ACT (Anderson 1983, 1993) and SOAR (Rosenbloom et al. 1993). New attempts at cognitive modeling must also be able to capture this feature.

To allow an agent to learn *continuously* from on-going experience in the world, we note that both implicit and explicit knowledge should be allowed to be acquired in such a gradual, on-going and concurrent way. Hence, on-going experience in the world gives rise to both types of knowledge on a gradual and continuous basis.

2.2 A Sketch of a Model

Given the voluminous evidence establishing the complex interaction between implicit and explicit processes, the questions now are: How can we better understand such an interaction? What are the *mechanisms* of the two types of processes and their interaction? I thus develop a model that accounts for the two types of processes and, more importantly, their interaction, constrained by the afore-detailed desiderata. In the subsequent subsections, I present an outline of the model: CLARION, which stands for *Connectionist Learning with Adaptive Rule Induction ON-line*. (Implementational details of the model are described in the next chapter.)

2.2.1 Representation

Let us first consider representations that can be used in a possible model incorporating the distinction between implicit and explicit processes. We notice that the inaccessible nature of implicit knowledge is best captured by subsymbolic distributed representations such as those provided by a backpropagation network (Rumelhart et al. 1986). This is because representational units in a distributed representation are capable of accomplishing tasks together but are subsymbolic and generally not individually meaningful (see Rumelhart et al. 1986, Sun 1994); that is, they generally do not have an associated semantic label. This characteristic of distributed representations accords well with the inaccessibility of implicit knowledge. (However, it is generally not the case that distributed representations are not accessible at all but they are definitely less accessible, not as direct and immediate as localist representations. Distributed representations may be accessed through indirect, transformational processes.) In contrast, explicit knowledge may be best captured in computational modeling by a symbolic or localist representations (Clark and Karmiloff-Smith 1993), in which each unit is easily interpretable and has a clear conceptual meaning, that is, a semantic label. This characteristic captures the property of explicit knowledge being accessible and manipulable (Smolensky 1988, Sun 1994). This radical difference in the representations of the two types of knowledge leads to a two-level (or two-tier) model CLARION, whereby each level using one kind of representation captures one corresponding type of process (either implicit or explicit).[5]

At each level of the model, there may be multiple modules (both *action-centered* modules and *non-action-centered* modules). At the bottom level, action-centered knowledge is known to be highly modular; thus, a number of backpropagation networks co-exist, each constitutes a module and is adapted to a specific modality, task, or input stimulus type. This is consistent with the well known modularity claim (Fodor 1983; Karmiloff-Smith 1986; Cosmides and Tooby 1994), and is also similar to Shallice's (1972) idea of a multitude of "action systems" competing with each other.[6] At the top level, the corresponding action-centered knowledge may reside in different modules, in correspondence with the bottom-level structure, but it may also reside in more centralized, coarser modules.

---

[5] Sun (1994, 1995, 1999), Dreyfus and Dreyfus (1987), and Smolensky (1988) presented theoretical arguments for such two-level models, which I will not get into here.

[6] Timberlake and Lucas (1993) specified a set of modules and their inter-relations and transitions for foraging related activities. Cosmides and Tooby (1994) listed a different set of modules for behaviors ranging from enforcing social contracts (catching cheaters) to understanding syntax of language (parsing sentences).

On the other hand, the non-action-centered modules (at both levels) represent more static, declarative, and generic types of knowledge. The knowledge there includes what is commonly referred to as "semantic" memory (i.e., general knowledge about the world in a conceptual, symbolic form; see Quillian 1968, Tulving 1972). We will not get into details of these modules in this work.

The reason for having both action-centered and non-action-centered modules (at each level) is that, as it should be obvious, action-centered knowledge (roughly, procedural knowledge) is not necessarily inaccessible directly, and non-action-centered knowledge (roughly, declarative knowledge) is not necessarily accessible directly. Although it was argued by some, for example, Anderson (1983), that all procedural knowledge is inaccessible directly and all declarative knowledge is directly accessible, such a clean mapping of the two dichotomies is untenable in my view.

Given explicit knowledge in symbolic or localist representations (e.g., in the form of rules) at the top level, a variety of explicit operations can be performed there. Such explicit operations may include forward chaining reasoning, backward chaining reasoning, and counterfactual reasoning (using given explicit representations of rules). These operations can be implemented on top of symbolic encoding or localist networks, for example, through controlling activation propagation (Sun 1997).

2.2.2   Learning

At the bottom level of the model, the learning of implicit action-centered knowledge can be done in a variety of ways consistent with the nature of distributed representations. In the learning settings where correct input/output mappings are available, straight backpropagation, a supervised learning algorithm, can be used for each network (Rumelhart et al. 1986). Supervised learning procedures require the a priori determination of a uniquely correct output for each input. In the learning settings where there is no such input/output mapping externally provided, reinforcement learning can be used instead, especially Q-learning (Watkins 1989) implemented using backpropagation networks. These learning methods are cognitively justified: For instance, Shanks (1993) showed that human instrumental conditioning was best captured by "associative" models (i.e., neural networks implementing backpropagation style learning algorithms), compared with a variety of rule-based models. Cleeremans (1997) argued that implicit learning could not be captured by symbolic models but neural networks.

At the top level, the action-centered explicit knowledge can also be learned in a variety of ways in accordance with localist (or symbolic) representations used. Because of the representational characteristics, one-shot learning based on hypothesis testing (e.g., Bruner et al. 1956, Busemeyer and Myung 1992, Nosofsky et al. 1994, Sun 1997) is needed. With such learning, agents explore the world, dynamically acquire representations along the way, and modify them as needed, reflecting the dynamic (on-going) nature of skill learning (Heidegger 1927a, Vygotsky 1962, Sun et al. 2001). The implicit knowledge already acquired in the bottom level can be utilized in learning explicit knowledge, through *bottom-up* learning. The basic process of bottom-up learning may be described as follows: If an action chosen (by the bottom level) is successful (i.e., it satisfies a certain success criterion), then a rule is extracted. Then, in subsequent interaction with the world, the rule is refined by considering its outcomes: if the outcomes are successful, the condition of the rule may be generalized to make it more universal; if the outcomes are not successful, then the condition of the rule should be made more specific and exclusive of the current case. This is an on-line version of hypothesis testing processes studied (in different contexts) by, for example, Bruner et al. (1956) and Nosofsky et al. (1994). Other types of learning are also possible, such as hypothesis testing without the help of the bottom level (for capturing *independent* explicit learning, as discussed in section 2; see also Sun et al. 2002).

In sum, the bottom level develops implicit skills using (mainly) the *Q-learning-Backpropagation* algorithm while the top level extracts explicit rules using (mainly) the *Rule-Extraction-Revision* algorithm. The learning difference of the two levels is somewhat analogous to that between the cortico-striatal "habit" system and the cortico-limbic "memory" system as proposed by Mishkin et al. (1984). The combination of multiple learning algorithms in this model is also similar to some extent to many machine learning models that utilize heterogeneous learning algorithms and techniques (such as Maclin and Shavlik 1994, Gelfand et al. 1989, Sun and Bookman 1994, Sun and Peterson 1998a), and ensemble approaches involving combining decision trees, backpropagation networks and other algorithms). However, in the present work, the motivation for such a combination is cognitive, rather than computational or mathematical, as is the case with most hybrid learning models.

2.2.3   Separation and Combination of the Two Levels

For making the final decision on which action to take, outcomes from both levels need to be incorporated. Specifically, we combine the corresponding values for an action from the two levels by a combination function (e.g., a weighted sum). In this way, with different parameters (different weights), we allow for different operational modes: for example, relying only on the bottom level, relying only on the top level, or combining the outcomes from both levels weighing them differently. These operational modes roughly correspond to the folk psychological notions of the reactive mode, the deliberative mode, and mixtures of the two (Dreyfus and Dreyfus 1987).

The relative contributions of the two levels in decision making may be manipulated to some degree. Performance can be affected when an agent is involved in more (or less) explicit processing. For instance, when an agent is forced to be more explicit, its top-level mechanisms may be more engaged and thus the performance may be enhanced to some extent, or unaffected, depending on circumstances. (The effect may be similar to that of a deeper level of processing; see, e.g., Craik and Lockhart 1972, Ahlum-Heath and DiVesta 1986, Squire and Frambach 1990.) When an agent is forced to be completely explicit, its top-level mechanisms may be fully engaged, but the bottom-level mechanisms may be hampered as a result (as has been observed by, e.g., Reber 1989) and thus the performance may be worsened (Reber 1989, Schooler et al. 1993, Berry and Broadbent 1984). On the other hand, when an agent is distracted by a secondary explicit task, its top-level mechanisms may be less active in relation to the primary task (i.e., the agent becomes more implicit), because such a manipulation is known to affect explicit processes more than implicit processes (Stadler 1995, Nissen and Bullemer 1987, Szymanski and MacLeod 1996). The CLARION model, through the use of the combination function, allows for such manipulations.

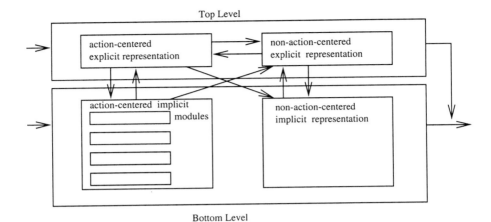

Figure 2.1. The CLARION architecture

2.2.4   Basic Theoretical Hypotheses

Summarizing the discussions thus far, we employed the following basic theoretical hypotheses in the model (see Figure 2.1):

- The separation and the co-existence of the two levels: One is explicit and the other is implicit.

- The representational difference of the two levels: The two levels involve two different types of representations and, as a result, have different degrees of accessibility.

- The learning difference of the two levels: Different learning methods are used at the two levels.

- The distinction of top-down learning versus bottom-up learning, with the former being learning implicit knowledge first and explicit knowledge from it later on (as in Anderson 1993) and the latter being learning implicit knowledge without the involvement of explicit knowledge and extracting explicit knowledge later on from implicit one (as in Sun 1997, 1999). When there is no sufficient a priori explicit knowledge available, learning is usually bottom-up.

- The separability of the two levels: The relative contributions of the two levels (in learning or performance) can be experimentally manipulated and thus studied (by using the dual task or the verbalization manipulation).

- The action-centered versus non-action-centered representations: Separate action-centered modules and non-action-centered modules coexist at the top level; similarly, action-centered modules and non-action-centered modules coexist at the bottom level.

These hypotheses together form our basic model (Sun 1997, 1999).

It should be emphasized that this dichotomous structure of two levels is minimally necessary (in the sense of a minimal innate architecture). The previous arguments show that there are qualitative and fundamental differences between the two types of processes. Given these differences, it is hard to imagine that one level can be derived from the other ontogenetically, without some minimal structure beforehand. Thus, the distinction should be viewed as innate somehow. Note also that most of the animal species are not capable of developing an elaborate and complete conceptual system with symbolic processing capabilities, whereas humans rarely fail to develop such a system. The constancy of this inter-species difference points to the innateness of such a difference and thus the innateness of the two-level structure. It is reasonable to hypothesize that the dichotomous structure is a given for humans, and thus should be incorporated into the model of the human cognitive architecture.

It is worth mentioning here the empirical work that verifies these theoretical hypotheses. In the experimental work that will be described later, a number of well known skill learning tasks were simulated based on CLARION, which spanned the spectrum ranging from simple reactive skills to complex cognitive skills (Sun et al. 2001, Sun et al. 2002). The tasks include serial reaction time tasks, process control tasks, and Tower of Hanoi (see Sun et al. 2002). In addition, extensive work on a minefield navigation task was carried out, in which both human experiments and simulation using CLARION were performed (see Sun et al. 2001, Sun and Peterson 1998a).

2.3   Summary

The CLARION model sketched out in this chapter highlights the interaction of implicit and explicit processes in human cognition. We aimed at the development of a unified cognitive model, by examining a wide variety of cognitive data and phenomena in this chapter. We captured the essence of these data and phenomena, through the CLARION model that included both implicit and explicit processes, with a particular emphasis upon their interaction.

Ultimately, the contribution of this work lies in a theory that meaningfully explains and predicts a wide range of human data through the use of the two types of processes. In this regard, I will undertake later detailed comparisons between human data and model data. I will describe a set of pertinent experiments that explore different effects of the implicit/explicit interaction and different ways of facilitating bottom-up learning.

The practical implication of this work is also intriguing (although I do not intend to get into this issue in this book). For example, based on the CLARION model, we may propose ways of optimizing individual training through best utilizing the synergy between implicit and explicit processes. We may come up with a set of parameters that can be tuned for adaptive training of human subjects with different ability levels and different inclinations of using implicit versus explicit processes.

Chapter 3

Current Implementations

> *Every possible case of reasoning involves the extraction*
> *of a particular partial aspect of the phenomena ......*
> *whilst Empirical Thought simply associates phenomena*
> *in their entirety, Reasoned Thought couples them by the*
> *conscious use of this extract.*
> — William James: *"Principles of Psychology"*

In this chapter, we look into the algorithmic implementation of the abstract version of the CLARION model as presented in the previous chapter. In particular, we look, in detail, into several major aspects in the implementation of CLARION. The major algorithms for implementing CLARION include learning at the bottom level using reinforcement learning, learning at the top level using rule extraction, plan extraction (as a variation of rule extraction), development of modular structures using spatial partitioning, and development of modular structures using temporal segmentation.

In this discussion, I focus mainly on these aspects individually, because each of them is a useful model in its own right. I discuss their respective *performance* advantages, in addition to justifying them as part of the CLARION implementation. Thus, there are not only cognitive motivations for these mechanisms (which was discussed previously), but also computational motivations for them in terms of dealing with complex learning tasks or explicating embedded learned knowledge. (In terms

33

of dealing with complex learning tasks, we consider tasks with large state spaces with complex value functions, or tasks with non-Markovian optimal action policies. In terms of explicating embedded knowledge, we consider extracting explicit rules and plans from implicit, closed-loop action policies.)

Because of the highly technical nature of this chapter, readers who are not prepared to get into details of reinforcement learning algorithms or do not want to get into them at this point may skip this chapter. They can safely do so without losing the thread of discussion.

3.1   The Overall Operation

CLARION consists of two levels (Sun 1997, Sun and Peterson 1998a, 1998b). Its overall operation of the two levels is as follows:

1. Observe the current state x.
2. Compute in the bottom level the Q values of x associated with each of all the possible actions a_i's: $Q(x, a_1)$, $Q(x, a_2)$, ..., $Q(x, a_n)$.
3. Find out all the possible actions $(b_1, b_2, ..., b_m)$ at the top level, based on the input x and the rules in place.
4. Consider the values of a_i's and b_j's, and choose an appropriate action b
5. Perform the action b, and observe the next state y and (possibly) the reinforcement r.
6. Update the bottom level in accordance with *Q-Learning-Backpropagation*.
7. Update the top level with *Rule-Extraction-Revision*.
8. Go back to Step 1.

The details of the two levels and their learning algorithms are discussed next.

3.2   Reinforcement Learning

In this section, we examine the implementation of the bottom level. In this level, a Q value is an evaluation of the "quality" of an action in a given state: $Q(x, a)$ indicates how desirable action a is in state x, which is described by sensory input. We can choose an action based on Q values. One easy way of choosing an action is to choose the one that maximizes the

Q value in the current state; that is, we choose a if $Q(x,a) = \max_i Q(x,i)$. To ensure adequate exploration, A stochastic decision process, for example, based on the Boltzmann distribution, can be used, so that different actions can be tried in accordance with their respective probabilities to ensure that various possibilities are all looked into.

To acquire the Q values, we use the *Q-learning* algorithm (Watkins 1989). In the algorithm, $Q(x,a)$ estimates the maximum (discounted) cumulative reinforcement that the agent will receive from the current state x on. The updating of $Q(x,a)$ is based on $\Delta(x,a) = \alpha(r + \gamma e(y) - Q(x,a))$, where γ is a discount factor, $e(y) = \max_a Q(y,a)$, and y is the new state resulting from action a. Thus, the updating is based on the *temporal difference* in evaluating the current state and the action chosen. In the above formula, $Q(x,a)$ estimates, before action a is performed, the (discounted) cumulative reinforcement to be received if action a is performed, and $r + \gamma e(y)$ estimates the (discounted) cumulative reinforcement that the agent will receive, after action a is performed; so their difference, the temporal difference in evaluating an action in a given state, enables the learning of Q values that approximate the (discounted) cumulative reinforcement. Through successive updates of the Q function, the agent can learn to take into account future steps in longer and longer sequences.

Reactive routines developed through reinforcement learning can exhibit sequential behavior (sequential decision making) without explicit (symbolic) planning. The agent accomplishes sequential behavior strictly on the basis of action decision making using moment-to-moment environmental input.

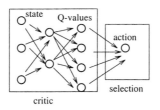

Figure 3.1. The Q-learning method

To implement Q-learning, a four-layered network is used, in which the first three layers form a backpropagation network for computing Q values and the fourth layer (with only one node) performs stochastic decision making. The network is internally subsymbolic. The output of the third layer (i.e., the output layer of the backpropagation network) indicates the Q value of each action (represented by an individual node), and the node in the fourth layer determines probabilistically the action to be performed based on a Boltzmann distribution (Watkins 1989):

$$p(a|x) = \frac{e^{1/\alpha Q(x,a)}}{\sum_i e^{1/\alpha Q(x,a_i)}}$$

where α controls the degree of randomness (temperature) of the decision-making process. (An annealing schedule may be used to determine α.) The training of the backpropagation network is based on minimizing the following:

$$error_i = \begin{cases} r + \gamma e(y) - Q(x,a) & \text{if } a_i = a \\ 0 & \text{otherwise} \end{cases}$$

where i is the index for an output node representing the action a_i. The backpropagation procedure (Rumelhart et al. 1986) is then applied to adjust weights.

The lookup table implementation of Q-learning is generally not feasible, because of likely continuous input spaces and, when discretized, huge state spaces. For example, in our navigation experiments as described in Appendix, there are more than 10^{12} states. Function approximators, such as backpropagation networks above, need to be used. In fact, multiple such networks may be employed (as will be discussed later).

This process of combined backpropagation and Q-learning performs, in an approximate manner, both structural credit assignment (with backpropagation), so that an agent knows which element in a state should be assigned credit/blame, as well as temporal credit assignment (with Q-learning), so that an agent knows which action leads to success or failure (in terms of reinforcement received). The combination of Q-learning and backpropagation enables the development of implicit knowledge based solely on the agent exploring the world on the continuous, on-going basis. It requires no external teacher or a priori domain-specific knowledge.

3.3   Rule Extraction

In the top level, a novel rule learning algorithm, *Rule-Extraction-Revision*, is devised. The basic idea is as follows: We perform rule learning (extraction and subsequent revision) at each step, which is associated with the following information: (x, y, r, a), where x is the state before action a is performed, y is the new state entered after an action a is performed, and r is the reinforcement received after action a. If some action decided by the bottom level is successful then the agent extracts a rule that corresponds to the decision and adds the rule to the rule network. Then, in subsequent interactions with the world, the agent verifies the extracted rule by considering the outcome of applying the rule: If the outcome is not successful, then the rule should be made more specific and exclusive of the current case ("shrinking"); if the outcome is successful, the agent may try to generalize the rule to make it more universal ("expansion"). Rules are generally in the following form: *conditions* $\longrightarrow$ *action*, where the left-hand side is a conjunction of individual elements each of which refers to a primitive: a value range (or a value) in a dimension of the sensory input.

At each step, we update the following statistics for each rule condition and each of its minor variations, that is, the current rule condition plus/minus one value, with regard to the action a performed: PM_a (i.e., Positive Match) and NM_a (i.e., Negative Match). Here, positivity/negativity is determined by the Bellman residual (the Q value updating amount) which indicates whether or not the action is reasonably good compared with similar actions in similar states. Based on these statistics, we calculate the information gain measure:

$$IG(A, B) = log_2 \frac{PM_a(A) + 1}{PM_a(A) + NM_a(A) + 2} - log_2 \frac{PM_a(B) + 1}{PM_a(B) + NM_a(B) + 2}$$

where A and B are two different conditions that lead to the same action a. This is a widely used measure. It is used, for example, in many Inductive Logic Programming systems. It is well justified on the empirical ground; see, for example, Lavrac and Dzeroski (1994) for a review. The measure essentially compares the percentage of positive matches under different conditions A and B (with the Laplace estimator; Lavrac and Dzeroski 1994). If A can improve the percentage to a certain degree over B, then A is considered better than B. In the algorithm, if a rule is better compared with, for example, the match-all rule (i.e, the rule with the condition that matches all inputs), then the rule is considered successful (for the purpose of deciding on expansion or shrinking operations).

We decide on whether or not to extract a rule based on a simple criterion which is determined by the current step (x, y, r, a):

- *Extraction*: if $r + \gamma \max_b Q(y, b) - Q(x, a) > threshold$, where a is the action performed in state x, r is the reinforcement received, and y is the resulting new state (that is, **if the current step is successful**), and if there is no rule that covers this step in the top level, set up a rule $C \longrightarrow a$, where C specifies the values of all the input dimensions exactly as in x.

The criterion for applying the *expansion* and *shrinking* operators, on the other hand, is based on the afore-mentioned statistical test. Expansion amounts to adding an additional value to one input dimension in the condition of a rule, so that the rule will have more opportunities of matching inputs, and shrinking amounts to removing one value from one input dimension in the condition of a rule, so that it will have less opportunities of matching inputs. Here are the detailed descriptions of these operators:

- *Expansion*: if $IG(C, all) > threshold1$ and $\max_{C'} IG(C', C) \geq 0$, where C is the current condition of a matching rule, *all* refers to the match-all condition (with regard to the same action specified by the rule), and C' is a modified condition such that $C' = C$ plus one value (i.e., C' has one more value in one of the input dimensions) (that is, **if the current rule is successful and the expanded condition is potentially better**), then set $C'' = argmax_{C'} IG(C', C)$ as the new (expanded) condition of the rule. Reset all the rule statistics.

- *Shrinking*: if $IG(C, all) < threshold2$ and $\max_{C'} IG(C', C) > 0$, where C is the current condition of a matching rule, *all* refers to the match-all condition (with regard to the same action specified by the rule), and C' is a modified condition such that $C' = C$ minus one value (i.e., C' has one less value in one of the input dimensions) (that is, **if the current rule is unsuccessful, but the shrunk condition is better**), then set $C'' = argmax_{C'} IG(C', C)$ as the new (shrunk) condition of the rule. Reset all the rule statistics. If shrinking the condition makes it impossible for a rule to match any input state, delete the rule.

During expansion, any existing rule covered by an expanded rule will be placed on its children list. The children list of a rule is created to keep aside and make inactive those rules that are more specific and thus covered by the rule. Later on, when the rule is deleted or shrunk, some or all of those rules on its children list may be reactivated if they are no longer covered.

In addition, the density parameter determines the minimum frequency of repetition necessary to keep a rule. For example, if this parameter is set at $1/n$, then at least one encounter of an input that matches a rule is necessary every n trials in order to maintain the rule. Otherwise, the rule will be deleted. The probability parameter determines how likely a rule will be extracted, given that all the necessary conditions are met.

Although we can directly use a symbolic rule representation, to facilitate correspondence with the bottom level and to encourage uniformity and integration, a localist connectionist encoding is used instead. Basically, the nodes representing elements in the condition of a rule are connected to the node representing the conclusion (Sun 1992). That is, the structure of a rule set is directly translated to that of a network. For each rule, a set of links are established, each of which connects an element (at the bottom level) involved in the condition of a rule to a node (at the top level) that represents the rule, which in turn is connected to the conclusion of the rule. If the element in the condition is in a positive form, the bottom-up link carries a positive weight w; otherwise, it carries a negative weight $-w$. The weight of the link connecting the rule node to the conclusion node is set uniformly at 1. Sigmoidal functions are used for node activation:

$$\frac{1}{1 + e^{-(\sum_i i_i w_i - \tau)}}$$

The threshold τ of a rule node is set to be $n * w - \theta$, where n is the number of incoming links (the number of elements in the condition of a rule), and θ is a parameter, selected along with w to make sure that the node has activation above 0.9 when all of its conditions are satisfied, and has activation below 0.1 when some of its conditions are not met. Activations above 0.9 are considered 1, and activations below 0.1 are considered 0. So rules are crisp (i.e., binary). See Figure 3.2. For more complex rule forms including predicate rules and variable binding, see the discussion in Sun (1992).

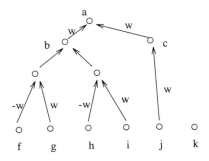

Figure 3.2. A network for representing rules
(1) $b \; c \longrightarrow a$, (2) $\neg f \; g \longrightarrow b$, (3) $\neg h \; i \longrightarrow b$, (4) $j \longrightarrow c$

In addition to cognitive necessity, rule extraction has some performance advantages, which make it useful in practice, as discussed in chapter 2. Extracted rules help to speed up learning. Rules also help to guide the learning of new situations. Rules can also help in communicating learned knowledge. See Appendix for experimental evidence that justifies claims of performance advantages. As analyzed in Sun and Peterson (1998a, 1998b), the performance advantages of the model could be attributed computationally to the following factors: (1) the complementary representations of the two levels: discrete versus continuous; (2) the complementary learning processes: one-shot rule learning versus gradual Q value approximation; as well as (3) the proper rule learning criteria used in CLARION.[1]

3.4   Combining Value Functions and Rules

For making the final decision of which action to take, two methods of combining outcomes from the two levels have been used. In the *percentage method*, in a random p percent of the steps, if there is at least one rule indicating an action for the current state, we use the outcome from the rule level; otherwise, we use the outcome of the bottom level (which is always available). When we use the outcome from the top level, we randomly select an action suggested by the matching rules. When we use the outcome from

---

[1] This type of on-line rule extraction is very different from rule extraction at the end of training a backpropagation network (Towell and Shavlik 1993), which requires a costly search process to find rules and does not benefit backpropagation learning per se.

the bottom level, we use the stochastic decision process described before for selecting an action. In the *stochastic method*, we combine the corresponding values for each action from the two levels by a weighted sum; that is, if the top level indicates that action a has an activation value v_a (which should be 0 or 1 as rules are binary) and the bottom level indicates that a has an activation value q_a (the Q value of a), then the final outcome is $w_1 * v_a + w_2 * q_a$. Stochastic decision making with Boltzmann distribution based on the weighted sums is then performed to select an action out of all the possible actions. Relative weights or percentages of the two levels can be automatically set based on the relative performance of the two levels through probability matching (Anderson 1990).

Putting everything together, implemented in a connectionist fashion, we now have an implementation of the whole CLARION model (Figure 3.3).

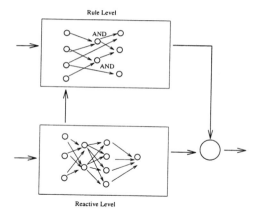

Figure 3.3. The implementation of the CLARION architecture

3.5   Plan Extraction

The above rule extraction method generates isolated rules, focusing on individual states, but not the chaining of these rules in accomplishing a sequential task. In contrast, the following plan extraction method generates a complete explicit plan that can by itself accomplish a sequential task (Sun and Sessions 1998).

By an explicit plan, we mean an action policy consisting of an explicit sequence of action steps, that does not require (or requires little) environmental feedback during execution (compared with a completely closed-loop action policy as represented by a Q value function). When no environmental feedback (sensing) is required, an explicit plan is an open-loop policy by definition. When a small amount of feedback (sensing) is required, it is a semi-open-loop policy. In either case, an explicit plan can lead to "policy compression", that is, it can lead to fewer specifications for fewer states, through explication of the closed-loop policy embedded in Q values. Explicit plans have been repeatedly demonstrated in various cognitive domains, especially in high-level cognitive skill acquisition (VanLehn 1995, Pfleger and Hayes-Roth 1997, Sacerdoti 1974).

Our plan extraction method (Sun and Sessions 1998) essentially turns learned Q values into a plan that is in the form of a sequence of steps. We do so by using beam search, to find the best action sequences (or conditional action sequences) that achieve a goal. Beam search works by iteratively performing the following, one step at a time: choosing the best possible actions for the present step in relation to the present states and figuring out the most likely resulting states (the outcomes of the actions) up to a fixed beam width. The beam search is guided by Q values. This is because the optimal Q value learned through Q-learning represents the total future probability of reaching the goal, provided that a reward 1 is given when and only when the goal is reached (Sun and Sessions 1998). Thus, Q values can be used as a guide in searching for explicit plans.

The following data structures are employed in plan extraction. The *current state set, CSS*, keeps track of the search beam step by step. At each step, it consists of multiple pairs in the form of $(x, p(x))$, in which the first item indicates a state $x \in S$ and the second item $p(x)$ indicates the probability of that state. At each step, for each state in CSS, a corresponding best action is identified. In so doing, the number of branches at each step has to be limited, for the sake of time efficiency of the algorithm as well as the representational efficiency of the resulting plan. The set CSS thus contains up to n pairs, where n is the branching factor in beam search. In order to calculate the best default action at each step, a second set of states CSS' is also included, which covers a certain number (m) of possible states not covered by CSS.

The algorithm is as follows:

Set the current state sets: $CSS = \{(x_0, 1)\}$ and $CSS' = \{\}$, where $x_0 \in S$ is the starting state

Repeat until the termination conditions are satisfied (e.g., *step* $> D$)

- For each action u, compute the probabilities of transitioning to each of all the possible next states (for all $x' \in S$) from each of the current states ($x \in CSS$ or $x \in CSS'$): $p(x', x, u) = p(x) * p_{x,x'}(u)$.[2]

- For each action u, compute its estimated utility with respect to each state in CSS: $Ut(x, u) = \sum_{x'} p(x', x, u) * \max_v Q(x', v)$. That is, we calculate the *probabilities* of reaching the goal after performing action u from the current state x.

- For each action u, compute the estimated utility with respect to *all* the states in CSS': $Ut(CSS', u) = \sum_{x \in CSS'} \sum_{x'} p(x) * p_{x,x'}(u) \max_v Q(x', v)$.

- For each state x in CSS, choose the action u_x with the highest utility $Ut(x, u)$: $u_x = argmax_u Ut(x, u)$.

- Choose the best default action u with regard to all the states in CSS': $u = argmax_{u'} Ut(CSS', u')$.

- Update CSS to contain n states that have the highest n probabilities, i.e., with the highest $p(x')$'s: $p(x') = \sum_{x \in CSS} p(x', x, u_x)$, where u_x is the action chosen for state x.

- Update CSS' to contain m states that have the highest m probabilities calculated as follows, among those states that are not in the new (updated) CSS: $p(x') = \sum_{x \in CSS \cup CSS'} p(x', x, u_x)$, where u_x is the action chosen for state x (either a conditional action in case $x \in CSS$ or a default action in case $x \in CSS'$), and the summation is over the old CSS and the old CSS' (before updating).[3]

In the measure Ut, we take into account the probabilities of reaching the goal in the future from the current states (based on the Q values), as well as the probability of reaching the current states based on the history of the paths traversed (based on $p(x)$'s). This is because what we are aiming at is the estimate of the overall success probability of a path.[4] In the

---

[2] $p_{x,x'}(u)$ denotes the probability of transitioning into state x' when action u is performed in state x.

[3] For both CSS and CSS', if a goal state or a state of probability 0 is selected, we may remove it and, optionally, reduce the beam width of the corresponding set by 1.

[4] $Ut(x, u)$ is the expected probability of reaching the goal (from the starting state), given the CSSs chosen so far and the corresponding actions for all the states in them. $Ut(CSS', u)$ is the expected probability of reaching the goal (from the starting state), given the CSS's chosen so far and their corresponding actions.

algorithm, we select the best actions (for $x \in CSS$ and $x \in CSS'$) that are most likely to succeed based on these measures.

Note that as a result of incorporating nonconditional default actions, nonconditional plans are special cases of conditional plans. If we set $n = 0$ and $m > 0$, we then in effect have a nonconditional plan extraction algorithm and the result from the algorithm is a nonconditional plan. On the other hand, if we set $m = 0$, then we have a purely conditional plan with no default action attached.

An issue is how to determine the branching factor (i.e., the number of conditional actions at each step). We can start with a small number, say 1 or 2, and gradually expand the search by adding to the number of branches, until a certain criterion, a termination condition, is satisfied. We can terminate the search when the estimated total probability of reaching the goal exceeds a certain threshold (i.e., $p(G) > \delta$, where δ is specified a priori) or when a time limit is reached (in which case failure is declared). Here is the algorithm:

Set the initial value for beam width n

Set the initial value for beam width m

Set the initial value for search depth D

Repeat until $p(G) > \delta$ (or the time limit expires)

- perform beam search (i.e., call the plan extraction algorithm), with n, m and D (where D is the termination condition of the plan extraction algorithm).

- calculate $p(G)$ resulting from the search,

$$p(G) = \sum_{x'} p(x')$$

where $x' = G$, each resulting from a different path.

- set $n := f_1(n)$ (e.g., $f_1(n) = n + 1$)

- set $m := f_2(m)$ (e.g., $f_2(m) = m$)

- set $D := f_3(D)$ (e.g., $f_3(D) = D * 2$)

The initial values of the parameters in the algorithm are set heuristically according to domain characteristics. Likewise, increments of these parameters can also be adjusted in accordance with domain characteristics. When we expand the search, we do not start all over again: The search can be partially based on the previous iteration; that is, at each step, we widen the search to explore additional branches, and we do not recompute the paths explored before. The algorithm is an *anytime* algorithm. At the end of any iteration, the result is a usable plan (or a failure in case the iterations up to the point failed to find a plan). It is not always necessary to wait until the very end of the algorithm, and this fact may reduce the complexity of planning in practice in many situations.

The advantage of extracting plans is that, instead of closed-loop policies that have to rely on moment-to-moment sensing, extracted plans can be used in an open-loop fashion, which is useful when feedback is not available or unreliable. They are also beneficial in the sense of saving sensing costs (even when reliable feedback is available). We demonstrated in our experiments that extracting plans can lead to "policy compression"; that is, it can lead to fewer specifications for fewer states (Sun and Sessions 1998). It thus leads to the saving of storage costs of policies. In addition, extracted plans can be used to help with further learning, for the sake of finding better sequences, adapting to changing environments, and so on, through setting up subgoals, constraining explorations, and other additional processing.

We can also show that the above algorithm is sound and complete with regard to probabilities of reaching goals (Sun and Sessions 1998). The usefulness of plan extraction is thus guaranteed in a practical sense. See Appendix for more details.

3.6   Modularity through Spatial Partitioning

In the bottom level, beyond the reinforcement learning algorithm described earlier, we also need methods for developing modular structures, so that different modules can specialize in dealing with different inputs, different sensory modalities, or different tasks. Modularization has been shown to be a cognitive necessity (Wolpert and Kawamoto 1998, Fodor 1983, Karmiloff-Smith 1986, Cosmides and Tooby 1994). Timberlake and Lucas (1993), Cosmides and Tooby (1994) and many other researchers have studied various sets of behavioral modules. Alternatively, modules may represent different concepts or categories, or different groups of concepts/categories (Tani and Nolfi 1998). Performance-wise, it is also important to develop modularity. In complex reinforcement learning tasks, partitioning a state (input) space into multiple regions helps to exploit differential characteristics of regions and to develop differential characteristics in modules assigned to these different regions, thus facilitating learning and reducing representational complexity (especially when function approximators are used). Usually local modules turn out to be a lot simpler than a monolithic, global module.

A region-splitting algorithm is developed to address automatic partitioning in complex reinforcement learning tasks, with multiple modules, without a priori domain-specific knowledge regarding task structures (Sun and Peterson 1999).

The algorithm adopts a learning/partitioning decomposition, separating the two issues and optimizing them separately, which facilitates both processes (as compared with on-line methods, such as Jacobs et al. 1991, Jordan and Jacobs 1994). Hard partitioning (with crisp region boundaries) is used, because due to decomposition, we do not need to calculate gradients of partitioning and hard partitioning (without involving gradient descent) is faster. A region is handled exclusively by a single module in the form of a backpropagation network.

This algorithm attempts to find better partitioning by splitting existing regions incrementally when certain criteria are met. The splitting criterion is based on the total magnitude of the errors that incurred in a region during training and also based on the consistency of the errors (the distribution of the directions of the errors, either positive or negative); these two considerations are combined.

Specifically, in relation to Q-learning, error is defined as the Q value updating amount (the Bellman residual). That is, $error_x = r + \gamma \max_{a'} Q_{k'}(x', a') - Q_k(x, a)$, where x is a (full or partial) state description, a is the action taken, x' is the new state resulting from a in x, r is the reinforcement received, k is the module responsible for x, and k' is the module responsible for x'. We select those regions to split that have high *sums of absolute errors* (or alternatively, high sums of squared errors), which are indicative of high total magnitude of the errors, but have low *sums of errors*, which together with high sums of absolute errors are indicative of low error consistency (i.e., that Q updates/Bellman residuals are distributed in different directions). That is, our combined criterion is

$$consistency(l) = |\sum_x error_x| - \sum_x |error_x| < threshold1$$

where x refers to the data points encountered during the previous training period that are within the region l to be split.

Next we select a dimension to be used in splitting, within each region to be split. Since we have already calculated the sum of absolute errors and it remains the same regardless of what we do, what we can do is to split a dimension to increase the overall error consistency (i.e., the sums of errors). Specifically, we compare for each dimension i in the region l the following measure: the increase in consistency if the dimension is optimally split, that is,

$$\Delta consistency(l, i)$$

$$= \max_{v_i}(|\sum_{x:x_i<v_i} error_x| + |\sum_{x:x_i\geq v_i} error_x|) - |\sum_x error_x|$$

where v_i is a split point for a dimension i, x refers to the points within region l on the one side or the other of the split point, when projected to dimension i. This measure indicates how much more we can increase the error consistency if we split a dimension i optimally. The selection of dimension i is contingent upon $\Delta consistency(l, i) > threshold2$. Among those dimensions that satisfy $\Delta consistency(l, i) > threshold2$, we choose the one with the highest $\Delta consistency(l, i)$. For a selected dimension i, we optimize the selection of a split point v'_i based on maximizing the sum of the absolute values of the total errors on both sides of the split point:

$$v'_i = argmax_{v_i}(|\sum_{x:x_i<v_i} error_x| + |\sum_{x:x_i\geq v_i} error_x|)$$

where v'_i is the chosen split point for a dimension i. Such a point is optimal in the exact sense that error consistency is maximized (Breiman et al. 1984).

Then, we split the region l using a boundary created by the split point. We create a split hyper-plane using the selected point $spec = x_j < v_j$. We then split the region using the newly created boundary: $region_1 = region \cap spec$ and $region_2 = region \cap \neg spec$, where $region$ is the specification of the original region.

The algorithm is as follows:

1. Initialize one partition to contain only one region that covers the whole input space
2. Train a module on the partition
3. Split the partition

4. Train a set of modules on the partition, with each region assigned to a different module

5. If no more splitting can be done, stop; otherwise, go to 3

To split a partition:

1. For each region l that satisfies $consistency(l) < threshold1$ do:

1.1.   Select a dimension j in the input space that maximizes $\Delta consistency$, provided that $\Delta consistency(l, j) > threshold2$

1.2. In the selected dimension j, select a point (a value v_j) lying within the region and maximizing $\Delta consistency(l, j)$

1.3. Using the selected value point in the selected dimension, create a split hyper-plane: $spec = x_j < v_j$

1.4. Split the region using the newly created hyper-plane: $region_1 = region \cap spec$ and $region_2 = region \cap \neg spec$, where $region$ is the specification of the original region; create two modules for handling these two regions by replicating the module for the original region

2. If the number of regions exceeds R, keep combining regions until the number is right: randomly select two regions (preferring two adjacent regions) and merge the two; keep one of the two modules responsible for these two regions and delete the other

The algorithm is domain independent in the sense that no a priori domain-specific knowledge (e.g., concerning which dimension to split and at which point) is needed. However, a priori domain-specific knowledge, when available, can be useful. For example, in a navigation setting, if we know a priori which input dimension (such as a particular instrument reading) is more important, then we can use that dimension first. In this way, we are more likely to find a good partition, and we also save much computation.

In the above algorithm, regions are made up of hypercubes, each of which is specified by a logical conjunction of simple inequalities each concerning values of inputs in one input dimension. Beside such a simple type of region, we can also use alternative types of regions, for example, hyper-spheres as specified by radial basis functions. We can also use a linear perceptron network for specifying regions. We can even extend to more general, arbitrarily shaped regions as, for example, specified by a backpropagation network, which can serve as a gating mechanism.

This method was experimentally tested and compared to a number of other existing algorithms. In our experiments, we found that the method outperformed single-module learning and on-line gradient descent partitioning, in terms of both speed of learning and result of learning (Sun and Peterson 1999). See Appendix for further details.

3.7   Modularity through Temporal Segmentation

To develop modular structures, instead of spatial regions, we may also generate temporal "regions", or sequential segments, during learning. These sequential segments may represent different routines (or subroutines) that agents learn. Our segmentation method (Sun and Sessions 1999a, 1999b, 2000) involves learning to segment action sequences to create hierarchical sequential modularity structures. Thus it resembles, to some extent, hierarchical planning methods studied in cognitive science and AI (e.g., Sacerdoti 1974, Knoblock et al. 1994). Proper segmentation is accomplished through comparing competing ways of segmentation in terms of total reinforcement received.

There are three types of learning modules used in this method:

- Individual action module Q: Each selects actions and learns through Q-learning to maximize its reinforcement.
- Individual controller CQ: Each CQ learns when a Q module (corresponding to the CQ) should continue its control and when it should give up the control, in terms of maximizing reinforcement. The learning is accomplished through (separate) Q-learning.
- Abstract controller AQ: It selects and learns abstract control actions, that is, which Q module to select under what circumstances. The learning is accomplished through (separate) Q-learning to maximize reinforcement.

The method works as follows:

1. Observe the current state x.
2. The currently active Q/CQ pair takes control. If there is no active one (when the system first starts), go to step 5.
3. The active CQ selects and performs a control action based on $CQ(x, ca)$ for different ca. If the action chosen by CQ is *end*, go to step 5. Otherwise, the active Q selects and performs an action based on $Q(x, a)$ for different a.
4. The active Q and CQ performs learning. Go to step 1.
5. AQ selects and performs an abstract control action based on $AQ(x, aa)$ for different aa, to select a Q/CQ pair to become active.

6. AQ performs learning. Go to step 3.

The learning rules of the three types of modules are as follows. First of all, a Q module learns its actions based on which action will lead to higher overall reinforcement (both by itself and by subsequent modules). For the active Q_k, when neither the current action nor the next action by the corresponding CQ_k is *end*, the usual Q-learning rule is used:

$$\Delta Q_k(x, a) = \alpha(r(x) + \gamma \max_{a'} Q_k(x', a') - Q_k(x, a))$$

where x' is the new state resulting from action a in state x. That is, when CQ_k decides to continue, Q_k learns to estimate reinforcement generated (1) by its current action and (2) by its subsequent actions, plus (3) the reinforcement generated later by other modules after Q_k/CQ_k relinquishes control (see the next learning rule). The value of Q_k is the sum of these estimates.

When the current action of CQ_k (in x) is *continue* and the next action of CQ_k (in x') is *end*, the Q_k module receives as reward the maximum value of AQ:

$$\Delta Q_k(x, a) = \alpha(r(x) + \gamma \max_{aa'} AQ(x', aa') - Q_k(x, a))$$

where x' is the new state (resulting from action a in state x) in which control is returned to AQ by CQ_k, and aa is any abstract action of AQ. As the corresponding CQ terminates the control of the current Q module, AQ has to take an abstract action in state x', the value of which is the (discounted) total reinforcement that will be received from that point on (by the whole system). So the Q module learns the (discounted) total reinforcement that will be received by the whole system thereon. Combining the explanations of the above two rules, we see that a Q module decides its actions based on which action will lead to higher overall reinforcement from the current state on both by itself and by subsequent modules.

Second, for the corresponding CQ_k, there are also two separate learning rules, for the two different actions. A CQ module learns its decisions based on whether giving up or continuing control may lead to more overall reinforcement. When the current action by CQ_k is *continue*, the learning rule is the usual Q-learning:

$$\Delta CQ_k(x, continue) = \alpha(r(x) + \gamma \max_{ca'} CQ_k(x', ca') - CQ_k(x, continue))$$

where x' is the new state resulting from action *continue* in state x and ca' is any control action by CQ_k. When CQ_k decides to continue, it learns to estimate reinforcement generated by the actions of the corresponding Q_k, assuming that CQ_k gives up control whenever *end* has a higher value, plus the reinforcement generated after Q_k/CQ_k relinquishes control (see the next learning rule). That is , CQ_k learns the value of *continue* as the sum of the expected reinforcement generated by Q_k until $CQ_k(end) > CQ_k(continue)$ and the expected reinforcement generated by subsequent modules thereafter.

When the current action by CQ_k is *end*, the learning rule is

$$\Delta CQ_k(x, end) = \alpha(\max_{aa} AQ(x, aa) - CQ_k(x, end))$$

where aa is any abstract control action by AQ. That is, when a CQ ends, it learns the value of the best abstract action to be performed by AQ, which is equal to the (discounted) total reinforcement that will be accumulated by the whole system from the current state on. Combining the above two learning rules, in effect, the CQ module learns to make its decisions by comparing whether giving up or continuing control will lead to more overall reinforcement from the current state on.

Finally, AQ learns to select lower-level modules based on which selection leads to more overall reinforcement. We have the following learning rule for AQ:

$$\Delta AQ(x, aa) = \alpha(ar(x) + \gamma^m \max_{aa'} AQ(x', aa') - AQ(x, aa))$$

where aa is the abstract control action that selects a Q module to take control, x' is the new state (after x) in which AQ is required to make a decision, m is the number of time steps taken to go from x to x' (used in determining the amount of discounting γ^m), and ar is the (discounted) cumulative reinforcement received after the abstract control action for state x and before the next abstract control action for state x' (that is, $ar(x) = \sum_{k=0,1,....,m-1} r(x_k)\gamma^k$, where $x_0 = x$ and $x_m = x'$). AQ learns the value of an abstract control action that it selects, which is the (discounted) cumulative reinforcement that the chosen Q module will accrue before AQ has to make another abstract action decision, plus the accumulation of reinforcement from the next abstract action on. In other words, AQ estimates the (discounted) total reinforcement to be accrued. So, in effect,

AQ learns to select lower-level modules based on which selection leads to more overall reinforcement from the current point on.

Let us look briefly into some possible variations of this method. As one may observe from the above explanation of learning rules, technically, we only need either CQs or AQ, but not both, since their values are closely related (if an identical input representation is given to them). Without AQ, the assignment of modules may be achieved through a competition among them (that is, using a "bidding" process, as described in Sun and Sessions 1999b). However, we may want to keep AQ and CQs separate if we have more than two levels, because otherwise it would be hard to create a hierarchical structure. Furthermore, if we adopt different input representations for different levels so that different information is relied on for decision making at different levels (Sun and Session 1999a), then we have to keep them separate in order to direct different information to them (even in case of two-level hierarchies).

In modules, we may need to construct temporal representations (e.g., to avoid excessive segmentation; Sun and Sessions 2000). One possibility of temporal representation is recurrent backpropagation networks (e.g., Elman 1990 and Giles et al. 1995). Recurrent networks have been used to represent temporal dependencies of various forms in much previous work. Recurrent networks have shortcomings, such as long learning time, possible inaccuracy, possibly improper generalizations, and so on. Theoretically, they can memorize arbitrarily long sequences, but practically, due to limitations on precision, the length of a sequence that can be memorized is quite limited (Lin 1993). As a more viable alternative, we may use decision trees, which splits a state if a statistical test shows that there are significant differences among the cases covered by that state, that is, if the state can be divided into two states by adding features from preceding steps and thereby provide more accurate assessment of the cumulative reinforcement that will be received (Sun and Sessions 2000).

This segmentation method automatically seeks out proper configurations of temporal structures (i.e., non-Markovian dependencies; Sun and Sessions 2000). This is done through maximizing overall reinforcement, because the proper ways of segmentation lead to higher total reinforcement. Our experimental results show that this method does help to improve learning. See Appendix for some details of experimental results.

Note that such automatic segmentation is different from reinforcement learning using (mostly) pre-given hierarchical structures. In the latter approach, a vast amount of a priori domain-specific knowledge has to be worked out by hand (a difficult, and sometimes impossible, task) and engineered into a system before learning starts (e.g., Dietterich 1997), which we aim to avoid.

3.8 Biological Interpretations

It is interesting to note some plausible biological correlates of the computational processes involved in the above implementation. The basal ganglia has been identified to be the locus of reinforcement learning (Schultz et al. 1997). The dopamine neurons in the basal ganglia predict reinforcement to be received and thereby drive the learning process using the discrepancy between the prediction and the actual reinforcement received (Houk et al. 1995, Schultz et al. 1997).

The central role of modularity in motor control learning and other sequential task learning has been argued from the neurophysiological standpoint (e.g., by Wolpert and Kawato 1998). Related to our implementation of partitioning or segmentation, it has been argued that modules, responsible for either spatial regions or temporal segments, reside mainly in the supplementary motor area, while the selection of modules is likely done in the basal ganglia (see, e.g., Bapi and Doya 2001).[5] The learning—updating of modules as well as updating of module selection mechanisms—is likely to be controlled by processes in the pre-supplementary motor area (Nakamura et al. 1998).

There has been indications that, in the human brain, the temporal lobe is often correlated with consciously controlled sequence learning (Keele et al. 1998). In implicit memory research, however, it was found that explicit recall of sequences was often correlated with frontal lobe activities (Posner et al. 1997). Thus, it may well be the case that the temporal lobe and the frontal lobe are both responsible for explicit processing, corresponding to the higher level of the CLARION model (with explicit rules or explicit plans). The lower level of the model, responsible for implicit processing, is distributed across a wide range of brain regions (Keele et al. 1998), including

---

[5] However, Houk et al. (1995) suggested that action modules resided in the basal ganglia in the form of matrix regions.

the pre-supplementary motor area, the supplementary motor area, and the motor cortex (Nakahara et al. 1997).

3.9 Summary

In this chapter, the implementation of the CLARION model was discussed. We looked into several key algorithms needed to make the model work. These algorithms cover the learning at the bottom level using reinforcement learning, the learning at the top level using rule extraction and plan extraction, as well as the development of modularity at the bottom level using spatial partitioning and temporal segmentation.

A word of caution is in order here: By no means is any of the afore-discussed algorithms final. They are merely reasonable options in implementing CLARION, the theoretical model. A great deal of painstakingly detailed experimental work has been done, and the current implementation is therefore reasonably mature. Nevertheless, there is much to be done in developing better, more sophisticated algorithms in relation to the theoretical model. Machine learning is still a relatively young and growing field. New advances in terms of paradigms, algorithms, and techniques can benefit the implementation of CLARION in many ways. With some luck, we may be able to translate, rather directly, new advances in reinforcement learning, rule learning, planning, and other types of algorithms into improved implementations for CLARION. I will be on the lookout for such possibilities.

3.10   Appendix

Appendix 1: Performance of the Basic CLARION Model

Described below are the experiments with the basic CLARION model, with Q-learning at the bottom level and rule extraction at the top level, as discussed earlier in sections 1-4. For further details of these experiments, the reader is referred to Sun and Peterson (1998a, 1998b).

Mazes

Extensive experiments have been done in a maze domain (Sun and Peterson 1998 b). In the maze, the agent has sensory inputs regarding its immediate left, front, and right side, indicating whether there is a wall, an opening, or the goal. As the maze has no location marker, the agent has no direct knowledge of its location. It has no information about the goal location. The agent can move forward, turn to the left, or turn to the right. An episode starts with an agent at the fixed starting location and ends when the agent reaches the goal (without time limit). The reward for an agent reaching the goal is 1, and the punishment for hitting a wall is -0.1.

Although in this case, because of the small state space we can use lookup tables for implementing Q-learning, we did not, because CLARION was not specifically designed for maze running but for sequential tasks in general, which more likely involve huge state spaces (e.g., as in the minefield navigation task discussed later).

Learning speed. We used a small maze shown in Figure 3.4 as the primary setting. When CLARION is compared with the bottom level alone (trained only with Q-learning), the differences in learning speed (averaged over 50 runs) is shown in Figure 3.5. In this experiment, we used fixed ratios in combining outcomes of the two levels. *Perc.x* refers to the versions using the percentage combination with rules being applied $x\%$ of the times. *Stoc.y* refers to the versions using the stochastic combination with rules being weighted at $y\%$. *Q* refers to the bottom level used alone with Q-learning as the sole learning method. The symbol *gen* indicates that generalization/specialization is performed; otherwise, generalization/specialization operations such as *expansion* and *shrinking* are omitted. It is clear from the figure that when rules are used frequently (e.g., with Perc.80 or Stoc.20), CLARION learns faster than the bottom level alone by large margins. A t test showed that the differences were significant with over 99% confidence ($p < 0.01$). The table indicates that the number of rules learned at the end of the 60 episodes is relatively stable (with a mean around 7 and a small standard error). Figure 3.6 shows a comparison of the learning curves of four different versions of CLARION and the bottom level alone with Q-learning.

Figure 3.4. The initial maze
The starting position is marked by 'S' in which the agent faces upward to the upper wall. The goal is marked by 'G'.

Trained performance. For the different models, the average number of steps needed to reach the target in one episode, after 60 episodes of training, are shown in Figure 3.7 in the *Moves* column. Again, CLARION outperforms the bottom level alone (trained only with Q-learning) by large margins. The t test showed over 99% confidence ($p < 0.01$).

Also reported are the average numbers of steps in one episode using only the top level (marked as *R-moves*) or using only the bottom level (marked as *Q-moves*), after both are trained together as part of CLARION. There is clearly a *synergy* between the top level and the bottom level: Comparing the three values horizontally on each line, the whole CLARION model always performs better than the top level alone or the bottom level alone in all the cases shown. Furthermore, comparing the *Q-moves* of different versions of CLARION with the *Q-moves* of the bottom level alone (trained only with Q-learning), that is, examining the *Q-Moves* column vertically, rule learning not only improves the performance of the whole system, but it also improves the bottom level per se when it is included as part of CLARION. Rules are learned from the bottom level, but in turn they help to improve it.

Transfer. We applied our trained models (after the training of 60

		Moves	Rules
Q-learning	Avg:	15348.48	n/a
	StdErr:	545.85	n/a
Perc.60	Avg:	4994.52	7.78
	StdErr:	288.64	0.50
Perc.80	Avg:	5840.14	7.28
	StdErr:	296.73	0.43
Perc.60.gen	Avg:	5164.36	8.50
	StdErr:	219.93	1.35
Perc.80.gen	Avg:	5040.84	9.12
	StdErr:	257.65	1.31
Stoc.15.	Avg:	4602.88	6.62
	StdErr:	768.28	0.35
Stoc.20	Avg:	4712.70	6.30
	StdErr:	218.89	0.32
Stoc.15.gen	Avg:	6539.04	6.82
	StdErr:	287.99	0.87
Stoc.20.gen	Avg:	5574.24	8.14
	StdErr:	358.07	1.38

Figure 3.5. A comparison of learning speeds
Moves indicate the total numbers of moves during training (averaged over 50 trials). *Rules* indicate the average numbers of rules at the end of training.

episodes) to a larger maze as shown in Figure 3.8 to assess transfer.[6] We are mainly concerned with comparing the transfer of the bottom level alone (trained only with Q-learning) versus that of CLARION. In Figure 3.9, as indicated by the *Moves* column, CLARION transfers much better than the bottom level alone (trained only with Q-learning) in terms of the average number of steps to reach the goal in one episode. Furthermore, by comparing the corresponding *Moves*, *Q-moves*, and *R-moves* on each line horizontally, we see that often learned rules alone perform better in transfer than either the bottom level (trained as part of CLARION) or the whole CLARION model. The superiority of R-moves in comparison with Q-moves demonstrates that, in this case, rule learning facilitates transfer

[6] Transfer occurs because of the similarity of the two mazes (e.g., the prevalence of left turns).

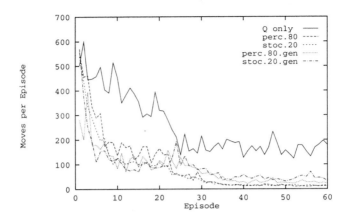

Figure 3.6. A comparison of learning curves

	Moves	Q-Moves	R-Moves
Q-learning	149.00	149.00	n/a
Perc.60	29.76	72.46	94.98
Perc.80	10.78	36.22	13.48
Perc.60.gen	42.06	118.24	189.18
Perc.80.gen	22.02	55.14	106.58
Stoc.15	28.42	102.70	44.74
Stoc.20	20.60	81.80	30.54
Stoc.15.gen	53.90	87.18	108.20
Stoc.20.gen	36.26	67.18	64.66

Figure 3.7. Trained performance

Here *moves* denotes the average number of steps in one episode for a whole model. *Q-moves* denotes the same number for the bottom level alone. *R-moves* denotes the same number for the top level alone.

to new and more complicated environments.[7]

Figure 3.8. The second maze

	Moves	Q-Moves	R-Moves
Q-learning	1681.48	1681.48	n/a
Perc.60	770.72	1782.16	559.96
Perc.80	492.14	1289.78	233.56
Perc.60.gen	766.38	2049.40	1030.66
Perc.80.gen	415.52	1581.62	722.48
Stoc.15	850.70	1481.34	405.94
Stoc.20	498.40	1586.88	392.08
Stoc.15.gen	703.80	1690.32	981.94
Stoc.20.gen	760.70	2028.24	956.50

Figure 3.9. Transfer to maze 2

Here *moves* denotes the average number of steps in one episode for a whole model. *Q-moves* denotes the same number for the Q-learning level alone. *R-moves* denotes the same number for the rule level alone.

Minefield Navigation

We tested CLARION on the simulated navigation task as shown in Figure 3.10. The agent has to navigate an underwater vessel through a minefield to reach a target location. The agent receives information only

[7] The differences between *R-moves* and *Q-moves* (or *Moves*) are significant in some cases, for example, in *Perc.60* and *Perc.80*.

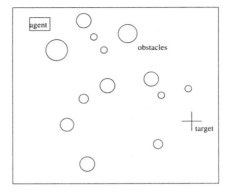

Figure 3.10. Navigation through a minefield

from a number of instruments. As shown in Figure 3.11, the sonar gauge shows how close the mines are in seven equal areas that range approximately from 45 degrees to the left of the agent to 45 degrees to the right. The fuel gauge shows how much time is left before fuel runs out. The bearing gauge shows the direction of the target from the present heading of the agent. The range gauge shows how far the target is from the current location. Based only on such information, the agent decides on (1) how to turn and (2) how fast to move. The time allotted to the agent for each episode is 200 steps. The agent, within an allotted time period, can either (1) reach the target (a success), (2) hit a mine (a failure), or (3) run out of time (a failure). Each episode starts with the agent on the one side of the minefield and the target on the other. An episode ends when (1) the target is reached, (2) the time runs out (200 steps), or (3) the agent hits a mine. A random mine layout is generated for each episode. The mines are randomly placed between the starting point of the agent and the target.

In CLARION, as input to the bottom level, each gauge is represented by a set of nodes. We tried both discrete and analog input values. In the case of discrete inputs, there are 41 inputs and thus more than 10^{12} states. In the case of analog inputs, each gauge is represented by one node, which takes on continuous values between the highest possible value and the lowest possible value, scaled to within $[0, 1]$. We compared the performance of these two types of inputs, and found no significant difference. We dealt with the problem of high input dimensionality. A lookup table implementation for Q-learning at the bottom level is not possible, because of the high dimensionality (Tesauro 1992, Lin 1992). A function approximator, a backpropagation network, is used (Bertsekas and Tsitsiklis 1996).

The action outputs in the bottom level consist of two clusters of nodes: one clusters of five nodes for five different values of "direction" (including *left, slightly left, straight, slightly right,* and *right*), and the other cluster of five nodes for five different values of "speed" (including *very fast, fast, normal, slow,* and *standstill*).

In the top level, as an alternative to using the same inputs as the bottom level, we also tried using some secondary (derived) high-level features as inputs. Although the secondary feature set led to more comprehensible rules, they had no significant impact on learning performance.

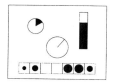

Figure 3.11. The navigation input
The display at the upper left corner is the fuel gauge; the vertical one at the upper right corner is the range gauge; the round one in the middle is the bearing gauge; the 7 sonar gauges are at the bottom.

The reinforcement for an agent is produced from two sources. One is the gradient reward, which is proportional to the change in the "range" readings (i.e, the change in the distance to the target).[8] The other is the end reward, which is determined by how successful the agent is at the end of an episode. The end reward is 1 if the agent reaches the target within the allotted time, and is inversely proportional to the distance from the target if the agent runs out of time or gets blown up.[9]

[8] When the agent is going toward the target, the reinforcement is $gr = 1/c * ((x_2 - x_1)/x)^4$, where $c = 7.5$, $x_2 - x_1$ is the distance traveled in the target direction in one step, and x is the maximum distance possible (which is 40). When the agent is going away from the target, the reinforcement is $gr' = -0.5gr$.
[9] When the agent runs out of time, the reinforcement is $er = 500/(500 + x) - 1$, where x is the distance to the target. When the agent gets blown up, the reinforcement is $er = 1/2 * 500/(500 + x) - 1$.

Learning speed. Figures 3.12, 3.13, and 3.14 show the data of CLARION (using the analog inputs in the bottom level and the secondary features in the top level). In terms of learning effectiveness, which is measured by the number of successful episodes out of a total of 1000 episodes of training (averaged over 10 runs), the "training" columns of these figures show the difference between CLARION and the bottom level alone (trained with only Q-learning). It appears that at higher mine densities (that is, in the more difficult settings), CLARION performed significantly better compared with the bottom level alone. In the 30-mine and 60-mine cases, the superiority of CLARION (over the bottom level alone with Q-learning only) is statistically significant (with t tests, $p < 0.05$). However, the performance is statistically undifferentiable in the 10-mine case.

Transfer. The right three blocks of Figures 3.12, 3.13, and 3.14 show the transfer data, where transfer is measured by the percentage of successful episodes in new settings by the trained models (each trained model is applied to minefields that contain a *different* number of mines for a total of 20 episodes; the data is averaged over 10 runs). The data generally follows the pattern that the higher the mine density is, the lower the success rate is. Moreover, the performance of a model is generally better if it is trained at a higher mine density. As also indicated by the tables, CLARION outperforms the bottom level alone (trained with Q-learning) in transfer at higher mine densities; the higher the mine density, the more pronounced the difference is. The differences are statistically significant in the 30-mine and 60-mine cases (using t tests, $p < 0.05$). Finally, comparing the transfer performance of the top level, the bottom level, and the whole system, after they are trained together, we notice that the whole system always performs much better than either level alone. There is definitely a synergy between the two levels. Learning rules does help to improve the transfer performance.

Trained performance. The right three blocks of Figures 3.12, 3.13, and 3.14 also contain the trained performance data: The 10-mine block in Figure 3.12 shows the trained performance after training in 10-mine minefields. The 30-mine block in Figure 3.13 shows the trained performance after training in 30-mine minefields. The 60-mine block in Figure 3.14 shows the trained performance after training in 60-mine minefields. Trained performance is defined to be the percentage of successful episodes in the

Model	Train	Mine Density During Training: 10								
		B+T	B	T	B+T	B	T	B+T	B	T
	10	10	10	10	30	30	30	60	60	60
CLARION	651.8	63.5	6.5	4.5	35.5	1.5	0.5	11.5	1.0	0.0
s.d.	31.3	34.4	4.5	6.9	21.0	2.3	1.5	9.5	2.0	0.0
Q	645.7	82.0			42.0			14.5		
s.d.	86.9	14.2			24.5			18.1		

Figure 3.12. Learning and transfer from 10-mine minefields
Q refers to the bottom level used alone with Q-learning as the sole learning method. *Train* indicates the total numbers of successful episodes during training. The next three blocks contain performance data (in percentage), in three different mine densities (10, 30, and 60) using the trained models with either the top level, the bottom level, or both together.

Model	Train	Mine Density During Training: 30								
		B+T	B	T	B+T	B	T	B+T	B	T
	30	10	10	10	30	30	30	60	60	60
CLARION	663.8	89.0	5.0	1.0	75.0	7.0	0.0	47.5	2.5	0.0
s.d.	48.4	26.5	3.2	2.0	23.6	5.6	0.0	24.9	2.5	0.0
Q	539.1	77.0			68.0			35.5		
s.d.	105.6	17.5			20.4			20.7		

Figure 3.13. Learning and transfer from 30-mine minefields
Q refers to the bottom level used alone with Q-learning as the sole learning method. *Train* indicates the total numbers of successful episodes during training. The next three blocks contain performance data in percentage, in three different mine densities (10, 30, and 60) using the trained models with either the top level, the bottom level, or both together.

same settings as used in training by the trained models (each trained model is applied to the minefields for a total of 20 episodes; the data is averaged over 10 runs). At higher mine densities, we notice that the trained performance of CLARION is better than the bottom level alone (trained only with Q-learning). Comparing the performance of the whole system and the two levels separately after the two levels are trained together, we again notice that the whole system performs much better than the bottom level and the top level alone, which strongly suggests a synergy between the two

Mine Density During Training: 60

Model	Train	B+T	B	T	B+T	B	T	B+T	B	T
	60	10	10	10	30	30	30	60	60	60
CLARION	581.4	99.5	9.5	2.0	96.0	8.5	0.0	76.0	6.0	0.0
s.d.	79.0	1.5	6.5	3.3	3.7	4.5	0.0	15.9	6.6	0.0
Q	495.8		71.5			67.5			47.5	
s.d.	137.9		11.6			16.8			24.3	

Figure 3.14. Learning and transfer from 60-mine minefields
Q refers to the bottom level used alone with Q-learning as the sole learning method. *Train* indicates the total numbers of successful episodes during training. The next three blocks contain performance data in percentage, in three different mine densities (10, 30, and 60) using the trained models with either the top level, the bottom level, or both together.

levels.

Appendix 2: Examples of Rule Extraction

Rules learned in the maze task. An example set of rules learned in the maze task is as follows:

> If left-corner, then turn right
> If right-opening, then turn left
> If blockage, then turn left
> If clear-front, then go forward
> If target-at-right, then turn right
> If corridor, then go forward
> If target-in-front, then go forward

where *blockage* means a wall right in front, *clear-front* means an opening in front, *corridor* means walls on both left and right sides, *left-corner* means walls on both the front and left sides, *target-at-right* means that the target is at right and either an opening in front or an opening at left (which happens to be the common configurations that the agent experiences; see Figure 3.4), *right-opening* means an opening at right (which is the starting situation of the agent), and *target-in-front* means that the target is right in front. One can easily verify that this is a good set of rules for navigating the maze.

Rules learned in minefield navigation. Due to lengths, only a subset of rules learned in the navigation task, which were extracted using derived secondary features, are shown here:

```
Bearing: straight ahead
LeastDense: center
FurthestMine: center
LeftAvgMineDistance: close
CenterAvgMineDistance: very far
RightAvgMineDistance: far
Direction: go straight, Speed: very fast

Bearing: straight ahead
LeastDense: center and right
FurthestMine: center
LeftAvgMineDistance: close
CenterAvgMineDistance: very far
RightAvgMineDistance: very far
Direction: go straight, Speed: very fast

Bearing: straight ahead
LeastDense: right
FurthestMine: right
LeftAvgMineDistance: close
CenterAvgMineDistance: far
RightAvgMineDistance: far
Direction: go straight, Speed: very fast

Bearing: straight ahead, right, far right, right behind or far left
LeastDense: right
FurthestMine: right
LeftAvgMineDistance: very close or close
CenterAvgMineDistance: close
RightAvgMineDistance: far
Direction: turn right, Speed: very fast

Bearing: far left, left or right behind
LeastDense: right
FurthestMine: right
LeftAvgMineDistance: very close or close
```

```
CenterAvgMineDistance: close
RightAvgMineDistance: far
Direction: turn right, Speed: standstill

Bearing: straight ahead
LeastDense: right
FurthestMine: right
LeftAvgMineDistance: very close
CenterAvgMineDistance: very close
RightAvgMineDistance: very close to far
Direction: turn slightly right, Speed: very fast

Bearing: far left
LeastDense: left
FurthestMine: left
LeftAvgMineDistance: far
CenterAvgMineDistance: close
RightAvgMineDistance: close
Direction: turn left, Speed: very fast

Bearing: far right
LeastDense: left
FurthestMine: left
LeftAvgMineDistance: far
CenterAvgMineDistance: close
RightAvgMineDistance: very close
Direction: turn left, Speed: very fast
```

The high-level features used in the above rules are self-explanatory.

Appendix 3: Formal Properties in Plan Extraction

Concerning the plan extraction algorithm, we have the following formal results:

Theorem 1. The time complexity of the plan extraction algorithm is $O(D * |A| * |S| * (m + n))$ where n and m are the pre-selected beam width, $|A|$ is the number of action choices, $|S|$ is the total number of states, and D is the number of steps searched (the search depth).

Concerning the iterative widening beam search algorithm, we have:

Theorem 2. Weak completeness I: If there exists a limited-depth conditional plan for a planning problem, then the algorithm will find a conditional plan for the problem (provided that we set the goal threshold at 0).

Theorem 3. Weak completeness II: If there exists a limited-depth nonconditional plan for a planning problem, then the algorithm will find a conditional plan and a nonconditional plan for the problem (if we set the goal threshold at 0).

Theorem 4. Strong completeness I: If there exists a limited-depth conditional plan for a planning problem that has a success probability $p > \delta$, then the algorithm will find a conditional plan with $p' > \delta$ (if we set the goal threshold to be δ).

Theorem 5. Strong completeness II: If there exists a nonconditional plan for a planning problem that has a success probability $p > \delta$, then the algorithm will find a (conditional and/or nonconditional) plan with $p' > \delta$ (if we set the goal threshold to be δ).

Theorem 6. Soundness: If the algorithm returns a conditional or nonconditional plan with an estimated success probability p, then the true success probability of the plan is greater than or equal to p.

A corollary is that a plan returned by the algorithm may not be the plan that has the highest probability of success, considering all the possible paths.

Appendix 4: Examples of Plan Extraction

We tested the plan extraction algorithm in several domains. Here I briefly examine two of them. Both are fairly simple, but together illustrate the idea.

Tower of Hanoi. The first domain is the three-disc version of the Tower of Hanoi problem, which is deterministic, and easy for plan extraction. It consists of three pegs, with peg 1 starting with the three discs. The goal of the task is to get the three discs from peg 1 to peg 3. Only the top disc on a peg can be moved. The three discs are of three different sizes and a larger disc may not rest on a smaller disc. There are six possible actions as shown in Figure 3.15, although at most only three can be performed at each move (due to the relative size constraint). These moves generate 27 allowable states (see Figure 3.16). As shown in Figure 3.16, there is only one goal state in this task. Figure 3.17 shows all possible state transitions resulting from all allowable actions (state transition probabilities are 1 as state transitions are deterministic).

A simple domain simulator was built along the line described above. Q-learning was then applied to learn closed-loop policies from interactions with the simulator. Plan extraction was then applied. Conditional plans are the same as nonconditional plans in this domain, and in the case of a conditional plan, increasing the number of conditional branches does not change it either. The goal can always be reached by an extracted plan with a 100% probability. Thus, I show only one example, a nonconditional plan, extracted from Q values. The plan steps are as follows:

> Step 1: moving the top disc from peg 1 to 3 (action 1). Step 2: from peg 1 to 2 (action 0). Step 3: from peg 3 to 2 (action 5). Step 4: from peg 1 to 3 (action 1). Step 5: from peg 2 to 1 (action 2). Step 6: from peg 2 to 3 (action 3). Step 7: from peg 1 to 3 (action 1).

Action	Description
A0	Peg 1 to Peg 2
A1	Peg 1 to Peg 3
A2	Peg 2 to Peg 1
A3	Peg 2 to Peg 3
A4	Peg 3 to Peg 1
A5	Peg 3 to Peg 2

Figure 3.15. The possible actions in the Tower of Hanoi task

Gripper. The second domain is the Gripper task, which is standard in the probabilistic planning literature (e.g., Kushmerick et al. 1995). In this task, a robot arm has to paint a block without getting itself dirty and to pick up the block in the end. There are three possible actions: paint, dry, and pickup. There are four binary features describing a state: BP (block painted), GD (gripper dry), HB (holding block), and GC (gripper clean); thus there are a total of 16 states (see Figure 3.18). Actions have probabilistic outcomes: For example, if the gripper is not dry, it may fail to pick up the block; if the block is painted while the gripper is holding the

State Number	Description
0	(123,0,0)
1	(23,1,0)
2	(23,0,1)
3	(13,2,0)
4	(13,0,2)
5	(12,3,0)
6	(12,0,3)
7	(3,12,0)
8	(3,0,12)
9	(3,1,2)
10	(3,2,1)
11	(2,13,0)
12	(2,0,13)
13	(2,1,3)
14	(2,3,1)
15	(1,23,0)
16	(1,0,23)
17	(1,2,3)
18	(1,3,2)
19	(0,123,0)
20	(0,23,1)
21	(0,13,2)
22	(0,12,3)
23	(0,3,12)
24	(0,2,13)
25	(0,1,23)
26	(0,0,123)

Figure 3.16. The possible states in the Tower of Hanoi task
State 0 is the starting state. State 26 is the goal state. In the description, pegs are separated by commas. "1" indicates the smallest disc, "2" the median-sized, and "3" the largest.

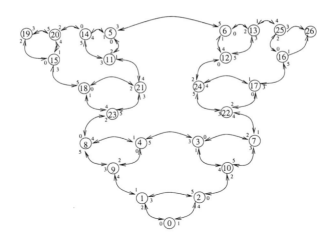

Figure 3.17. State transitions in the Tower of Hanoi task

States are indicated in circles. Actions are marked on arcs. The state transitions are deterministic.

block, the gripper will likely get dirty; drying the gripper may not always lead to a dry gripper; and so on. The state transition probabilities, as given in Kushmerick et al. (1995), are shown in Figure 3.19. This task is interesting for probabilistic planning because it involves nondeterministic state transitions, and because of the existence of anti-goals (the states in which the block gets dirty are the anti-goal states because there is no possibility of recovery from that).

We applied Q-learning to learn closed-loop policies in this task, from interacting with a domain simulator (which was as specified above). Plans were extracted after Q-learning. The conditional plan can be paraphrased as follows:

> Step 1: from the starting state 4, do *paint* (action 2). Step 2: if the current state is 12, do *dry* (action 1); otherwise, the plan fails. Step 3: if the current state is 13, do *pickup* (action 0); otherwise, do *dry* (action 1) again. Step 4: if the current state is not 15, do *pickup* again (action 0). Step 5: if the current state is not 14 or 15, do *pickup* (action 0) again.

The nonconditional plan is simply as follows:

Step 1: paint. Step 2: dry. Step 3: pickup. Step 4: pickup.[10]
Step 5: dry. Step 6: pickup.

There is a clear tradeoff between the accuracy of a plan and
its simplicity. Figure 3.20 shows a comparison of estimated success
probabilities of plans and running times of the plan extraction algorithm
with different numbers of branches. Comparing our algorithm with
Kushmerick et al. (1995), we noticed that on average our algorithm
performed much faster, although the comparison was rough by nature due
to variations in implementation.

The extracted plans achieve "policy compression" to varying degrees.
The nonconditional plan achieves the highest degree of compression, since
it has no conditional branch. While the original closed-loop policy requires
specifying actions for 16 states, the nonconditional plan only requires
specifying a sequence of 6 actions. It thus saves representational cost. It
can be executed without sensory input, which means that (1) it also saves
sensing cost and (2) it works even when sensory input is not available (e.g.,
due to faulty sensors).

Appendix 5: Examples of Spatial Partitioning

To test the region-splitting algorithm, we looked into two maze tasks, one
easy and one hard. For each task, we varied the size of the layout. Maze 1
of the small size is shown in Figure 3.21. Maze 2 of the small size is shown
in Figure 3.22. The medium size is twice the original size, and the large
size is three times the original size.

The task setting is as follows: An agent has views of five sides: left,
soft left, front, soft right, and right, and can tell in each direction whether
there is an obstacle or not, up to a distance of two cells away. It has also
the information of the distance and the bearing to the goal. There is a total
of 20 binary inputs (and thus more than 10^6 possible inputs). An agent
can move by selecting two output parameters: turn (left, right, or no turn)
and speed (0 or 1). The information used for region specification consists
of x-y coordinates. Reinforcement is provided when the target is reached,
the value of which is 1.

---

[10] This is done only if previous pickup failed, because otherwise the plan would have
been terminated already.

State Number	Feature Description
0	(not BP, not GC, not HB, not GD)
1	(not BP, not GC, not HB, GD)
2	(not BP, not GC, HB, not GD)
3	(not BP, not GC, HB, GD)
4	(not BP, GC, not HB, not GD)
5	(not BP, GC, not HB, GD)
6	(not BP, GC, HB, not GD)
7	(not BP, GC, HB, GD)
8	(BP, not GC, not HB, not GD)
9	(BP, not GC, not HB, GD)
10	(BP, not GC, HB, not GD)
11	(BP, not GC, HB, GD)
12	(BP, GC, not HB, not GD)
13	(BP, GC, not HB, GD)
14	(BP, GC, HB, not GD)
15	(BP, GC, HB, GD)

Figure 3.18. The possible states in the Gripper task
State 4 is the starting state. States 14 and 15 are the goal states. The anti-goal
states include states 8, 9, 10, and 11. States 0, 1, 2, and 3 are impossible to reach.

We compared the region-splitting method (denoted as RS) with some
other algorithms. These algorithms include: a variation of region-splitting
with the weighted averaging of multiple modules for each region (with
combination weights determined through gradient descent in each region;
denoted as MRS), weighted averaging of multiple (diversified) modules
without partitioning (with different initial weights and learning rates
in each, with combination weights determined through gradient descent
learning, denoted as WA; Breiman 1996), gating (on-line, soft partitioning,
a simple extension of Jacobs et al. 1991; denoted as G), a GA-based
algorithm (denoted as GA, in which crossover and mutation are done on
region specifications), as well as single-module Q-learning (denoted as Q).

Figure 3.23 shows the learning performance (success rates) of RS as
compared with single-module Q-learning. We see clearly that partitioning
helps to improve learning: RS achieved higher success rates when task

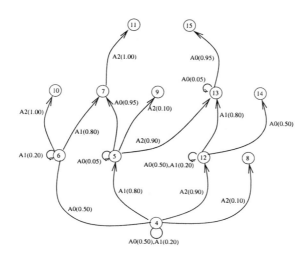

Figure 3.19. State transitions for the Gripper task

State 4 is the starting state. States 14 and 15 are the goal states. States are represented in circles and state transition probabilities are indicated in parentheses along with actions. A0 = Pickup, A1 = Dry, and A2 = Paint.

n	CPU time	success rate
0	6.0	79%
1	6.0	85%
2	6.1	87%
3	6.1	90%
5	6.1	90%
10	6.1	90%

variation	CPU time	success rate
KHW (F)	7.9	90%
KHW (Q)	9.0	90%
KHW (N)	150.2	90%
KHW (R)	430.6	90%

Figure 3.20. A comparison of running times

The left table contains the CPU running times of the algorithm (excluding Q-learning) and the success probabilities of the resulting plans as a function of the number of branches. The times (in ms) were estimated on a 266 MHz Pentium II PC. The right table contains the running times of the four algorithms in Kushmerick et al. (1995).

Figure 3.21. The easy maze

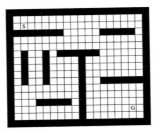

Figure 3.22. The hard maze

settings were difficult (with large sizes and difficult layouts). RS requires
no more training than Q (1000 episodes in total).

RS:

level/size	1x	2x	3x
easy	100.0(0.0)	94.6(5.1)	96.8(2.3)
hard	89.0(3.5)	57.6(8.3)	42.8(6.5)

Q:

level/size	1x	2x	3x
easy	100.0(0.0)	95.0(6.6)	90.0(7.1)
hard	73.8(12.5)	34.6(14.3)	15.6(5.5)

Figure 3.23. Learning performance

Performance is measured by the average number of successful episodes out of 100
test episodes. The standard deviations are in parentheses. RS is compared with
regular Q-learning.

In Figure 3.24, we compared all of the different algorithms mentioned
earlier. We focused mostly on difficult settings, which differentiated these
algorithms. We see RS fared well: It performed better than all of

these other algorithms, while it required a less or comparable amount of training compared with these other algorithms, because in RS there was no overlapping regions or multiple partitions to deal with. GA performed reasonably close to RS, but MRS, WA, and G all performed worse than RS in hard mazes.

	1xEasy	1xHard	2xHard	3xHard
RS	100.0(0.0)	89.0(3.5)	57.6(8.3)	42.8(6.5)
MRS	100.0(0.0)	79.0(4.9)	36.2(4.3)	20.8(4.3)
WA	100.0(0.0)	56.6(16.3)	22.0(6.2)	10.6(1.5)
GA	97.2(5.6)	86.6(8.6)	49.4(8.5)	21.8(13.2)
G	100.0(0.0)	60.2(8.3)	22.8(7.7)	13.0(4.7)

Figure 3.24. Comparisons of different algorithms
Performance is measured by the average number of successful episodes out of 100 test episodes. The standard deviations are in parentheses. See text for explanation.

The point of using different modules for different regions is to be able to specialize each learning module to a different region, in order to exploit differential characteristics of regions and to develop differential characteristics in the corresponding modules, and thus to reduce the complexity of individual modules. Comparing different modules (each for a different region), we found that the average Q values of different modules were different, which implied that different action policies were formed. Each module was indeed specialized to its corresponding region because its Q values were specifically concerned with actions in that specific region. See Sun and Peterson (1999) for a detailed analysis.

Using multiple modules may reduce the complexity of individual modules. With a backpropagation network, the complexity of a module is determined by the number of hidden units in the network. Our data (see Figure 3.25) shows that when we gradually reduced the number of hidden units in Q (a single-module algorithm) and RS (a multi-module algorithm) respectively, Q performed worse and worse, but the performance of RS was hardly affected.

The learning curves are shown in Figures 3.26 and 3.27. Figure 3.28 shows a partition of regions and trajectories through a maze to reach the

algorithm/hidden units	1xHard	2xHard	3xHard
Q /15	85.2 (11.8)	23.8 (3.3)	19.2 (3.3)
Q /7	73.8 (12.5)	34.6 (14.3)	15.6 (5.5)
Q /3	61.8 (12.4)	26.0 (2.8)	13.8 (7.4)
Q /2	41.0 (18.0)	12.9 (9.5)	2.4 (1.9)
RS /15	86.4 (5.5)	61.0 (15.4)	42.0 (9.6)
RS /7	89.0 (3.5)	57.6 (8.3)	42.8 (6.5)
RS /3	83.2 (5.7)	73.4 (6.7)	49.6 (10.9)
RS /2	79.8 (10.3)	55.8 (15.7)	52.4 (16.0)

Figure 3.25. The effect of number of hidden units
The success rates are shown here. The standard deviations are in parentheses.

goal, at the end of learning using RS.

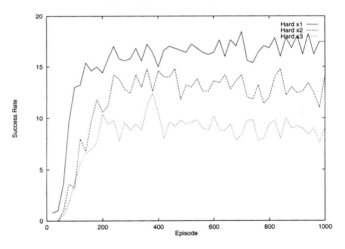

Figure 3.26. The learning curves in three hard mazes

Appendix 6: Examples of Temporal Segmentation

Let us look into two simple examples that illustrate the idea of temporal segmentation.

Maze 1. In this maze, there are two possible starting locations and one goal location. The agent occupies one cell at a time and at each step obtains

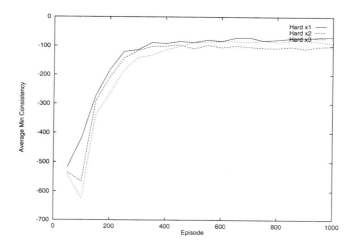

Figure 3.27. The consistency measure during learning in the three hard mazes

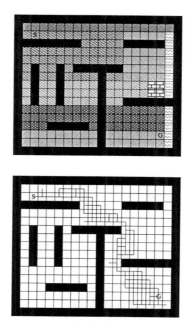

Figure 3.28. A partition of regions and 10 sample trajectories through these regions

local information concerning the four adjacent cells regarding whether each is an opening or a wall. It can make a move to any adjacent cell at each step (either go left, go right, go up, or go down). See Figure 3.29, where "1" indicates the starting cells. Each number indicates an input state as perceived by the agent. In this domain, the minimum path length (i.e., the number of steps of the optimal path from either starting cell to the goal cell) is 6. The reward for reaching the goal location is 1, and no other reward (or punishment) is given. When not all the paths are optimal, the average path length is a measure of the overall quality of a set of paths.

As shown in Figure 3.29, the three cells marked as "5" are perceived to be the same by the agent. However, different actions are required in these cells in order to obtain the shortest path to the goal. Likewise, the two cells marked as "10" are perceived to be the same but require different actions. In order to remove non-Markovian dependencies, we can divide up each possible sequence (from one of the starting cells to the goal) into a number of segments so that, when different modules are used for these segments, a consistent Markovian policy can be adopted in each module.

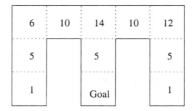

Figure 3.29. A maze requiring segmentation

Each number (randomly chosen) indicates an unique input state as perceived by the agent.

As confirmed by the results of our experiments, a single module (with atemporal representation) cannot learn the task at all (i.e., the learning curve is flat), due to oscillations (and averaging) of Q values. Adding temporal representation (i.e., memory) may partially remedy the problem, but this approach has difficulty dealing with long-range dependencies. Thus it was not used. On the other hand, as confirmed by the experiments, we can segment sequences to remove non-Markovian dependencies. In this domain, it can be easily verified that a minimum of two Q/CQ

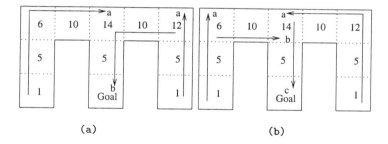

Figure 3.30. Different segmentations
(a) two pairs of modules are used. (b) three pairs of modules are used. Each
arrowed line indicates an action (sub)sequence produced by a pair of modules.

pairs are needed in order to remove non-Markovian dependencies in each
module. See Figure 3.30. However, finding the optimal paths using
only two pairs of modules is proven difficult, because the algorithm has
to be able to find switching points (between the two modules) that are
exactly right for a sequence. In general, in this domain, the more modules
there are, the easier the segmentation can be done (i.e., the faster the
learning is). This is because the more modules there are, the more
possibilities (alternatives) there are for a proper segmentation that removes
non-Markovian dependencies. An ANOVA analysis (number of pairs
of modules × block of training) shows that there is a significant main
effect of number of modules ($p < 0.05$) and a significant interaction
between number of modules and block of training ($p < 0.05$), which
indicates that the number of pairs of modules has a significant impact on
learning performance. The performance of the resulting systems is shown
in Figure 3.31, under two conditions: using the completely deterministic
policy in each module, or using a stochastic policy (with the Boltzmann
distribution action selection with $\tau = 0.006$). In either case, as indicated
by Figures 3.31, there are significant performance improvements in terms
of percentages of the optimal path traversed and in terms of the average
path length, when we go incrementally from 2 pairs of modules to 14 pairs
of modules. Pairwise t tests on successive average path lengths confirmed
this conclusion ($p < 0.05$). See Figure 3.31 for the test results.

As a variation, to reduce the complexity of this domain and thus to
facilitate learning, we limit the starting location to one of the two cells. This

# modules	Perc.Opt.Path $\tau = 0$	Perc.Opt.Path $\tau = 0.006$	Avg Length $\tau = 0.006$	t test $T(> 2.33)$
2	32%	30%	17.32	
3	46%	44%	10.54	5.387
4	66%	59%	9.50	4.959
6	83%	70%	9.33	3.649
10	90%	76%	8.88	2.617
14	92%	81%	8.10	2.184
18	93%	84%	7.50	1.207
22	96%	87%	7.53	0.175

Figure 3.31. The effect of number of pairs of modules
The effect is measured by the performance after learning, in terms of the percentage of optimal paths and the average path length (with the maximum length of 24 imposed on each path).

setting is easier because there is no need to be concerned with the other half of the maze (see Figure 3.32). The learning performance is indeed enhanced by this change. We found that this change led to better learning performance using either two, three, or four pairs of modules. Another possibilities for reducing the complexity is to always start with one module. Again, the learning performance is enhanced by this change. Therefore, segmentation performance is determined to a large extent by the inherent difficulty of the domain that we deal with. The performance changes gradually in relation to the change in the complexity of task domains.

In all, the above experiments demonstrated that proper segmentation was indeed possible. Through learning a set of Markovian processes (with atemporal representations), the algorithm removed non-Markovian dependencies and handled sequences using a (learned) chain of Markovian processes.

Maze 2. In this maze, there is one starting location at one end (marked as "2") and one goal location at the other. However, before reaching the goal location, the agent has to reach the top of each of the three arms. At each step, the agent obtains local observation concerning the four adjacent cells regarding whether each is an opening or a wall. See Figure 3.33, where each number indicates an input state as perceived by

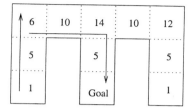

Figure 3.32. A possible segmentation using two pairs of modules
In this case, only one starting location is allowed.

the agent. The agent can make a move to any adjacent cell at each step
(either go left, go right, go up, or go down). The reward for reaching the
goal location (after visiting the tips of all the three arms) is 1.

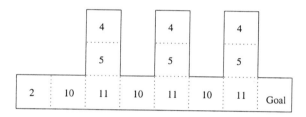

Figure 3.33. A maze requiring segmentation and reuse of modules
Each number (randomly chosen) indicates an input state as perceived by the
agent.

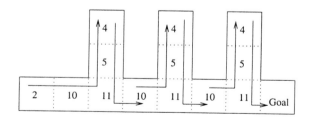

Figure 3.34. A segmentation using two pairs of modules
Each arrowed line indicates an action sequence produced by a pair of modules.
The two pairs of modules alternate.

In this domain, the shortest path has 19 steps. A minimum of two

Q/CQ pairs are needed (using atemporal input representation), in order to remove non-Markovian dependencies through segmentation and thus to obtain the shortest path. As confirmed by the results of our experiments, a single module with atemporal representation cannot learn the task at all. With two pairs of modules, there is exactly one way of segmenting the sequence (considering only the shortest path to the goal): switching to a different module at the top cell of each arm (marked as "4") and switching again at the middle cell between any two arms (marked as "10"). See Figure 3.34. This segmentation allows repeated use of the same modules along the way to the goal. When more modules are added, reuse of modules might be reduced: A third pair of module, for example, can be used in place of the second use of the first pair (Figures 3.34 and 3.35).

# modules	Perc.Opt.Path $\tau = 0$	Perc.Opt.Path $\tau = 0.001$	Avg Length $\tau = 0.001$	t test $T(> 2.33)$
2	60%	52%	22.51	
3	43%	38%	23.85	8.600
4	27%	20%	24.85	4.010
5	27%	22%	25.42	1.281

Figure 3.35. The effect of number of modules
The effect is measured by the performance after learning, in terms of the percentage of optimal paths and the average path length (with a maximum length of 39).

In all, the experiments in this domain further demonstrate the point made earlier regarding the feasibility of self-segmentation. Non-Markovian dependencies are handled through a set of Markovian processes (with atemporal representations). Furthermore, the experiments demonstrate the reuse of a module (in several different places) in a sequence or, in other words, the possibility of subroutines that can be called into use any number of times. Reuse of modules has significant advantages. It leads to the compression of descriptions of sequences. Moreover, it allows the handling of sequences that cannot be (efficiently) handled otherwise. For example, the above task could not be handled by simpler models in which segmentation was limited to a linear chaining of a small number of modules without any way of reusing modules (Wiering and Schmidhuber 1998).

Chapter 4

Accounting for Human Data
Qualitatively

> *He shapes the situation, but in conversation with it, so*
> *that his own methods and appreciations are also shaped*
> *by the situation. The phenomena that he seeks to*
> *understand are partly of his own making; he is in the*
> *situation that he seeks to understand.*
> — Donald Schon: *"Educating the Reflective Practitioner"*

In relation to the CLARION model, in this chapter, I discuss a number of general phenomena of human cognition that are related to the implicit/explicit interaction. The power of CLARION lies in accounting for many such phenomena. The focus of this chapter is on qualitative match between the human data and the model. The following phenomena are looked into: dissociation and division of labor between implicit and explicit learning, difference between implicit and explicit knowledge, interaction between implicit and explicit learning, and interaction between their resulting knowledge.

4.1 Dissociation

Can implicit and explicit learning be empirically separated as two different processes? Human learning data indicates that the answer to this question is yes. Berry and Broadbent (1988) demonstrated this point using two process control tasks that differed in the degree to which the pattern of correct responding was salient to subjects.[1] Subjects in the two different conditions learned the tasks in different ways: Subjects in the non-salient condition learned the task implicitly while subjects in the salient condition learned the task more explicitly (as demonstrated by the difference in questionnaire scores). Lee (1995) showed a similar difference, but in relation to task complexity instead of saliency. A.Cohen et al. (1990) described another similar situation in serial reaction time tasks. When complex hierarchical relations were needed in order to predict next positions, subjects tended to use implicit learning, while explicit learning was more evident when simpler relations were involved. In artificial grammar learning tasks, there were also dissociations between learning simple (pairwise) relations and learning complex hierarchical relations (Reber 1989, Mathews et al. 1989). Lee (1995) further demonstrated a reverse dissociation between implicit and explicit learning across two conditions: one with explicit instructions and the other without. With instructions, subjects did better on explicit tests than on implicit tests; without instructions, subjects did better on implicit tests than on explicit tests. There were also other corroborating findings to such dissociation results. For example, in learning physics, subjects could show different knowledge in different contexts: They showed incorrect knowledge while making explicit judgments; they nevertheless showed correct knowledge while actually performing a task (see Seger 1994).

Another line of evidence resulted from contrastive manipulations of implicit and explicit processes. First of all, through explicit search instructions, a more explicit mode of learning may be employed by subjects. The effect of such a mode change varies, depending on task difficulty. In the case of salient relations/regularities in the stimulus materials, explicit search may be more successful and thus improve performance (Reber et al. 1980, A.Cohen et al. 1990). In the case of nonsalient relations, explicit search may fail and thus lead to worsened performance (Berry and Broadbent 1988, Owen and Sweller 1985). This contrast accentuates the differences between the two types of processes: Some tasks are more

---

[1] In the salient version, the computer responded in accordance with the subjects' immediately preceding response. In the non-salient version, the computer responded in accordance with the response prior to the immediately preceding response.

amenable to explicit processes than others. Second, through verbalization, a more explicit learning mode may likewise be employed, as verbalization focuses subjects' attention explicitly on the relations and regularities in stimulus materials and thereby helps to bring them out explicitly. Verbalization usually leads to comparable or improved performance (Gagne and Smith 1962, Reber and Allen 1978, Stanley et al. 1989, Sun et al. 1998), but may sometimes lead to worsened performance (Schooler 1993, Sun et al. 2001). Third, through using dual-task conditions, a more implicit mode of learning may be attained. This is because, as has been established in the literature, such manipulation affects explicit processes more than implicit processes (Stadler 1995, Nissen and Bullemer 1987, Hayes and Broadbent 1988, Szymanski and MacLeod 1996, Dienes and Berry 1997). Dual-task conditions usually lead to worsened performance that reflects the reduction of contribution from explicit processes (Nissen and Bullemer 1987). Moreover, under dual-task conditions, the performance difference between subjects with explicit knowledge and those without may disappear (Curran and Keele 1993). Contrasting these three manipulations, we see the role played by explicit processes: Enhancing explicit processes helps performance and weakening explicit processes hinders performance. Similar changes may be attained by using other methods, some of which may also serve to illustrate the separation of the two types of processes.

Posner et al. (1997) reviewed evidence from brain imaging research that indicated the possibility of different brain regions being associated with implicit and explicit learning and memory. Such evidence relates biological findings to psychological constructs and lends additional support to the hypothesized separation of implicit and explicit processes. Keele et al. (1998) reviewed evidence from brain imaging studies and further delineated the nature of two separate learning processes. Mishkin et al. (1984) studied the contrast between (explicit) one-shot learning and (implicit) repetitious routine formation learning, using brain lesioned primates, which clearly showed physiological separation of these two types of processes. The studies involving brain damaged amnesic human patients (such as by Nissen and Bullemer 1987) indicated also that such patients were able to learn as well as normals in task settings where implicit learning was assumed to be dominant, but not in settings where explicit learning was required, which also lent support for the physiological separation of the two types of processes.

This accords well with the CLARION model. With the model, one can select one type of learning or the other, by engaging or disengaging the top level (and its learning mechanisms), or the bottom level (and its learning mechanisms). The question is how a subject decides this on the fly. I address this question next.

4.2   Division of Labor

A general pattern discernible from human data, especially those reported in the implicit learning literature, is that, if the to-be-learned relations are simple and the number of input dimensions are small (in other words, if the relations are salient to the subjects), explicit learning usually prevails; if more complex relations and a large number of input dimensions are involved, implicit learning becomes more prominent (Seger 1994, Mathews et al. 1989, Reber 1989). This pattern has been demonstrated in artificial grammar learning tasks, serial reaction time tasks, and process control tasks (e.g., sugar factory control), as reviewed earlier. Seger (1994) further pointed out that implicit learning was biased toward structures with a system of statistical relations, as indicated by the results of Kersten and Billman (1992) and Stadler (1992). The upshot of this is that the implicit learning mechanism appears more structurally sophisticated and able to handle more complex situations (e.g., Lewicki et al. 1992).

This phenomenon can be accounted for by CLARION. While explicitness of knowledge at the top level allows a variety of explicit processing, it does not lend itself easily to the learning of complex structures because of the crisp representations and the selective hypothesis-testing learning processes (Hayes and Broadbent 1988). On the other hand, in the bottom level, the distributed representation in the backpropagation network (that incorporates gradedness and temporal information through Q-learning) handles complex relations (including complex sequential relations) and high dimensionalities better. A specific instance of this complexity (salience) difference effect is as follows. In correspondence with the psychological findings that implicit learning of sequences is biased toward sequences with a high level of statistical structure, as has been shown by Elman (1990), Cleeremans and McClelland (1991), and Dienes (1992), backpropagation networks (either feedforward or recurrent) perform well in capturing complex sequences (in, e.g., serial reaction time tasks and process control tasks). On the other hand, also in correspondence with available human data, the rule learning mechanism used in the top level of CLARION has trouble handling complex stochastic sequences, due to limitations of hypothesis testing and crisp representations (as will be demonstrated later in chapter 5). Therefore, in such circumstances, while both components are present, the bottom level of the model prevails. This correspondence supports the two-level framework of CLARION. (Other instances of this difference abound, such as in terms of number of sequences, number of input dimensions, or distance of dependencies; see Sun et al. 2002).

This explanation implies that it is not necessary to deliberately and a priori decide when to use implicit or explicit learning. When complex relations and high dimensionalities are involved and the top level fails to learn (or is slow to learn), then we can expect a reliance on implicit learning at the bottom level. When the stimulus materials involved are simple, the top level may handle them better and therefore be more readily utilized. This accords well with the fact that, in most situations, both types of learning are involved with varying amounts of contributions from each (Seger 1994, Sun et al. 1998, 2001).

There have also been other views concerning division of labor, for example, in terms of procedural versus declarative processes (Anderson 1983, 1993), in terms of non-selective versus selective processing (Hayes and Broadbent 1988), in terms of algorithms versus instances (Stanley et al. 1989), or in terms of the uni-dimensional versus the multi-dimensional system (Keele et al. 1998). However, these alternative views are not as generically applicable as the implicit/explicit difference, although each of them may be supported by data in specific contexts (see chapter 9 for further discussions).

4.3 Bottom-Up Learning

As reviewed earlier, subjects' ability to verbalize is often independent of their performance on implicit learning (Berry and Broadbent 1988). Furthermore, performance typically improves earlier than explicit knowledge that can be verbalized by subjects (Stanley et al. 1989). For instance, in process control tasks, although the performance of subjects quickly rose to a high level, their verbal knowledge improved far slower:

Subjects could not provide usable verbal knowledge until near the end of their training (Stanley et al. 1989). This phenomenon has also been demonstrated by Reber and Lewis (1977) in artificial grammar learning. It appears that explicit knowledge is separable from implicit skills (or routines) and, furthermore, it is easier to acquire implicit skills (or routines) than to acquire explicit knowledge—hence the delay in the development of explicit knowledge. In addition, the delay indicates that explicit learning may be triggered by implicit learning, and the process may be described as delayed *explication* of implicit knowledge. In such cases, explicit knowledge is in a way extracted from implicit skills. Explicit learning can thus piggyback on implicit learning.

In the context of discovery tasks, Bowers et al. (1990) showed evidence of explication of implicit knowledge. When subjects were given patterns to complete, they showed implicit recognition of what a proper completion might be, although they did not have explicit recognition of a correct completion. The implicit recognition improved over time and eventually an explicit recognition was achieved. Siegler and Stern (1998) also showed in a arithmetic problem that children's strategy shifts often occurred several trials earlier than their explicit recognition of their strategy changes. Stanley et al. (1989) and Seger (1994) suggested that, due to the fact that explicit knowledge lagged behind but improved along with implicit knowledge in process control tasks (Stanley et al. 1989), explicit knowledge could be viewed as obtained from implicit knowledge. Cleeremans and McClelland (1991) also pointed out this possibility in analyzing their data.

Several developmental theorists have considered a similar delayed explication process in child development. Karmiloff-Smith (1986) suggested that developmental changes involved "representational redescription": In children, first low-level implicit representations of stimuli were formed and used; then, when more knowledge was accumulated and stable behavior patterns developed, through a redescription process, more abstract representations were formed that transformed low-level representations and made them more explicit. This redescription process repeated itself a number of times and a verbal form of representation emerged. Karmiloff-Smith (1986) proposed four representational forms: implicit, primary explicitation, secondary explicitation, and tertiary explicitation. A three-phase process was hypothesized, in which the first phase used only implicit representations and focused on input/output mappings, the second phase focused instead on gaining control over internal representations and resulted in gains in accessibility of representations, and the third phase was characterized by a balance between external information and internal knowledge. Mandler (1992) proposed a different kind of "redescription": From perceptual stimuli, relatively abstract "image-schemas" were extracted that coded several basic types of movements. Then, on top of such image-schemas, concepts were formed utilizing information therein. Based on data on perceptual analysis and categorization in infants, she suggested that an infant gradually formed "theories" of how his/her sensorimotor procedures worked and thereby gradually made such processes explicit and accessible. Although the mechanism of explicit representations had always been there (at least after the central nervous system matured), it was only with increasingly detailed perceptual analysis that such representations became detailed enough (filled up with extracted "theories") to allow conscious access. In a similar vein, Keil (1989) viewed conceptual representations as composed of an associative component (with frequency and correlational information) and a "theory" component (with explicit knowledge). Developmentally, there is a shift from associative to theory-based representations. In the data concerning learning concepts (of both natural and nominal kinds) under a variety of conditions, simple similarity-based or prototype representations dominated at first, but gradually more explicit and focused "theories" developed and became prominent. Keil (1989) pointed out that it was unlikely that "theories" developed independently, but rather they developed somehow from associative information that was already available. These theoretical models and their associated data testify to the ubiquity of implicit-to-explicit transitions.

CLARION captures this kind of bottom-up process. In the model, the bottom level develops implicit skills (or routines), on its own, using *Q-learning-Backpropagation* while the top level extracts explicit rules using *Rule-Extraction-Revision* (see chapter 3 for details). Thus, bottom-up learning naturally falls out of the model.

As reviewed earlier, there is also evidence that explicit knowledge may develop independently (with little or no correlation with implicit skills), under some circumstances. Willingham et al. (1989) reported data that were consistent with the parallel development of implicit skills and explicit knowledge. It was shown that explicit knowledge might be acquired in the absence of implicit knowledge and vice versa. Correspondingly, CLARION accounts for this phenomenon, because explicit hypothesis testing can be employed for learning rules in the top level, independent of the bottom level (as explained in chapter 2), when the to-be-learned materials are not too complex.[2]

4.4   Differences in Representation of Resulting Knowledge

Although there have been suggestions that implicit and explicit learning and performance are based on the same knowledge base, recent data support the position that the two have separate, although content-wise overlapping, knowledge bases (as hypothesized in chapter 2; see also Sun 1994, 1995). Let us see how CLARION can account for such phenomena.

In implicit learning, Reber (1989) showed that implicit learning functioned by the induction of an underlying *tacit* (i.e., implicit) representation that mirrored the structure intrinsic to the interaction of agents with the world. Seger (1994) showed that, in implicit learning, subjects developed *abstract* but *instantiated* representations. By instantiated, it is meant that representations are tied to the specific sensory modalities of stimuli; by abstract, it is meant that that the knowledge represented can be transferred or generalized to novel stimuli. On the other hand, the representation of explicit knowledge is universally accepted to be symbolic (Stanley et al. 1989, Logan 1988, Nisbett and Wilson 1977, Smolensky 1988, Dulaney et al. 1984).

CLARION captures the differing characteristics of the two types of representations. At the bottom level, an "instantiated" representation is used for the input layer of the backpropagation networks, which directly represents the modality-specific input stimuli (Rumelhart et al. 1986, Bower 1996). This type of network is also "abstract" in Seger's sense, because the distributed representations in the network provide some generalization

---

[2] Such hypothesis testing, as mentioned before, is similar to models proposed by Bruner et al. (1956), Haygood and Bourne (1965), and more recently Nosofsky et al. (1994). In AI research, many symbolic models for learning rules using hypothesis testing were proposed, such as Michalski (1983), Quinlan (1986), and Quinlan (1990), which may also be adapted for the top level of CLARION.

ability (see chapter 5; see also Rumelhart et al. 1986, Sun et al. 2001). The network is also "tacit" because of the lack of direct interpretability of the distributed representations in the networks. On the other hand, at the top level of CLARION, rules that are more abstract, less tacit, and less tied to specific sensory modalities are learned (due to generalization in rule learning) and represented symbolically, which capture subjects' explicit knowledge (Smolensky 1988, Sun 1994, 1997, 1999).

4.5 Differences in Accessibility of Resulting Knowledge

It has also been argued that some knowledge (i.e., implicit knowledge) is, for the most part, not consciously accessible (Reber 1989, Lewicki et al. 1992, Seger 1994). There is some disagreement concerning what experimentally constitutes accessibility.[3] Despite such difficulties, it is generally agreed that at least some part of skilled (routine) performance is not conscious under normal circumstances (by whatever experimental measures and whatever operational definitions) (cf. Reber 1989, Dulaney et al. 1984, Reber et al. 1985). Reber (1989) pointed out that "although it is misleading to argue that implicitly acquired knowledge is completely unconscious, it is not misleading to argue that implicitly acquired epistemic contents of mind are always richer and more sophisticated than what can be explicated".

Consistent with the idea of bottom-up learning, Reber (1989) further pointed out: "Knowledge acquired from implicit learning procedures is knowledge that, in some raw fashion, is always ahead of the capability of its possessor to explicate it." For example, Mathews et al. (1989) asked their subjects in a process control task to periodically explicate the rules that they used, and the information was then given to yoked subjects who were then tested on the same task (see also Stanley et al. 1989). Over time, the original subjects improved their performance and also their verbalization of explicit knowledge, as evidenced by the improvement of performance by the later groups of yoked subjects. However, yoked subjects never caught up with original subjects, thus suggesting both the hypothesis of

---

[3] It is also difficult to distinguish between explicit knowledge that is used consciously when the task is being performed and explicit knowledge that is retroactively attributed to the task performance at a later time, for example, when verbal reports are given (Nisbett and Wilson 1977, Kelley and Jacoby 1993, Sun et al. 2001).

delayed explication (as discussed before) and that of relative inexplicability of implicit skills.

Such results are explained by the CLARION model, in which delayed explication is the result of the bottom-up learning process and inexplicability of implicit skills is the result of distributed representations used in backpropagation networks at the bottom level, which is always richer and more complex than crisp, explicit representations used in the top level.

4.6   Differences in Flexibility, Generalizability, and Robustness

It has been shown that implicit learning entails less flexibility in resulting knowledge than explicit learning (Seger 1994, Berry and Broadbent 1988, Stanley et al. 1989, Karmiloff-Smith 1986). As mentioned earlier, implicit learning results in knowledge that is more tied to specific stimulus modalities and other specifics of learning environments (Seger 1994, Dienes and Berry 1997), less reflective (e.g., lacking meta-knowledge due to the implicitness; Chan 1992), and less adaptable to changing situations (Hayes and Broadbent 1988). In a similar vein, based on psycholinguistic data, Karmiloff-Smith (1986) observed that with the growth of explicit representations, more and more flexibility was shown by subject children.

CLARION accounts for the higher degree of flexibility of explicit knowledge as follows: With explicit (i.e., localist) representations at the top level of CLARION, a variety of explicit manipulations can be performed that are not available to the bottom level. For example, backward and forward chaining reasoning, counterfactual reasoning, explicit hypothesis testing learning, and so on can be used individually or in combination. These capacities lead to heightened flexibility of the top level. Thus, CLARION explains the observed difference in flexibility between the two types of processes.

As observed in many experiments, following implicit learning, subjects are able to handle novel stimuli, or in other words, to generalize. In artificial grammar learning, Reber (1967, 1976) found good transfer to strings involving different letters but based on the same grammar. Berry and Broadbent (1988) showed that subjects trained on one process control task could transfer to another that had a similar cover story and an identical underlying relation. As shown by Vokey and Brooks (1992) and others, both the similarity between a novel stimulus and learned stimuli and more abstract commonalities between them (such as grammars and common category assignments) were employed in generalization.

The bottom level of CLARION, which contains backpropagation networks, has the ability to capture generalization exhibited in implicit learning. Generalization has been amply demonstrated in backpropagation networks in various contexts: Elman (1990) reported good generalization of sequences by recurrent backpropagation networks in artificial grammar learning; Pollack (1991) found generalization of such networks to arbitrarily long sequences; Cleeremans and McClelland (1991) and Dienes (1992) modeled data in artificial grammar learning with such networks. As in human learning, generalization in networks is based in part on similarity of old and new sequences but also in part on certain structures exhibited by the sequences. Explicit processes in the top level of CLARION can also generalize, albeit following a different style via explicit hypothesis formation and testing. This alternative style of generalization has been investigated by hypothesis-testing psychology (e.g., Bruner et al. 1956, Haygood and Bourne 1965, Dominowski 1972).

It has also been observed that implicit processes are more robust than explicit processes (Reber 1989) in the face of internal disorder and malfunctioning. For example, Hasher and Zacks (1979) found that encoding of frequency information (an implicit process) was correctly performed by clinically depressed patients, although they could not perform explicit tasks. Warrington and Weiskrantz (1982) found that amnesics were more successful in performing implicit rather than explicit memory tasks. Implicit processes are also more robust in the face of dual-task distractions, as shown by Curran and Keele (1993).

This effect of differing degrees of robustness can be explained within the dual-representation framework of CLARION: While the top level employs localist representations and is thus more vulnerable to malfunctioning, the bottom level utilizes distributed representations that are more resistant to distractions, damages and faults, as demonstrated amply in connectionist modeling (e.g., Rumelhart et al. 1986, Plaut and Shallice 1994).

4.7   Initiation of Performance

What are the respective roles of explicit and implicit processes in skilled (routine) performance? Existing evidence indicates that implicit processes often, if not always, initiate actions in advance of explicit awareness. Libet (1985) reported that electrophysiological "readiness potentials" (RPs) always preceded conscious initiation of an act that was fully endogenous and voluntary. The onset of conscious, explicit intention to act was 350 ms behind the initiation of RPs. After a conscious intention to act appeared, whether the action actually took place or not could still be decided explicitly within a time period somewhere between 100 and 200 ms. As suggested by Libet (1985), the role of explicit processes was not to initiate a specific course of action, but to control and influence implicitly selected and initiated actions. Kelley and Jacoby (1993) also showed that an important function of explicit processes was to oppose, or counterbalance, the influence of the implicit.

This view is also consistent with voluminous data on the ever-present role of implicit (unconscious) processes in various kinds of tasks, such as lexical priming, semantic processing, visual attention, perception, and so on (as discussed in Velmans 1991, Marcel 1983). Velmans (1991) summarized evidence for the existence of implicit (preconscious) analysis of input stimuli, implicit processing of semantic content (Lewis 1970), and implicit processing of bilingual messages (Treisman 1964). Some of these implicit processes happened not only in unattended channels (i.e., modalities that had no conscious focus of attention) but also in the attended channel (involving messages that were consciously attended to). Most of the findings supported the possibility that implicit processes started before explicit processes took hold. For example, in a word recognition experiment, a word might not be explicitly processed until it was recognized as an English word. However, before any such recognition happened, a series of implicit acoustic and semantic comparisons took place in preparation for the recognition (Velmans 1991).

Willingham et al. (1989) posited that, in skilled (routine) performance, the effects from the two types of processes were "superimposed" on each other, so that they complemented each other. This was accomplished through using explicit knowledge to affect, alter, and rectify implicit processes that were in direct control of actions.

CLARION embodies this phenomenon by its design, in that the bottom level, which captures implicit processes, works independently and initiates processing without the involvement of the top level. However, along with the initiation of an action, the activation of the relevant nodes representing sensory inputs at the bottom level can lead to the activation of the corresponding representations at the top level (if they exist), by the bottom-up information flow. The activated explicit representations and their associated explicit knowledge (if such knowledge is available) can in turn influence implicit processing at the bottom level, in ways of modifying its outcomes. Thus, implicit processes, which directly control actions in skilled performance, incorporate outcomes of explicit processes to achieve skilled performance.

4.8   Knowledge Interaction

Interaction of various sorts between implicit and explicit processes exists. Let us look specifically into the interaction of implicit and explicit knowledge in learning and in performance.

With regard to the use of explicit knowledge to affect implicit processes (top-down information), the existing literature suggests that explicit knowledge may help subjects to learn when it directs subjects to focus on relevant features, or when it heightens subjects' sensitivity to relevant information (see, e.g., Reber et al. 1980 and Howard and Ballas 1980). Explicit knowledge may also help subjects to deal with high-order relations (Premack 1988). However, as Reber (1976, 1989) has discussed, explicit knowledge may also hamper implicit learning, especially (1) when explicit prior instructions induce an explicit learning mode in subjects performing a task for which explicit learning is not suitable (e.g., Schooler et al. 1993), or (2) when explicit knowledge is contradictory to the implicit learning that subjects are undergoing and the tacit representations used by the subjects (see Dulaney et al. 1984). Owen and Sweller's (1985) findings that learning might be hampered when certain explicit processes such as means-ends analysis were encouraged also supported this idea.

On the other hand, we know less about how implicit knowledge is used to affect explicit processes (bottom-up information). We posit that implicit knowledge *is* used in explicit learning and explicit performance (e.g., in certain verbalization), and this reverse influence, given proper circumstances, can be at least as strong as the case of top-down influences. As indicated by the discussion earlier, implicit processes handle more complex relations (Berry and Broadbent 1988, Lewicki et al. 1992), and can thus help explicit processes by providing them with relevant information. Implicit processes are also better at keeping track of frequency statistics and may use them to aid explicit processes in useful ways (Hasher and Zacks 1979, Gluck and Bower 1988, Lewicki et al. 1987).

However, there is a tendency for subjects, during explicit tasks (e.g., verbal reasoning), to ignore the outcomes of implicit processes when they contradict explicit knowledge or explicit mental models that subjects hold (Seger 1994). For example, Murphy and Medin (1985)'s experiments demonstrated that concept formation was not merely a feature similarity based implicit process. Explicit prior theory played an important part and could overwrite feature similarity based decisions. Rips (1989) demonstrated a similar point. Wisniewski and Medin (1994) further delineated the possible ways in which such interaction might happen. Stanley et al. (1989) interpreted the difficulty their subjects had with verbalizing their knowledge used in task performance as the interference of subjects' explicit, prior domain knowledge (or mental models) upon the explication (verbalization) of their implicit knowledge.[4]

As detailed in chapter 2, the interaction of explicit and implicit processes is captured in CLARION with the dual-representation framework and the inter-level interaction mechanism, which allows a proper mixture of the top level and the bottom level through stochastic selection that captures the "superimposition" of the effects of the two levels. Conflicts between the two types of knowledge occur either when the development of explicit knowledge lags behind the development of implicit one, or when standalone hypothesis testing learning methods are used in the top level to acquire its knowledge independent of the bottom level (chapter 2). When conflicts occur, the interaction mechanism of CLARION allows it to ignore the bottom level (in explicit reasoning), or to ignore the top level (in implicit performance), in ways consistent with human data.

---

[4] As discussed by Nisbett and Wilson (1977), such mental models are composed of cultural rules, causal schemata, causal hypotheses generated on the fly, and so on.

4.9   Synergy

Why are there two separate (although interacting) systems? There need to be reasons other than mere redundancy (e.g., for the sake of fault-tolerance). The discussion in section 2 concludes that there is a division of labor between explicit and implicit processes. We may further hypothesize that there may be a synergy between the two types of processes (on the basis of dissociation between the two types of knowledge as discussed in section 1). Such a synergy may show up, under right circumstances, in ways of speeding up learning, improving learned performance, and facilitating transfer of learned skills.

As mentioned earlier, there is indeed some psychological evidence in support of this hypothesis. In terms of speeding up learning, Willingham et al. (1989) found that those subjects who acquired full explicit knowledge in serial reaction time tasks appeared to learn faster than those who did not have full explicit knowledge. Stanley et al. (1989) reported that in a process control task, subjects' learning improved if they were asked to generate verbal instructions for other subjects during learning (i.e., verbalization). That is, a subject is able to speed up his/her own learning through an explication process that generates explicit knowledge. Reber and Allen (1978) showed similar effects of verbalization. Mathews et al. (1989) showed that a better performance could be attained if a proper mix of implicit and explicit learning was used (in their case, through devising an experimental condition in which first implicit learning and later explicit learning was encouraged). See also Biederman and Shiffrar (1987).

In addition, in terms of learned performance, Willingham et al. (1989) found that subjects who verbalized while performing serial reaction time tasks were able to attain a higher level of performance than those who did not verbalize, as the requirement that they verbalized their knowledge prompted the formation and utilization of explicit knowledge. Squire and Frambach (1990) reported that initially, amnesic and normal subjects performed comparably in a process control task and equally lacked explicit knowledge. However, with more training, normals achieved better performance than amnesics and also better scores on explicit knowledge measures, which pointed to the conjecture that it was the fact that normal subjects were able to learn explicit knowledge, which amnesics could not learn, that helped them to achieve better performance. Consistent with this conclusion, Estes (1986) suggested that implicit learning alone could not lead to optimal levels of performance. Even in high-level skill acquisition, similar effects were observed. Gick and Holyoak (1980) found that good problem solvers could better state rules that described their actions in problem solving. Bower and King (1967) showed that verbalization improved performance in classification rule learning. Gagne and Smith (1962) showed the same effect of verbalization in learning Tower of Hanoi. This phenomenon may be related, to some extent, to the self-explanation effect reported in the cognitive skill acquisition literature (Chi et al. 1989): Subjects who explained the examples in physics textbooks more completely did better in solving new problems. In all of these cases, it could be the explication process and the use of explicit knowledge that helped the performance.

In terms of facilitating transfer of learned skills (routines), Willingham et al. (1989) obtained some suggestive evidence that explicit knowledge facilitated transfer of skilled performance. They reported that (1) subjects who acquired explicit knowledge in a training task tended to have faster response times in a transfer task; (2) these subjects were also more likely to acquire explicit knowledge in the transfer task; and (3) these subjects who acquired explicit knowledge responded more slowly when the transfer task was unrelated to the training task, suggesting that the explicit knowledge of the previous task might have interfered with the performance of the transfer task. In high-level domains, Ahlum-Heath and DiVesta (1986) found that the subjects who were required to verbalize while solving Tower of Hanoi problems performed better on a transfer task after training than the subjects who were not required to verbalize. Berry (1983) similarly showed in Watson's selection task that verbalization during learning improved transfer performance.

It has been demonstrated in our experiments (see Sun et al. 1998, 2001) that CLARION can produce similar synergy effects as identified above (along with other effects in different settings), through comparing various training conditions, such as comparing the verbalization condition and the non-verbalization condition (whereby the verbalization condition encourages explicit learning), or comparing the dual-task condition and the single-task condition (whereby the dual-task condition discourages explicit learning). See chapter 5 for more details. Although the idea of synergy has been mentioned before (e.g., Mathews et al. 1989), CLARION demonstrated in computational terms the very process by which synergy was created (Sun and Peterson 1998b, Sun et al. 2001), which had a lot to do with differing characteristics of the two levels (sections 4–6).

Note that these synergy effects are dependent on experimental settings. They are not universal. Even so, it should still be recognized that explicit processes play important cognitive functions. Cleeremans and McClelland (1991) and Gibson et al. (1997) both pointed to the need to include explicit processes even in modeling typically implicit learning tasks. Explicit processes also serve additional functions such as facilitating verbal communication and acting as gate-keepers (e.g., enabling conscious veto; Libet 1985).

4.10 Summary

To sum up, in this chapter, I discussed the following issues through qualitatively examining a variety of data: (1) the separation of two types of processes (in sections 1 and 2), and how CLARION captures it; (2) the differing characteristics of the two types of processes (in sections 4–6), and how they correspond with CLARION; (3) the possible ways of interaction between the two types of processes (in sections 3, 7, and 8), and how CLARION captures them; and finally (4) the possible consequences of the interaction (in section 9), and how CLARION captures them as well.

Through this discussion, I argued for the following points:

- the usefulness of incorporating both explicit and implicit processes in theorizing about cognition,
- the importance of the interaction of the two types of processes in learning and in performance, and the importance of their synergy resulting from the interaction,
- the psychological plausibility of bottom-up learning through the interaction of the two types of processes.

Now I will move on to demonstrate some *quantitative* match between the model and human data.

Chapter 5

Accounting for Human Data Quantitatively

Nevertheless, it is by no means easy to decide just what is meant by reason, or how the peculiar thinking process called reasoning differs from other thought-sequences which may lead to similar results.
— William James: *"The Principles of Psychology"*

The qualitative match between CLARION and human data has been described in the previous chapter. To substantiate these points, we conducted simulations of human data using CLARION. We have found some substantial quantitative match between CLARION and human data (Sun et al. 2001, Sun et al. 2002). In this chapter, I describe a set of experiments, and the quantitative match that we have found, in a wide range of tasks.

5.1 Introduction

In order to generate a quantitative match between the model and human data, a number of well known learning tasks were chosen to be simulated with CLARION. The set of tasks spans the spectrum of different degrees of cognitive involvement, ranging from simple reactive tasks to cognitively more complex tasks. These simulated tasks include serial reaction time (SRT) tasks, artificial grammar learning (AGL) tasks, process control (PC) tasks, the Tower of Hanoi (TOH) task, and the minefield navigation (MN) task. Sun et al. (1998, 2001) and Sun et al. (2002) contain the full discussion of the simulations of these tasks. I will discuss a few of these simulations in this chapter to highlight the quantitative match between the model and the human data.

Let me mention a few generic issues concerning all of these simulations. In simulating these tasks, we used the same *Q-Learning-Backpropagation* (QBP) and *Rule-Extraction-Revision* (RER) algorithms at the bottom and the top level of CLARION respectively, although some details varied from task to task as appropriate. Although alternative encodings and algorithms (such as recurrent backpropagation networks at the bottom level) were also possible, I felt that our choices were reasonable ones, supported by existing theories and data (Sun et al. 2002).

We focused on capturing the interaction of the two levels in the human data, whereby the respective contributions of the two levels were discernible through various experimental manipulations of learning settings that encouraged differential emphases on the two levels. We wanted to see how these data could be captured and interpreted using a two-level interactive and bottom-up perspective.

We looked into a number of experimental manipulations that led to what we interpreted as the synergy effects. These manipulations, or experimental conditions, are:

- The explicit search instruction condition, in which subjects were encouraged to perform explicit search for regularities in stimuli that might aid in task performance. See, for example, Reber et al. (1980), Owen and Sweller (1985) and Schooler et al. (1993).

- The explicit how-to instruction condition, in which subjects were told specifically how the tasks should be performed, including providing detailed information concerning regularities in stimulus materials. See, for example, Stanley et al. (1989) and Berry and Broadbent (1988).

- The verbalization condition, in which subjects were asked to verbalize (to specify, explain, or justify) what they did, either concurrently with task performance or afterwards. See, for example, Stanley et al. (1989) and Berry (1983).

- The dual-task condition, in which, while performing a primary task, subjects were also required to perform a secondary, distracting task. See, for example, Gagne and Smith (1962), Reber and Allen (1978), and Stanley et al. (1989).

The synergy effects (and the detrimental effects) can be discerned by comparing single-task versus dual-task conditions, instructed versus uninstructed conditions, or verbalizing versus non-verbalizing conditions. The relative contributions of the two levels are manipulated through these conditions. The verbalization condition, compared with no verbalization, tends to reflect more of explicit processes, that is, a higher degree of contribution from the top level (Ahlum-Heath and DiVesta 1986, Squire and Frambach 1990, Stanley et al. 1989). It may lead to enhanced performance, but may also lead to worsened performance when too much verbalization is involved (Sun et al. 2001). Dual-tasks interfere with top-level explicit processes, compared with single-task conditions, and may lead to the slow-down of learning that reflects more the working of implicit processes (Nissen and Bullemer 1987, Dienes and Fahey 1995). Explicit how-to instructions help to enhance top-level processes, and thus may lead to improved performance (Stanley et al. 1989). Explicit search instructions, on the other hand, may emphasize more top-level activities and lead to improved performance, but may also weaken bottom-level implicit processes and lead to worsened performance for certain types of tasks (Reber et al. 1980, Owen and Sweller 1985, and Schooler et al. 1993).

To capture each individual manipulation, we do the following:

- The explicit how-to instruction condition is modeled using the explicit encoding of the given knowledge at the top level (prior to the training).

- The verbalization condition is captured in simulation through changes in parameter values that encourage more top-level activities, compared with non-verbalization conditions, consistent with existing understanding of the effect of verbalization (that is, subjects become more explicit).

- The explicit search condition is captured through changes in parameter values that encourage more reliance on top-level rule learning activities, in correspondence with what we normally observe in subjects.

- The dual-task condition is captured through changes in parameter values that reduce top-level activities, because, when distracted by a secondary (explicit) task, top-level processes will be less active in relation to the primary task (Stadler 1995, Nissen and Bullemer 1987,

Szymanski and MacLeod 1996, Dienes and Berry 1997).[1]

- Finally, given same conditions, subjects may differ in terms of the explicitness of their resulting knowledge after training (some are more aware of their knowledge, while other less aware; Willingham et al. 1989, Curran and Keeele 1993). The individual difference in degree of awareness is captured by different parameter settings: More aware subjects have parameter settings that allow more rule learning to occur.

Note that for modeling each of these manipulations, usually only a few rule learning parameter values were changed. I will specify these parameters later on when describing experiments.

Many parameters in the model were set uniformly: Network weights were randomly initialized between -0.01 and 0.01; the Q-value discount rate was 0.95; the temperature (randomness parameter) for stochastic decision making was set at 0.01; no gradual lowering of temperature or learning rates was used; no limit on the size of rule sets was used; the combination weights were set at $w_1 = 0.2$ and $w_2 = 0.8$. The density parameter was set at 1/50; the probability parameter was set at 1. In this work, these values were not free parameters, because they were set in an a priori manner and not varied to match human data.

Some other parameters are domain-specific because they are likely adjusted in relation to domain characteristics. For example, the numbers of input, output, and hidden units are set in a domain specific way. The same goes for the external reward, the rule learning thresholds, the backpropagation learning rate, and the momentum. These values are generally optimized (in some way) with respect to each domain, and not varied to match human data. The true free parameters, however, are those used to capture variations of experimental conditions, such as the rule learning thresholds, which have been mentioned earlier and will be described more later.

This set of experiments highlights the importance of the interaction of implicit and explicit processes in human cognition. They reveal something new in the existing data: We show that synergy (as well as detrimental effects) may result from interaction, through examining a variety of relevant

---

[1] There have been alternative interpretations of dual-task conditions, for example, in terms of mixed modality sequences (Keele et al. 1998). However, such alternatives are not very well established.

data and through capturing the data in our simulation. With fairly detailed comparisons between the human and the model data, these simulations shed light on the plausible ways these data might be generated. The contribution of this work lies not only in capturing a range of human data through the interaction of the two types of processes, but also in demonstrating the psychological plausibility of bottom-up learning as embodied in CLARION.

The emphasis here is not on fine-grained modeling of each task involved, but a broad-stroke coverage of a variety of tasks. The scope is broader and thus the model is coarser, by necessity. The simulation may overlook a few phenomena in these tasks that we consider to be of secondary importance, or may focus on only a few data sets of a task instead of all. This "oversight" may actually be beneficial. As in any function approximation or data fitting situations, we have to strike a balance between fitting data faithfully and avoiding fitting noise in the data (that is, overfitting). Coarser-grained modeling may be beneficial in this regard. Finally, a broad-scoped but coarse-grained synthesis of a range of data is essential to the goal of understanding the general principles of cognition, which is what I aim for in this work.

5.2   Simulating Serial Reaction Time Tasks

In this type of task, we aim to capture (1) the degree of awareness effect, (2) the salience difference effect, (3) the explicit how-to instructions effect, and (4) the dual-task effect. We utilize the human data reported in Lewicki et al. (1987), and Curran and Keele (1993).

Some technical details concerning model setup were as follows. For this type of task, we used a simplified QBP in which temporal credit assignment was not used. This was because we predicted one position at a time, with immediate feedback, and thus there was no need for backwards temporal credit assignment. $Q(x, a)$ computes the likelihood of the next position a, given the information concerning the current and past positions x. The actual probability of choosing a as the current prediction (of the next position) is determined based on the Boltzmann distribution (described earlier in chapter 3). The error signal used in the simplified QBP for updating the network is as follows:

$$\Delta Q(x, a) = \alpha(r + \gamma \max_{b}(x, b) - Q(x, a)) = \alpha(r - Q(x, a))$$

where x is the input, a is one of the outputs (the current prediction), $r = 1$ if a is the correct prediction, $r = 0$ if a is not the correct prediction, and $\gamma \max_b(x, b)$ is set to zero.[2]

5.2.1 Simulating Lewicki et al. (1987)

The serial reaction time task used in Lewicki et al. (1987) was based on matrix scanning: Subjects were to scan a matrix, determine the quadrant of a target digit (the digit 6) and respond by pressing the key corresponding to that quadrant. Each experimental block consisted of six identification trials followed by one matrix scanning trial. In identification trials, the target appeared in one of the quadrants and the subject was to press the corresponding keys. In matrix scanning trials, the target was embedded among 36 digits in a matrix but the subject's task was the same. See Figure 5.1. In each block of 7 trials, the actual location of the target in the 7th (matrix scanning) trial was determined by the sequence of the 6 preceding identification trials (out of which 4 were relevant). 24 rules were used to determine the location of the target on the 7th trial. Each of these rules mapped the target quadrants in the 6 identification trials to the target location on the 7th trials in each block. 24 (out of a total of 36) locations were possible for the target to appear. The major dependent variable, the variable that we wanted to predict, was the reaction time on the 7th trial in each block.

The whole experiment consists of 48 segments, each of which consists of 96 blocks (so there are a total of 4,608 blocks). During the first 42 segments, the afore-mentioned rules are used to determined target locations. However, on the 43rd segment, a switch occurs that reverses the outcomes of the rule set: The upper left is now replaced by the lower right, the lower left is now replaced by upper right, and so on. The purpose is to separate unspecific learning (e.g., motor learning) from prediction learning (i.e., learning to predict the target location on the 7th trial).

The reaction time data of three subjects were obtained by Lewicki et al. (1987). See Figure 5.3. Each curve showed a steady decrease of reaction

---

[2] This simplified version is in fact similar to straight backpropagation (except that we only update one of the outputs at each step—the output that is used as the current prediction). We also tried the full-fledged QBP instead of the simplified version described above. We obtained comparable results from this alternative approach as well.

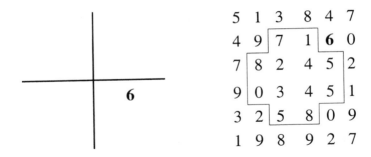

Figure 5.1. The simple identification trial and the matrix scanning trial

times up until the switch point. At that point, there was a significant increase of reaction times. After that, the curve became gradually lowered again. Lewicki et al. (1987) pointed out that the result showed that the subjects learned to predict the locations of the 7th trials. Hence the decrease in reaction time up to the 42nd segment and the increase after the switch (which thwarted their predictions).

Here are some details of the model setup for simulating this experiment (Sun et al. 2002). The simplified QBP was used. Inputs represented sequences of 6 elements, with each element having 4 values (for 4 different quadrants). (A sequence of 6 elements was assumed to be within the capacity of the short-term working memory.) Outputs represented predictions of 7th elements in sequences. Thus, 24 input units (representing 6 elements, with 4 values each), 24 output units (one for each possible location of the 7th element of a sequence), and 18 hidden units were used. The model was trained by presenting the stimulus materials in the same way as in the human experiment described above, without any further embellishments or repetitions of the materials. We tried various parameter settings.

Because in this experiment there were a total of 4^4 sequences with each consisting of 7 elements, it was too complex for subjects to discern the sequence structures explicitly, as demonstrated in human experiments through explicit tests by Lewicki et al. (1987). Computationally, no rule was extracted in the model, because the large number of sequences entailed the lack of sufficient repetitions of any particular sequence throughout the experiments, which prevented the model from extracting any rule. The density parameter was set to be 1/50; that is, at least one repetition (of a sequence) was necessary every 50 trials. In this task, there were 4,608 presentations of sequences and there were 4^4 sequences, and thus on average the repetition rate was only 0.004504. Therefore, our simulation involved only the bottom level of the model (with the simplified QBP).

We were able to create an error rate curve going downwards resembling Lewicki's reaction time curves (averaged over 10 runs, to ensure its representativeness). See Figure 5.2. The model succeeded in predicting with 100% accuracy the target positions in all the sequences at the end of the 42 segments. The question is how we should translate error rate into reaction time.

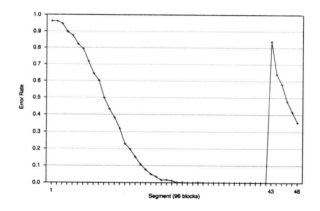

Figure 5.2. The model prediction errors

One way of translation is through a linear transformation from error rate to reaction time (as argued for by, e.g., Mehwort et al. 1992 and as used in many existing simulations); that is, $RT_i = a * e_i + b$, where RT_i is the reaction time (in ms), e_i is the error rate, and a and b are two free parameters. For each set of human data, we adjust the parameters to match the data. One possible interpretation of linear transformation is that it specifies the time needed by a subject to search for a target item and the time needed by a subject to respond to a target item without searching (through correctly predicting its location); that is,

$$RT_i = ae_i + b = b(1 - e_i) + (a + b)e_i$$

where b is interpreted as the time needed to respond to an item without searching, since $1 - e_i$ is the probability of successfully predicting the location of a target item, and $a + b$ is interpreted as the time needed to respond to an item by first searching for it and then responding to it after finding it. So, instead of relying on additional functions and parameters (as in, e.g., Ling and Marinov 1994), this method relies only on error rate to account for human performance in terms of reaction time.

Another way of generating reaction time from prediction accuracy is through an alternative formula (used by Ling and Marinov 1994):

$$RT_i = t_1(1 - e_i) + t_2 e_i + B\alpha^{-t}$$

where t_1 is the time needed to respond when there is no search (using correct predictions), t_2 is the time needed to respond when search is necessary, B is the initial motor response time, and α is the rate at which the motor response time decreases. The third term is meant to capture unspecific practice effects (mostly resulting from motor learning). In other words, in this formula, we separate the motor response time from the search time and the prediction time (as represented by t_1 and t_2 respectively). Note that, if we set $B = 0$, we have $t_1 = b$ and $t_2 = a + b$ and thus this equation becomes the same as the previous one. This formula takes into account the independent nature of motor learning, as separate from the learning of prediction of target locations. However, it involves two more free parameters.

Using the linear transformation (without the power function), we generated three sets of data from the error rate curve reported earlier, one for matching each human subject in Lewicki et al.'s (1987), using different a and b values for each subject. As shown in Figure 5.4, the model outcomes fit the human data well up to the point of switching (segment 41). When the switch to a random sequence happened, the model's reaction time became much worsened whereas the subject's reaction time suffered only slightly.

Subject 1:	$a = 320$	$b = 430$
Subject 2:	$a = 860$	$b = 620$
Subject 3:	$a = 170$	$b = 530$

Figure 5.3. Parameters for matching Lewicki's data

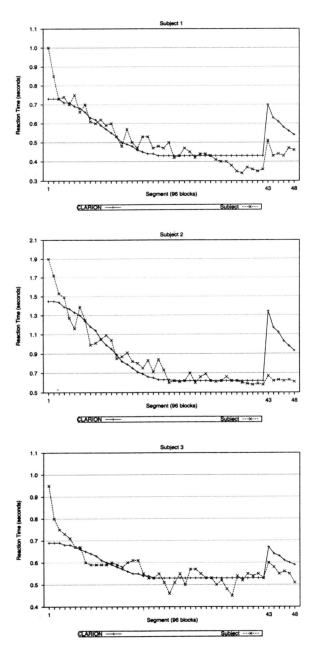

Figure 5.4. Matching Lewicki's data using linear transformation

Therefore, we added the power function. After adding the power function, we re-fit the parameters. The effect of adding the power function was that we reduced the contribution from the model prediction (i.e., the error rates e_i) because we took into consideration the contribution from the power function. In this way, we obtained a much better match of the human data after the switch while maintaining a good match before the switch. This comparison suggested that the amount of benefit the human subjects got from their predictions (by lowering e_i) was, although significant, relatively small. Significant benefit was gained through the improvement of motor response as represented by the power function. See Figure 5.6. Note that in the figure, we used exactly the same parameter settings (for a, b, B, and α) as in Ling and Marinov (1994). These parameters could be further optimized, which, in our experiments, led to a slightly better fit but the difference was not significant (Sun et al. 2002).

Subject 1:	$t_1 = 150$	$t_2 = 350$	$B = 700$	$\alpha = 0.33$
Subject 2:	$t_1 = 150$	$t_2 = 350$	$B = 1600$	$\alpha = 0.33$
Subject 3:	$t_1 = 100$	$t_2 = 210$	$B = 800$	$\alpha = 0.19$

Figure 5.5. Parameters for matching Lewicki's data with power functions

The match between our model and the human data was excellent, as measured by the sum-squared error. Compared with Ling and Marinov's match, CLARION (with the power function) did better on two of the three subjects, using the same parameters as Ling and Marinov for transformation. See Figure 5.7 for a comparison.

Along with the simulation of Curran and Keele's (1993) data (see the next subsection), the simulation of Lewicki et al.'s (1987) data demonstrated in some way the salience difference effect. That is, when the stimuli were highly non-salient as in Lewicki et al.'s experiments, the learning process was completely implicit. On the other hand, when the stimuli were more salient as in Curran and Keele's (1993) experiments, some explicit learning was involved, as described below.

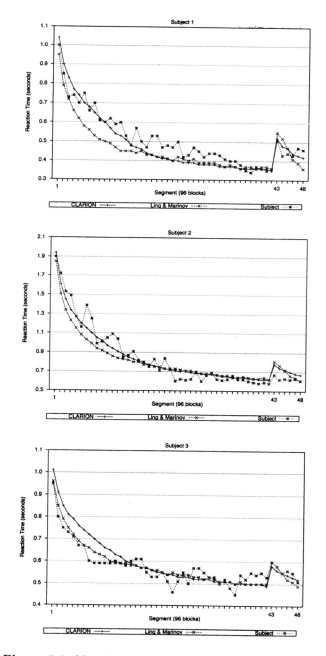

Figure 5.6. Matching Lewicki's data with power functions

	Subject 1	Subject 2	Subject 3
CLARION w/o power function	0.30	1.85	0.14
CLARION w/ power function	0.07	0.25	0.05
Ling& Marinov (1994)	0.14	0.43	0.04

Figure 5.7. Comparing the goodness of fit

5.2.2   Simulating Curran and Keele (1993)

The experiments of Curran and Keele (1993) consisted of presenting a repeating sequence of X marks, each in one of the four possible positions. The subjects were instructed to press the key corresponding to the position of each X mark. Reaction times of the subjects were recorded. The experiment was divided into three phases (in succession): dual task practice, single task learning, and dual task transfer. In the first phase (consisting of two blocks of 120 trials each), the positions of X marks were purely random to allow subjects to get used to the task setting, under a dual-task condition. The second phase was where learning occurred: There were five sequence blocks (blocks 3-6 and 8), where the positions followed a sequential pattern of length 6, and one random block (block 7). Each block consisted of 120 trials. The third phase tested transfer to a dual-task condition (with a secondary tone counting task): Three random blocks (blocks 9, 10, and 12) and a single sequence block (block 11) were presented. A total of 57 subjects were tested.

   Three groups of subjects were identified in the analysis of data: "less aware", "more aware", and "intentional". The "intentional" subjects were given explicit instructions about the exact sequence used before learning started. The "more aware" subjects were those who correctly specified at least four out of six positions in the sequence (which measured the amount of explicit knowledge), and the rest were "less aware" subjects. The difference in reaction time between the random block (block 7) and the sequential blocks (blocks 6 and 8) was used to measure the amount of learning. ANOVA (intentional vs. more aware vs. less aware × sequential vs. random) was done. The analysis showed that, while the "intentional" group performed the best, the "more aware" group performed close to the "intentional" group, both significantly better than the "less aware" group, demonstrating the effect of explicit knowledge. However, during the transfer to the dual-task condition, all three groups performed poorly. There was notably no significant difference between the three groups. However, there was significant difference between the random blocks (blocks 10 and 12) and the sequential block (block 11). So learning did occur despite the poor performance. See Figure 5.8 for the reaction time data for the three groups. The finding of primary interest here is that the difference in explicit knowledge led to the difference in performance during phase 2 and the performance difference dissipated under the dual-task condition during phase 3, which was known to suppress explicit knowledge.

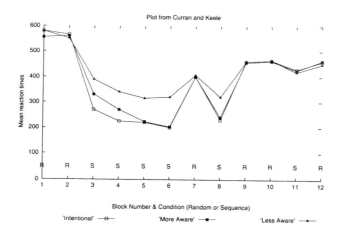

Figure 5.8. The reaction time data from Curran and Keele (1993)

In the simulation model (Sun et al. 2002), the simplified QBP were used at the bottom level as in the simulation of Lewicki et al. We used a network with 7 × 6 input units and 5 output units for handling both the SRT primary task and a secondary tone counting task. Seven groups of input units represented a moving window of seven steps preceding the current step (with seven being roughly the size of the working memory).[3] In each group, there were six input units. The first four units were used to encode inputs for the SRT task, one for each possible position of lights. The other two input units were used for the tone counting task (low tone versus high tone). The output consisted of four units for predicting the

---

[3] We tried increasing the size of the working memory. The results remained essentially the same.

next light position, and also a unit for indicating whether a high tone was detected. Twenty hidden units were used.

Rule learning was used at the top level. The detail of rule learning was as follows: The criterion for rule extraction was based on "reward" received after each button press, which was determined by whether the prediction made was correct or not: If it was correct, a reward of 1 was given; otherwise 0 was given. If 1 was received, a rule might be extracted; otherwise, no rule could be extracted. The positivity criterion used in calculating IG measures was set to be the same as the rule extraction criterion.

The difference between "less aware" and "more aware" subjects was captured by the difference in rule learning thresholds. To simulate less aware subjects, we used higher thresholds so that they were less likely to develop explicit knowledge (although they could develop some).[4] To simulate more aware subjects, we used lower thresholds. To simulate the "intentional" group, we coded the given sequence as a set of a priori rules, before the training started, with the rule learning thresholds set at the same levels as the more aware subjects.

To simulate the dual-task condition, we interleaved the presentations of tones and lights (as in Curran and Keele's experiment) to the backpropagation network, which handled both the secondary tone counting task and the primary task. Consistent with existing knowledge of the effect of dual tasks (Nissen and Bullemer 1987, Cleeremans and McClelland 1991, Stadler 1995, Szymanski and MacLeod 1996, Dienes and Berry 1997), we hypothesized that the dual task interfered with, and thus reduced, top-level activities. Thus, we chose to increase the rule learning thresholds to reduce top-level activities (since rule learning was more effortful than rule application).[5]

We ran 19 model runs for each group, in rough correspondence with the number of subjects in the human experiments. For these model "subjects", we randomly set the seeds for random number generators (used in initializing weights and in decision making), analogous to random selection of human subjects. We used a linear transformation ($a = 600, b = $

[4] Alternatively, we could assume they had a lower probability of extracting rule (when the thresholds for rule learning were reached). This method worked as well.
[5] We tried some alternatives: reducing the weighting of the top level (in combining the outcomes of the two levels), to reduce the impact of the top level. We also tried adding noise at the top level, which served the same purpose. Both worked as well.

100) that turned error rates into reaction times. The result is shown in Figure 5.9, which captured well the characteristics of the human data. A non-linear transformation with a power function as described in the previous subsection produced an even better fit.

We performed ANOVA (intentional vs. more aware vs. less aware × sequential blocks vs. random blocks) in correspondence with the analysis of human data in this task. The random block was block 7 and the sequential blocks were blocks 6 and 8. The results showed that there was a significant interaction between group and block, indicating a significant effect of explicit knowledge, similar to what was found in the human data. The "more aware" group and the "intentional" group performed significantly better than the "less aware" group, as was in the human data.

For the transfer to the dual-task condition, We performed another ANOVA (intentional vs. more aware vs. less aware × sequential vs. random). The analysis showed that there was no significant difference between the three groups, showing the disappearance of the effect of explicit knowledge under the dual-task condition, as was in the human data. However, ANOVA revealed that there was a significant difference between the random blocks (blocks 10 and 12) and the sequential block (block 11), indicating that some learning occurred, again the same as in the human data.

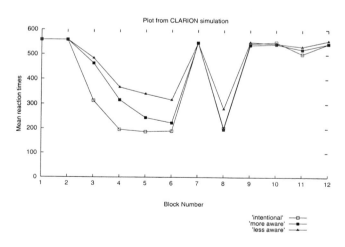

Figure 5.9. The simulation of Curran and Keele (1993)

In this simulation, we captured the following effects related to the interaction of the two levels: (1) the explicit instruction effect, as demonstrated by the "intentional" group, (2) the degree of awareness effect, (3) the synergy effect, as a result of capturing the above two effects, since explicit processes, in the forms of given instructions or heightened awareness, led to improved performance, and (4) the dual-task effect, as shown by the dual-task transfer data in which the differences due to instructions or awareness disappeared because of the interference of the secondary task. The dual-task effect also lent support to the synergy effect, because it showed that less involvement of explicit processes led to worsened performance. The simulation of this task suggested that the division of labor between the two levels and the bottom-up learning, as hypothesized in CLARION, were important for capturing human performance.

5.3   Simulating Process Control Tasks

In this type of task, we aim to capture (1) the verbalization effect, (2) the explicit how-to instruction effect, (3) the explicit search effect, and (4) the salience difference effect. Due to capturing the verbalization effect and the explicit search effect, we capture the synergy effect, which can be discerned through contrasting these two conditions with the conditions in which there is no verbalization and no explicit search, which indicates that the enhancement of the top level leads to better performance. Through the simulation of this task, we show that the division of labor between, and the interaction of, the two levels is important, and that bottom-up learning can be used to capture performance in this task.

We use QBP at the bottom level, because there is no teacher input (supervision) but there is feedback regarding the outcome of an action decision. The input consists of a moving window of past input and output levels, as well as the target level.[6]

Because rules for this task are mostly numerical relations that cannot be generalized or specialized the same way as before (e.g., a rule may be: "choose the input to be halfway between the current output and the target output"), we use *independent rule learning* as mentioned in chapter 2— hypothesizing rules and then testing them through experience. Initially, we

---

[6] The moving window is necessary because agents need a trace of past activities on which they base their action decisions.

hypothesize rules of a certain form to be tested. When the IG measure of a rule falls below the shrinking threshold, we delete the rule. Whenever all the rules of a certain form are deleted, a new set of rules of a different form are hypothesized, and the cycle repeats itself. In hypothesizing rules, we progress from the simplest rule form to the most complex, in the order as shown in Figure 5.10, in accordance with those numerical relations commonly used in human experiments (Berry and Broadbent 1988, Stanley et al. 1989). The IG measure is calculated based on the immediate reward at each step. It involves comparing a rule in question and the random rule (which selects actions randomly according to uniform distribution). This is analogous to the calculation of IG in RER.

$$P = aW + b$$
$$P = aW_1 + b$$
$$P = aW + cP_1$$
$$P = aW_1 + bP_2$$

Figure 5.10. The order of rules to be tested
$a = 1, 2$, $b = -1, -2, 0, 1, 2$, $c = -1, -2, 1, 2$, P is the desired system output level (the goal), W is the current input to the system (to be determined), W_1 is the previous input to the system, P_1 is the previous system output level (under W_1), and P_2 is the system output level at the time step before P_1. (Other rule forms can be easily added to the hypothesis testing process.)

To capture the verbalization effect, we change the rule learning thresholds at the top level to encourage more rule learning activities. In this task, only the rule deletion (i.e., shrinking) threshold matters. The hypothesis is that, as explained earlier, verbalization tends to increase top-level activities, especially rule learning activities. To capture the explicit search effect, we again change the rule deletion/shrinking threshold at the top level to encourage more activities, as well as increasing the weighting of the top level in combining outcomes. The hypothesis is that explicit search instructions tend to increase the reliance on top-level activities, especially rule learning activities. To capture the explicit how-to instruction effect, several different manipulations can be used in correspondence with the forms of explicit instructions given (see details later). To capture the salience difference effect, we do not need to change any parameter: The effect falls out of the salience difference of the stimulus materials presented to subjects.

5.3.1   Simulating Stanley et al. (1989)

Two versions of the PC task were used. In the "person" version, subjects were to interact with a computer simulated "person" whose behavior ranged over 12 levels, from "very rude" to "loving", and the task was to maintain the behavior at "very friendly" by controlling his/her own behavior, which could also range over the 12 levels, from "very rude" to "loving".

In the sugar production factory version, subjects were to interact with a simulated factory to maintain a particular production level, out of a total of 12 production levels, through adjusting the size of the workforce, which has also 12 levels.

In either case, the behavior of the simulated systems was determined by $P = 2*W - P_1 + N$, where P was the current system output, P_1 was the previous system output, W was the input to the system by a subject, and N was noise. Noise (N) was added to the output of the system, so that there was a chance of being up or down one level (a 33% chance respectively).

There were four groups of subjects. The "original" group was required to verbalize: Subjects were asked to verbalize after each block of 10 trials. Explicit instructions were presented in various forms to some other groups of subjects. To the "memory training" group, a series of 12 correct input/output pairs was presented. To the "simple rules" group, a simple heuristic rule ("always select the response level half way between the current production level and the target level") was given. The control group was not given any explicit instruction and not asked to verbalize. The subjects were trained for 200 trials (20 blocks). The numbers of subjects varied across groups. 12 to 31 subjects were tested in each group.

The exact target value plus/minus one level was considered on target. The mean scores (numbers of on-target responses) per trial block for all groups were calculated. Analysis showed that the score of the original group was significantly higher than that of the control group. Analysis also showed that the scores of the memory training group and the simple rule group were significantly higher than that of the control group as well. See Figure 5.11.

The model was set up as described earlier. We used 70 input units,

Human Data		
	Sugar Task	Person Task
Control	1.97	2.85
Original	2.57	3.75
Memory Training	4.63	5.33
Simple Rule	4.00	5.91

Figure 5.11. The human data for the PC task from Stanley et al. (1989)

Model Data		
	Sugar Task	Person Task
Control	2.01	2.23
Original	2.85	3.97
Memory Training	4.21	5.52
Simple Rule	4.10	5.67

Figure 5.12. The model data for the PC task of Stanley et al. (1989)

30 hidden units, and 12 output units. There were 2 groups of input units constituting a time window; each group contained 24 units, in which half of them encoded the 12 output levels and the other half encoded the 12 input levels at a particular step. In addition, there was a group of 12 units encoding the target level, and another group of 10 units encoding the serial position (within a block). The 12 output units encoded the 12 output levels.

To capture the verbalization effect, the rule deletion (shrinking) threshold was altered under that condition to increase top-level rule learning activities. To capture explicit how-to instructions, in the "memory training" condition, each of the 12 examples was wired up at the top level as a set of rules; in the "simple rule" condition, the simple rule as described earlier was wired up at the top level. A reward of 1 was given when the system output was on target. When the output was not on target, a negative reward inversely proportional to the deviation was given. Each run lasted for 200 trials, the same as in the human experiments.[7]

Our simulation captured the verbalization effect in the human data

[7] In the person task, to capture the prior experience subjects likely had with this type of situation, a pre-training of 200 trials was conducted. There was no pre-training for the sugar factory task.

well. See Figures 5.11 and 5.12.   ANOVA (control vs. original) showed that there was a significant difference between the control and the original group, analogous to the human data.   Our simulation also captured the explicit how-to instruction effect, as shown in Figure 5.12.   ANOVA showed that there was a significant difference between the simple rule group and the control group, analogous to the human data. The finding concerning the memory training group was similar.

In all, the simulation and the human data both confirmed the verbalization effect and the explicit instruction effect.   They also demonstrated the match between the two and thus the validity of the CLARION model.

5.3.2   Simulating Berry and Broadbent (1988)

The task of Berry and Broadbent (1988) was similar to the computer "person" version in Stanley et al. (1989). Subjects were to interact with a computer simulated "person" whose behavior ranged from "very rude" to "loving" and the task was to maintain the behavior at "very friendly" by controlling his/her own behavior, which could also range from "very rude" to "loving". In the salient version of the task, the behavior of the computer "person" was determined by the immediately preceding input of the subject: It was usually two levels lower than the input ($P = W - 2 + N$). In the non-salient version, it was determined by the input before the immediately preceding one and again two levels lower than that input ($P = W_1 - 2 + N$). Noise (N) was added to the output of the computer "person" so that there was a chance of being up or down one level (a 33% chance respectively).

Four groups of subjects were used: salient experimental, salient control, non-salient experimental, and non-salient control. The experimental groups were given explicit search instructions after the first set of 20 trials and, after the second set of 20 trials, were given explicit how-to instructions in the form of an indication of the relevant input that determined the computer responses. 12 subjects per group were tested.

The same as before, the exact target value plus/minus one level was considered on target. The average number of trials on target was recorded for each subject for each set of 20 trials. Figure 5.13 shows the data of the four groups of subjects during the three sets of trials. Analysis showed that on the first set, neither of the two experimental groups differed significantly from their respective control groups; however, on the second set, the salient experimental group scored significantly higher than the salient control group, but the non-salient experimental group scored significantly less than the non-salient control group. On the third set, both experimental groups scored significantly higher than their respective control groups. The data clearly showed (1) the explicit search effect—improving performance under the salient condition and worsening performance under the non-salient condition, and (2) the explicit instruction effect—improving performance in all conditions, as well as (3) the salience difference effect (under the explicit search condition).

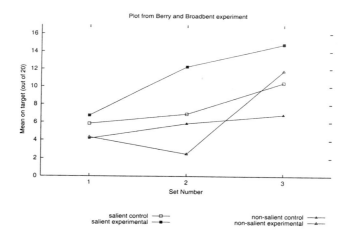

Figure 5.13. The data of Berry and Broadbent (1988)

The simulation model was set up as described earlier for simulating Stanley et al. (1989).   To capture the explicit search effect, the rule deletion (shrinking) threshold was altered to increase learning activities in the top level, and the weighting of the top level was increased in combining outcomes. To capture the explicit how-to instructions given in this task, only rules that related the critical variable to the system output were hypothesized at the top level: that is, $P = aW + b$, where $a = 1, 2$, $b = -2, -1, 0, 1, 2$, and W was the critical variable indicated by the instructions.

We captured in the simulation of this task the following effects exhibited in the human data: the salience difference effect, the explicit search effect, and the explicit how-to instruction effect. The results of the simulation is shown in Figure 5.14.

Following the analysis of human data, we performed t tests on respective sets. The analysis showed that on the first set, neither of the two experimental groups differed significantly from their respective control groups. However, on the second set, the salient experimental group (which was given explicit search instructions) scored somewhat higher than the salient control group (which was not given explicit search instructions), but the non-salient experimental group (which was also given explicit search instructions) scored less than the non-salient control group. On the third set, both experimental groups (which were given explicit how-to instructions) scored significantly higher than their respective control groups. These results demonstrated the consistency between the model and the human performance.

The data and the simulation together demonstrated the match between the CLARION model and the human data with regard to the explicit search effect (improving performance in the salient condition and worsening performance in the non-salient condition), the explicit instruction effect (improving performance in all conditions), and the salience difference effect, as discussed earlier. Together, they also lent support to the hypothesis of the synergy effect.

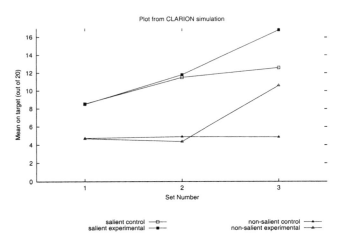

Figure 5.14. The simulation of Berry and Broadbent (1988)

5.4 Simulating High-Level Cognitive Skill Learning Tasks

We use the Tower of Hanoi task as an example of high-level cognitive skill learning, since it has been used extensively in cognitive skill acquisition research and is typical of the type of task addressed in such research (Sun et al. 2002). (In the next subsection, I will discuss a simulated minefield navigation task as a further example.)

In the Tower of Hanoi task, there were three pegs. At the beginning, a stack of disks were on one of the pegs. The goal was to move these disks to another (target) peg. Only one disk could be moved at a time, from one peg to another. These disks were of different sizes, and larger disks could not be placed on top of smaller disks. Initially, the stack of disks was arranged in a proper order from the smallest disk at the top to the largest at the bottom.

In the experiment of Gagne and Smith (1962), subjects were given 2-disk, 3-disk, 4-disk, and 5-disk versions of the task in succession, each version running until a final, best solution was found, and their mean numbers of moves (and excess moves) were recorded. Some subjects were instructed to verbalize. They were asked to explain why each move was made. The performance of the two groups of subjects (verbalization versus no verbalization) was compared. Thus, in this task, the verbalization effect was captured. The verbalization effect lent support to the synergy hypothesis.[8]

Figure 5.15 shows the performance of the two groups in terms of mean number of excess moves (in excess of the minimum required numbers of moves). Comparing the verbalization group and the no verbalization group in the figure, the advantage of verbalization is apparent. Analysis indicated that there was a significant difference between verbalization and no verbalization.

In the simulation model, at the bottom level, we used QBP. We used $6 \times 6 \times 3 = 108$ input units, 30 hidden units, and 6 output units. The input units encoded the current state of the pegs: There were 3 banks of input nodes, each encoding one peg. In each bank, there were 6 groups of nodes, with each group encoding one disk, and thus the 6 groups encoded up to 6

---

[8] Because of the lack of data on other effects, we did not simulate them. Among them, the salience difference effect did not apply. The explicit how-to instruction effect was obvious. There was no data on the dual-task effect or the explicit search effect.

Condition/No. of discs	2	3	4	5
No verbalization	0.0	2.1	4.3	21.2
Verbalization	0.0	0.0	0.9	1.3

Figure 5.15. The data of Gagne and Smith (1962)

disks. Within each group, 6 nodes encoded up to 6 different sizes. The 6 output units indicated 6 possible actions, each for moving a disk on top of any peg to the top of another peg.

At the top level, RER rule learning was used. To capture the verbalization condition, we used lowered rule learning thresholds, to encourage more activities at the top level, in correspondence with what we knew about the effect of verbalization.

Reward (which was 1) was given at the end when the goal state was reached. If an illegal move was selected (such as moving a large disk to the top of a small disk), a penalty of -0.1 was given.

The result of our simulation is shown in Figure 5.16. Comparing the simulation data with the corresponding human data, we found no significant difference between model performance and human performance. Consistent with the analysis of the human data, ANOVA (number of disks × verbalization vs. no verbalization) indicated that in the simulation data, there was a significant difference between verbalization and no verbalization, analogous to the human data, confirming again the verbalization effect we discussed.

Condition/No. of discs	2	3	4	5
No verbalization	0.0	1.9	4.2	17.0
Verbalization	0.0	0.0	0.6	0.8

Figure 5.16. The simulation of Gagne and Smith (1962)

5.5   Simulating the Minefield Navigation Task

In the minefield navigation task, we capture the following effects resulting from various manipulations of experimental conditions (Sun et al. 2001): (1)

the dual-task effect, (2) the verbalization effect, and (3) the synergy effect, as a result of considering both the dual-task effect and the verbalization effect, which indicates the beneficial role of the top level. That is, the enhancement of the top level often leads to better performance, and the weakening of the top level leads to worse performance.

In this task (Gordon et al. 1994), subjects were seated in front of a computer monitor that displayed an instrument panel containing several gauges that provided current information of the minefield. See Figure 5.17. At the bottom of the screen, the sonar gauges showed how close the mines were in 7 local areas in front of the vessel that the subjects were supposed to steer, ranging from approximately 45 degrees to the left of the vessel to approximately 45 degrees to the right. Right above the sonar gauges, the bearing gauge showed the direction of the target from the present heading of the vessel. Above and to the left, the fuel gauge showed how much time was left before fuel ran out. To the right was the range gauge, which showed the distance to the target. Subjects used a joystick to navigate the vessel and decided (1) how much to turn and (2) how fast to move. In each trial, the subjects could either (a) reach the target (a success), (b) hit a mine (a failure), or (c) run out of fuel (a failure).

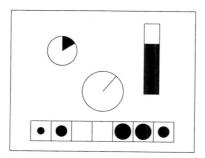

Figure 5.17. The navigation input
The display at the upper left corner is the fuel gauge; the vertical one at the upper right corner is the range gauge; the round one in the middle is the bearing gauge; the 7 sonar gauges are at the bottom.

Three training conditions were used (Sun et al. 2001). In the standard training condition, subjects received five blocks of 20 trials on each of five consecutive days (100 trials per day). In each trial, the minefield contained

60 mines. The subjects were allowed 200 steps to navigate the minefield. The verbalization training condition was identical to the standard training condition except that subjects were asked to step through slow replays of selected trials and to verbalize what they were thinking during the trial. In the dual-task condition, subjects performed the navigation task while concurrently performing a category decision task. Ten subjects were used for each condition. The data for each group, averaged over the 10 subjects of the group, are shown in Figures 5.18 and 5.19 (the top panels).

The data showed that the standard (single-task) condition led to significantly better performance than the dual-task condition; the verbalization condition led to significantly better performance than the standard condition. They showed that explicit processes helped to improve learning. (See Sun et al. 2001 for additional conditions and data.)

Here are some details of the model setup. In CLARION each gauge was represented by a set of nodes. One node was used to for "fuel", one node for "range", six nodes for "bearing", and five nodes for each of the seven sonars. This setup yielded a total of 43 input units. The outputs consisted of two clusters of nodes: one cluster of five nodes represented five different values of "turn" and the other cluster of four nodes represented four different values of "speed". Reward was determined by how successful the agent was at the end of a trial. The end reward was 1 if the agent reached the target within the allotted time, and was inversely proportional to the distance from the target if the agent ran out of time or exploded.

The QBP algorithm was used at the bottom level. The RER algorithm was used at the top level.

The dual-task effect was captured in CLARION by increasing rule learning thresholds so that less activities could occur at the top level. To capture the verbalization effect, we used reduced rule learning thresholds to encourage more rule learning.

Ten model "subjects" were compared to ten human subjects in each condition. The model data are shown in Figures 5.18 and 5.19 (the bottom panels). To compare human and model performance under single versus dual-task training, an ANOVA (human vs. model × single vs. dual-task) was performed (with success rates averaged in each condition), which indicated that the standard (single-task) condition led to significantly better performance than the dual-task condition, and that human and model subjects were highly similar in this regard. See Figure 5.18.

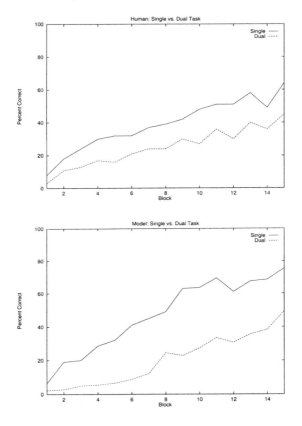

Figure 5.18. Single versus dual-task training
The top panel contains averaged human data, and the bottom panel averaged
model data.

To discern the effect of verbalization, averaged success rates across each
of these 4 days were subjected to an ANOVA (day × human vs. model
× verbalization vs. no verbalization). The analysis indicated that both
human and model subjects exhibited a significant increase in performance
due to verbalization, but that the difference associated with the effects of
verbalization for the two groups (human versus model) was not significant.
See Figure 5.19.
In addition, the human and model subjects were compared under the

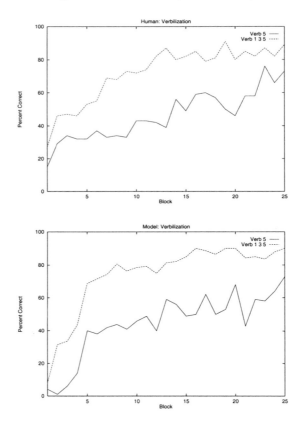

Figure 5.19. Verbalization versus no verbalization
The top panel contains averaged human data, and the bottom panel averaged model data.

standard, the verbalization, and the dual-task condition. They were highly similar. The model data were within the standard error of the human data. The two corresponding sets of data in each condition were both best fit by power functions. A correlation coefficient was calculated for each pair, which yielded high positive correlations (r ranged from .82 to .91), indicating a high degree of similarity between human and model subjects in how practice influenced human and model performance in each condition (Sun et al. 2001).

    In summary, in both human performance and model simulation, the standard (single-task) condition led to significantly better performance than the dual-task condition. The verbalization condition likewise led to significantly better performance than the no verbalization condition. This result supported the point that explicit processes at the top level helped to improve learning, or in other words, the synergy effect.

5.6   Discussions

5.6.1   Uniqueness of the Model

There may be alternative interpretations of the data presented that do not involve the assumption of two levels and may be more or less equally compelling. However, alternatives notwithstanding, the two-level approach provides a coherent, theoretically motivated (Smolensky 1988, Sun 1994, 1997, 1999), and principled framework. The model succeeds in interpreting many important findings that have not yet been adequately captured in computational modeling and points to ways of incorporating such findings in a unified model. This is where the significance of the model lies.

It is seldom, if ever, the case that human data can be used to demonstrate the *unique* validity of a model. We need to rely on converging evidence from various sources, including philosophical accounts, to justify a model. By such a standard, CLARION fares well.

5.6.2   Simulating Other Effects

Beside the cognitive effects simulated as described above (such as the verbalization effect, the how-to instruction effect, the explicit search effect), there are other established effects in the skill learning literature, such as the stimulus-response compatibility effect, the set size effect, the practice effects, the Stroop effects, and so on (see Proctor and Dutta 1995). We have tackled many of these effects as well. We are continuing to work on simulating an even wider range of tasks and many more cognitive effects and phenomena.

5.6.3   Factors in Division of Labor

What determines the explicitness/implicitness of processing when an agent faces a particular task? How and why is a task "assigned" to one level or the other (or both)? Although we touched upon this issue in chapter 4 appealing to a generic notion of complexity, we need to explicate this notion and thus draw a more detailed picture of the "division of labor" between the two levels.

We can speculate on the following factors in determining complexity:

- Number of input dimensions. The higher the number, the more prominent implicit learning will be (i.e., the more "holistic" the processing will be). For example, see the review of data in Seger (1994).

- Number of output dimensions. The higher this number, the more prominent implicit learning will be, by analogy to input dimensions.

- Multiplicity of correct input/output mappings. The more such mappings there are, the more likely that explicit learning will be prominent. This is because the more correct mappings there are, the easier a learning task become. See, for example, Sun et al. (2001).

- Stochasticity. The more stochastic a task is, the more likely that implicit learning will be prominent. See, for example, DeShon and Alexander (1996) and Cleeremans and McClelland (1991).

- Sequentiality (that is, whether a task is sequential, how long a typical sequence is, and how complex sequential dependency relations are).[9] The more sequential a task is, the more prominent implicit learning will be. We can compare Lewicki et al. (1987) and Willingham et al. (1989): Although similar tasks were used, the sequences were longer and more complex in Lewicki et al. and thus there was more implicit learning there. The same goes for Mathews et al. (1989), in which using complex finite state grammars led to more implicit learning while using simple correspondence rules led to more explicit learning. See also Reber (1989) and Berry and Broadbent (1988) for similar results.

- Complexity of correct input/output mappings in a task.[10] Obviously, the more complex input/output mappings of a task are, the more prominent implicit learning will be. We can again, for example,

---

[9] Sequences can be characterized roughly by the types of "language" that they belong to: regular, context-free, context-sensitive, and so on. Finer distinctions can also be made.

[10] Complexity may be measured by, for example, the minimum encoding length and the learnability of explicit knowledge necessary for performing a task explicitly. The latter measures the complexity of learning while the former the complexity of the outcome of learning. See Mitchell (1998).

compare Lewicki et al. (1987) and Willingham et al. (1989): There needed to be a lot more input/output mapping rules in Lewicki et al., and there was more implicit learning there. See also Stanley et al. (1989), Berry and Broadbent (1988), and Lee (1995) for demonstrations of this factor. Complexity of input/output mappings is highly correlated with the other factors listed above.

• Amount and type of instructions given prior to task performance. Generally speaking, the more instructions given about a task, or the more explicitly focused the instructions are, the more prominent explicit learning will be. See, for example, Stanley et al. (1989) and Sun et al. (2001) for human data demonstrating this factor.

• Single task versus dual tasks. Generally speaking, under dual-task conditions, implicit learning becomes more prominent. See, for example, Sun et al. (2001), Stadler (1995), and Nissen and Bullemer (1987) for human data demonstrating this factor.

Our experimental findings with CLARION thus far are highly consistent with the above conjectures.

5.6.4   Why Synergy in the Model?

How is the synergy between the two separate but interacting components of the mind (the two types of processes) generated? CLARION may shed some light on this issue, by allowing systematic experimentations with the two corresponding levels in the model.

Sun and Peterson (1998a) did a thorough computational analysis of the source of synergy between the two levels of CLARION in learning and in performance. The conclusion, based on a systematic analysis, was that the explanation of synergy between the two levels rests on the following factors: (1) the complementary representations of the two levels (discrete versus continuous); (2) the complementary learning processes (one-shot rule learning versus gradual Q value tuning); and (3) the bottom-up rule learning criterion used in CLARION. I will not repeat the lengthy analysis here. The reader is referred to Sun and Peterson (1998a) for further details.

It is very likely, in view of the match between the model and human performance, that the corresponding synergy in human performance results also from these same factors. In chapter 4, we identified distinct characteristics of the two levels of the human mind similar to the above three factors. It is conceivable that these same characteristics contribute to the generation of synergy in the human data.

5.7 Summary

In this chapter, I described a set of experiments that showed a quantitative match between the CLARION model and data of human cognition, on top of the qualitative match described previously in chapter 4. To recapitulate the main points, I highlighted the interaction of implicit and explicit processes in cognition, and I showed that synergy might result from such interaction. I demonstrated the psychological plausibility of bottom-up learning as well.

Now that we have established the cognitive validity of the CLARION model, let us turn to examine the theoretical underpinnings and implications of this model, especially in relation to its emphasis on two-level interaction and on bottom-up learning. We shall look into its theoretical implications in terms of the following issues: symbol grounding, intentionality of representation, situated cognition, consciousness, and sociocultural factors in cognition. As we will see, these issues are intrinsically interconnected, and should be dealt with in a unified theoretical framework. Any true solution to one of these issues will inevitably lead to the solutions to the other issues. These issues will be dealt with in chapters 6, 7, and 8.

Chapter 6

Symbol Grounding and Situated Cognition

> Thinking does not produce usable practical wisdom.
> Thinking does not endow us directly with the power to
> act.
>
> — Martin Heidegger: "Thinking"

6.1 Introduction

Symbols and symbol manipulation have been central to cognitive science.
But the disembodied nature of traditional symbolic systems has been
troubling many cognitive scientists; see, for example, the writings of Searle
(1980), Churchland (1986), Dreyfus and Dreyfus (1987), Winograd and
Flores (1987), Waltz (1990), Wertsch (1991), Bickhard (1993), Varela
et al. (1993), Sun (1994), and Freeman (1995). One remedy that has
been proposed by some of them (e.g., Harnad 1990, Barsalou 1999) is
symbol grounding, that is, connecting symbols to lower-level sensory-motor
processes and thus rooting the abstract in the concrete.

In this chapter, I take a detailed look at this issue. Based on
the afore-discussed computational cognitive model, I hope to further our
understanding on this issue. CLARION offers a new perspective on matters
related to this issue and beyond. The new ideas offered by this model
include dual processes and bottom-up learning. I also go back in time, to

link up with traditional philosophical accounts relevant to this issue, such as Heidegger (1927a).

My main points can be summarized as follows. Symbols should be grounded, as has been argued for years. But I insist that they should be grounded not only in subsymbolic activities (subsymbolic "representation"), but also in direct interaction between agents and the world. The point is that concepts and categories, which symbols represent, are not formed in isolation (from the world), in abstraction, or objectively. They are formed in relation to the life-world of agents, through the perceptual/motor apparatuses of agents, linked to their goals, needs, and actions (Milner 1999). This view can be argued on the basis of Heideggerian philosophy, which emphasizes the primacy of direct, unmediated interaction between agents and the world. Symbolic representation and concepts are derived from such direct interaction. Precisely in this sense, can symbols really be grounded. I will show how this can be achieved computationally.

The remainder of this chapter is a detailed account that extends from computational mechanisms to philosophical abstractions. In the next section, I review the traditional notions of symbols, representation, and so on, and identify their important properties. In section 3, I offer a theoretical perspective on these issues that remedies shortcomings of traditional approaches, drawing ideas from Heideggerian philosophy. In section 4, the computational underpinnings of this perspective are analyzed. In section 5, the framework outlined is analyzed in light of the issues raised in the first section. In section 6, further discussions are given.

6.2   Symbols and Representation

In this section, I review some background notions needed in our discussion, including the notions of symbols and representation. I try to clarify a few possible confusions and lay the foundation for the synthesis of a new perspective. In so doing, I identify relevant properties of each of these notions, which will be utilized later on.

6.2.1   Symbols

Symbols have been a mainstay of cognitive science, ever since its early incarnations as information processing psychology and artificial intelligence in the 1950s. The idea is based on the notion of computation as commonly understood in early days of computer science. (So, in some sense, it is based on a simplistic and narrowly conceived notion of computation.) Computation generally consists of input, output, retrieval, storage, and manipulation of symbols (as in a digital computer); a sequence of specified steps accomplishes a computational task, such as numerical calculation. Cognition is understood in much the same way, as consisting of input/output, storage/retrieval, and symbol manipulation. The most important part of this is, of course, the manipulation of symbols that changes symbol structures that stand for mental states. Because of the use of this computer metaphor, cognition is perceived as a sequence of explicit and clear-cut steps involving nothing but symbols.

Later, the *physical symbol system hypothesis* introduced by Newell and Simon (1976) clearly articulated this "vision" and called for a concentrated research program along the symbol manipulation line. They claimed that "symbols lie at the root of intelligent action". They defined, as the fundamental building block of the science of the mind, *physical symbol systems*:

> A physical symbol system consists of a set of entities, called symbols, which are physical patterns that can occur as components of another type of entity called an expression (symbol structure). Thus a symbol structure is composed of a number of instances (or tokens) of symbols related in some physical way (such as one token being next to another).

They further claimed that symbols could designate arbitrarily: "a symbol may be used to designate any expression whatsoever"; "it is not prescribed a priori what expressions it can designate." "There exist processes for creating any expression and for modifying any expression in arbitrary ways". Based on that, they concluded: "A physical symbol system has the necessary and sufficient means for general intelligent action", which is the famed physical symbol system hypothesis (where we take "general intelligent action" to mean the full range of human intelligent behavior). Clearly, a physical symbol system is an abstracted view of a digital computer (that is, it is an instance of a Turing machine, which is hypothesized in turn by Turing to be able to capture any "computational process"; see Turing 1950). Now the loop is almost complete: If you believe in some kind of universality of "computation" (especially in cognition), and if you believe in Turing's hypothesis (the universality of Turing machines), then you are naturally inclined to believe in the physical symbol system hypothesis (because physical symbol systems, as defined by Newell and Simon, are Turing equivalent).

The physical symbol system hypothesis has spawned, and was used to justify, enormous research effort in traditional AI and cognitive science. This approach (i.e., classical cognitivism) typically uses discrete symbols as primitives, and performs symbol manipulation in a sequential and deliberative manner. Although this view came to dominance in AI and cognitive science for a while, it has been steadily receiving criticisms from various sources (for example, Dreyfus 1972, Searle 1980, Dreyfus and Dreyfus 1987, Winograd and Flores 1987, and Bickhard 1993). They focused on the disembodied abstractness of this approach. In response to such criticisms, Vera and Simon (1993) presented a modified version of physical symbol systems as follows: "A physical symbol system is built from a set of elements, called symbols, which may be formed into symbolic structures by means of a set of relations." "A physical symbol system interact with its environment in two ways: (1) it receives sensory stimuli from the environment that it converts into symbol structures in memory; and (2) it acts upon the environment in ways determined by symbol structures that it produces." It "has a set of information processes that form symbol structures as a function of sensory stimuli" as well as "produce symbol structures that cause motor actions". Clearly, in this new version, they tried to put more emphases on sensory-motor connections, through which (they hoped) symbols could be put in contact with the world. Can either of these two versions of the physical symbol system hypothesis justify the claim to universality? Can the new version sustain better the claim?

In this regard, let us look into a basic question: What are symbols after all? "Symbols are patterns", according to the new version of Vera and Simon (1993), in the sense that "pairs of them can be compared and pronounced alike or different." Patterns are symbols when "they can designate or denote". Then, the question becomes: What is the difference between symbols and, say, pictures? According to the old version of the physical symbol system hypothesis, their answer would be that symbols, different from non-symbols such as pictures, can designate arbitrarily; according to the new version, however, their answer is likely that there is really no difference. The old version seems overly restrictive: Why do we restrict ourselves to a particular type of pattern and forego the others? How can we believe that such a restricted type of pattern is necessary and sufficient for cognition? The new version seems overly liberal: If anything is a symbol, then of course cognition can be modeled by symbol manipulation; it becomes a tautology and thus trivially true.

In order to pinpoint precisely what a symbol is, we should abstract its essential characteristics. Those characteristics that are at issue here are the following: (1) arbitrariness: whether a pattern (or a sign) has an intrinsic meaning or not; and (2) syntacticity: whether a set of patterns (or signs) can be arbitrarily and systematically combined in a language-like manner (i.e., whether they have the properties of compositionality and systematicity found in human languages). These two characteristics constitute necessary conditions for a pattern (or a sign) to be a symbol.[1] It is important to emphasize the distinction between the two different notions: signs (generic patterns) and symbols, which Peirce made clear a century ago (Peirce 1955). To quote from Peirce (1955):

> A sign is either an icon, an index, or a symbol. An icon is a sign which would possess the character which renders it significant, even though its object has no existence; such as a lead-pencil streak as representing a geometrical line. An index is a sign which would, at once, lose the character which makes it a sign if its object were removed, but would not lose that character if there were no interpretant. Such, for instance, is a piece of mould with a bullet-hole in it as sign of a shot...... A symbol is a sign which would lose the character which renders it a sign if there were no interpretant. Such is any utterance of speech which signifies what it does only by virtue of its being understood to have that signification.

[1] This had been the way symbols were commonly conceived in the cognitive science community (Collins and Smith 1988, Posner 1989), until the emphasis on symbols and the physical symbol system hypothesis begun to come under attack from connectionists (Chalmers 1990, Bechtel and Abrahamsen 1991, Clark 1993, Sun and Bookman 1994) and situated cognition advocates (Suchman 1987, Lave 1988, Agre 1988, Brooks 1991, Brooks and Stein 1994). Then, all of a sudden, the definition of symbols was drastically altered and enlarged, which renders the notion useless.

Because of the nonsensical consequence of the new version of "symbols", we will have to rely on the old version of Newell and Simon (1976).

Whether symbols are necessary and sufficient for accounting for cognition is not a settled matter. However, almost nobody disputes that some form of symbols, in connectionist, classical, or some other ways, is needed for accounting for high-level cognition, for example, language and reasoning. Even radical connectionists accept that symbols may emerge from dynamic interactions of elements of a network, or a dynamic system in general (Bechtel and Abrahamson 1991). I do not make any claim here as to what form symbols should be in, but that there should be symbols of some form, for obvious reasons (Sun 1994).

6.2.2   Representation

Classical cognitivism believes that an agent has an internal copy, an explicit model of some sort, of the external world. In that model, there are internal states that encode external states in the world (Fodor and Pylyshyn 1988). Cognition is accomplished by developing, maintaining, and modifying these internal states, aka, representation. This is the basic tenet of representationalism. According to the analysis by Peirce (1955), a representational system consists of, or can be analyzed into, representational media, representational entities (i.e., what constitutes a representation), representational semantics (or references, i.e., what is being represented).

To understand characteristics of internal (explicit) representation (as in traditional cognitive science as described by Fodor 1975 and Collins and Smith 1988), we can identify the following syntactic properties: First of all, such representation is explicit. This is because, without this requirement of explicitness, everything is a representation and thus the tenet of representationalism becomes meaningless. For example, a tennis ball has a representation of forces hitting it and trajectories it flies through, because it can respond to forces and fly through space; a car has a representation of roads and driving movements of its driver, because it can follow the driver's direction and stay on the road (Port and van Gelder 1995). Thus, the representation thesis (representationalism) becomes trivially true in this way. Second, explicit representation is punctate: It consists of clearly delineatable items. Third, it is also elaborate: It contains much detail, although it may not be a complete model.[2] Forth, explicit representation, as traditionally used, is symbolic and compositional. Note that, although explicit representation *need not* be symbolic in the full sense of the term (exceptions include imagery, analogue, and so on), almost all the existing representational systems in traditional cognitive science were symbolic (e.g., Anderson 1983, Minsky 1983, Klahr et al. 1987).[3] In addition, explicit representation is semantically specifiable: Each particular representation can have a specific meaning as (arbitrarily) designated. Meanings are compositional as well.

There are many possibilities in terms of manipulating internal (explicit) representation. Symbol manipulation is the prime candidate for such a task. The compositionality of the syntax and the semantics of explicit representation makes it easy to devise a symbolic procedure to manipulate representation and keep track of references and meanings. There are also other possibilities; for example, connectionist models (or neural networks) can somehow be suitable for manipulating representation as well (see Chalmers 1990, Bechtel and Abrahamsen 1991, Clark 1993, Sun and Bookman 1994).

6.2.3 Intentionality

One of the most important questions concerning representation is the following: In virtue of what does representation have or acquire its meanings or signification? How does it come to represent what it purports to represent?[4] As we discussed earlier, it is doubtful that an arbitrarily constructed symbolic representation can suffice, by itself, to account for cognition, when only complex relations among symbols are involved (Newell and Simon 1976). Clearly, meanings can hardly lie solely in symbols and their interrelations. How is it possible to move from the notion of meaning as arbitrary designation to a notion of "intrinsic" meaning? In other words,

[2] A particular version of representationalism advanced by Fodor (1980) is that mental states are represented by propositional attitudes, which consist of propositions and the agent's relations to them, described in sentential (linguistic) forms.

[3] Note that if a representational system is symbolic, it must be compositional; if it is not symbolic, it can still be, and often is, compositional, as we see in existing models.

[4] We could, for example, use the word "party" to mean anything from "a political organization" to "an informal gathering", or even "highway construction" (if we decide to interpret it arbitrarily).

how do we relate representation to whatever is out there in the world, in an intrinsic way? No argument more clearly demonstrates this point than Searle's Chinese Room argument (Searle 1980). The issue brought to light by this argument is *intentionality*. That is, our mental states and mental representation are *about* something. Mere symbols, as pointed out by Searle (1980), have no intentional content and therefore cannot adequately capture cognition.

Cognitive science has been grappling with the issue of intentionality ever since the publication of Searle's (1980) original argument. Where may an answer to these questions lie? I would venture to suggest a few possible places that we may go to look for answers. These places include: (1) existential experience of cognitive agents, individually or collectively, especially (but not exclusively) their everyday activities; (2) their functional pre-dispositions in such activities, acquired through evolutionary and other processes, involving biological substrates that embody their representational structures, functional capacities, and behavioral propensities.[5] Symbol grounding in the sense of linking symbols (symbolic representation) to lower-level (subsymbolic) processes (Harnad 1990) provides a partial answer to the intentionality question. But it does not fully answer it. This is because the issue of *how* grounded symbols, and associated subsymbolic processes, acquire their intentional content remains. I would argue that, instead of being narrowly conceived, symbol grounding should be understood in a generalized way in order to fully address the intentionality question, which is at the heart of the matter.

Let us look into some details of this position.

6.3   Everyday Activities and Symbol Grounding

What is the structure of everyday experience of cognitive agents? How is representation acquired in that experience? Where does its meaning lie?

Let us draw some ideas from phenomenological philosophers such as Martin Heidegger (1927a, 1927b) and Maurice Merleau-Ponty (1962, 1963). (Also see the work of Dewey 1958, Gibson 1950, 1979, Rorty 1979, 1991, Bruner 1995.) What is particularly interesting is the notion of *being-in-*

---

[5] This position is similar to, but considerably weaker than, Searle's own view. He believes that biological systems have some special properties that are the basis of their intentionality, which cannot be captured by computational systems.

the-world (Heidegger 1927a, Dreyfus 1992). The idea is that our existence in the world, or being-in-the-world, is fundamental. *Being-in-the-world* entails that we constantly interact with the world in an immediate and non-reflective (i.e., reflexive) way, in everyday activities in the world. It is believed that "mindless" everyday activities, or coping with the world, on top of biological pre-endowment, is the basis of high-level conceptual thinking and its intentionality.[6]

According to Heidegger, everyday coping with the world presupposes a background of common everyday practices (Dreyfus 1972, 1982, 1992). The "background of practices" (Dreyfus 1992) is not represented in an explicit and elaborate fashion (such as what we see, e.g., in the rule base of an "expert" system), which spells out every detail and every minute variation of every possible situation (Carnap 1969), but is assumed in our *comportment* toward the world. In other words, the most important and fundamental part of the mind is *embodied* and *embedded*, not explicitly represented, and thus it is not directly and explicitly accessible to critical reflection.

Another important theoretical notion is behavioral *structure* (or *form*; Merleau-Ponty 1963, Madison 1981). Maurice Merleau-Ponty extended Heidegger's notions, emphasizing the importance of the structural whole in the understanding of agents. It is not just external situations and internal reactions, but the structural connection that links the two that matters. In Gibsonian parlance, they are the affordance and the effectivity (Turvey 1992). They are linked on the basis of their shared participation in structures that are comprised of agents and the world. Temporal and spatial patterns (or structures) are formed that involve various external situations and various reactions. The patterns/structures thus formed constitute the foundation of cognition of agents. For further discussions of this point, see also Ballard (1991), Zhang and Norman (1994), Hammond et al. (1995), Hutchins (1995), and Agre and Horswill (1997). According to Merleau-Ponty, in such structures there lies the key to the meanings or signification of an agent's behavior.

---

[6] The term "everyday activities" as used here does not include *all* everyday activities, but those that are reactive and routinized. Certain activities that we perform everyday may rely heavily on high-level conceptual thinking, for example, if we discuss mathematics everyday. I do not consider such exceptions here (the same as in Dreyfus 1992).

6.3.1   Comportment

Heidegger (1927a, 1927b) suggested that there is a primordial kind of *comportment* in an agent that directly involves the agent with the world, without the mediation of (explicit) representation. This term was meant to capture this direct interaction, that is, the "dialectics" (Merleau-Ponty 1963). It is a pattern of two-way interaction between the agent and its environment. As he put it, "comportment has the structure of directing-oneself-toward, of being-directed-toward" (Heidegger 1927b).

Let us explore this notion further to better appreciate the interaction, and the mutual dependency, between an agent and its world. First of all, comportment is direct and unmediated. Thus it is free from representationalist baggage. In other words, comportment does not involve, or presuppose, (explicit) representation and all the problems and issues associated with explicit representation (as discussed earlier). To the contrary, (explicit) representation, and relations between mental states and their objects, presuppose the presence of comportment. Direct, unmediated comportment is in fact the condition of possibility of all representation. Comportment, according to Heidegger (1927a), "makes possible every intentional relation to beings" and "precedes every· possible mode of activity in general", prior to (explicit) beliefs, prior to (explicit) knowledge, and prior to (explicit) conceptual thinking (Heidegger 1927a). That is, comportment is primary. The mistake of traditional approaches to cognitive science lies in the fact that they treat (explicit) knowledge and its correlates as primary instead, and in so doing, they turn the priority upside-down: "Every act of directing oneself toward something receives [wrongly] the characteristics of knowing" (Heidegger 1927b). This is in essence the problem of classical cognitivism, including its difficulty with nature of representation, language of thought, intentionality, consciousness, and other theoretical issues. In contrast, in the real world, agents "fix their beliefs not only in their heads but in their worlds, as they *attune* themselves differently to different parts of the world as a result of their experience" (Sanders 1996).

Heidegger's philosophy eschewed the traditional internal/external dichotomy (Bechtel 1988, Pollack 1989) and, in its stead, posited a primordial way of interaction, direct and unmediated, as a foundation upon which all cognitive processes (including high-level conceptual processes) can function. Being-in-the-world thus serves as a focal point of a different way of approaching cognition. However, this is not at all to deny the existence of (explicit) representation. To the contrary, high-level conceptual processes involving (explicit) representation, as studied extensively in cognitive science and AI, do occur, but they are not as prevalent and as basic as assumed by classical cognitivism.

It might be useful to point out that the comportment we are talking about is not exactly the same as "embodiment" that has been advocated by some as the key to understanding human cognition. Lakoff and Johnson (see Lakoff and Johnson 1980 and Johnson 1987) have been putting forth a view that cognition is largely determined by the bodily basis of cognitive agents: The bodily schemata are abstracted and mapped onto all other domains and all other cognitive processes. Interpreted based on that position, an object should not be understood and represented in terms of its shape, color, or any other static features, but should be approached in terms of what an agent can do with it (Glenberg 1997). However, although these ideas are on the right track, they leave open too many possibilities. For example, there are too many different uses we can make of a cup: We can drink from it, we can use it to store coffee, tea, water, powder, coins, paper clips, or business cards, we can hold it in our hands, we can put it on top of our heads, we can stand on it, or we can play tricks with it. Its uses are unlimited. How can an agent structure its understanding around so many different possibilities? The key here, I would argue, is what an agent *usually*, *routinely*, *reflexively*, and *habitually* do with an object in its everyday life, amidst its "contexture of functionality". What is important is the common and routine dealing with an object, which is what we call comportment (of an agent) toward an object, or being-with-things as termed by Heidegger (1927a). Such comportment, or routine and habitual dealing, with objects is the basis of how an agent approaches objects.

Direct and unmediated comportment has been variously referred to as reactive routines, habitual routines, reactive skills, routine activities, everyday coping, ongoing interaction, and so on, in the work of, for example, Agre (1988, 1997), Lave (1988), Chapman (1991), and Dreyfus (1992). They have also been characterized as subconceptual "representation", in the broadest sense of the term "representation", as I have been using in the previous chapters (Smolensky 1988, Sun 1994).

6.3.2   Conceptual Processes and Representation

Evidently, comportment is intentional only in the sense that it directs an agent to objects in the world as part of a "natural" structure (Merleau-Ponty 1963). Such intentionality of an agent is not qualitatively different from that of a tennis ball or a car (see the discussion of both earlier). This kind of "pre-representational" (i.e., implicit) pattern of interaction with the world serves as the foundation of how an agent relates to its environment in its everyday activities and, more importantly, serves as the foundation of more complex forms of intentionality. Explicit representation can be formed only on top of primordial comportment; thus, explicit representation is secondary, or derivative, and its intentional content is *derived* from direct comportment with the world.

As argued in chapter 2 early on, there is ample psychological evidence pointing to "bottom-up" learning that goes from comportment to conceptual, symbolic representation. Several areas of research have demonstrated that agents can learn complex activities without first obtaining (a large amount of) explicit knowledge. As reviewed before, in the research on implicit learning, for example, Berry and Broadbent (1988), Willingham et al. (1989), and Reber (1989) demonstrated a dissociation between explicitly represented knowledge and routinized performance in a variety of tasks, including dynamic control tasks (Berry and Broadbent 1988), artificial grammar learning tasks (Reber 1989), and serial reaction time tasks (Willingham et al. 1989). Berry and Broadbent (1988) argued that agents could learn to perform a task without being provided a priori explicit knowledge and without being able to explicitly verbalize the rules they used to perform the task.   There are also indications that explicit knowledge may arise from routinized activities in some circumstances (Stanley et al. 1989).   Using a dynamic control task, Stanley et al. (1989) found that the development of explicit knowledge paralleled but lagged behind the development of skilled performance.   Similar claims concerning the development of performance prior to the development of explicit knowledge have been made in a number of other research areas, as mentioned in earlier chapters, and provide strong support for the bottom-up process.

Generation of low-level comportment during ontogenesis is determined by, at a minimum, the following two important factors: (1) structures in the external world as perceived by the agent, which, to some degree, depend on existent structures in the agent and therefore on the (ontogenetic and phylogenetic) history of agent/world interaction, and (2) innate "biases", or built-in constraints and predispositions, which clearly depend on the (ontogenetic and phylogenetic) history of agent/world interaction. In turn, the generation of high-level structures (i.e., conceptual representation, with symbols) is, to a significant extent, determined by low-level structures, as well as signs/symbols employed in a given culture.

Therefore, according to this perspective, high-level conceptual, symbolic representation is rooted, or grounded, in low-level comportment, from which it obtains its meanings or signification and for which it provides support and explanations. The rootedness/groundedness is guaranteed by the way high-level representation is formed: It is to a very significant extent a transformation and explication of low-level behavioral structures and processes. Even culturally transmitted signs/symbols have to be linked up, within the mind of an individual agent, with low-level processes in order to be effective.

It is worth noting that conceptual, symbolic representation so formed is, in general, formed in a functionally relevant way, in relation to everyday activities of agents. In other words, in general, it must bear certain existential and/or biological significance to agents and be in the service of agents' activities. The world is of such a high (or even an infinitely high) dimensionality, and thus there can be no totally objective way of perceiving/conceiving it, except in relation to what an agent has to do with it in everyday activities. Forming symbolic representation on the basis of comportment provides an agent with a viable way of basing its conceptual representation on its everyday activities in a functionally relevant way.[7]

The existence of internal explicit representation, or at least its importance, has been downplayed by some advocates of strong forms of situated cognition views (e.g., Agre 1988, Brooks 1991, Port and van Gelder 1995). The existence of explicit representation (but not its paramount role)

---

[7] In addition, of course, biological pre-endowment in agents (acquired through evolutionary processes) may also provide them with some ways of picking out relevant information (Pinker 1994, Cosmides and Tooby 1994, Shepard 2001). The two aspects may interact closely in forming conceptual representation.

has in fact been argued for by a number of researchers, persuasively, I believe. See, for example, Smith et al. (1992) and Markman and Dietrich (1998) for such arguments. Here I take a more "eclectic" position, which acknowledges that representation is important while maintaining that it is mediated by direct comportment.

6.3.3   A Dual Process Theory

This analysis boils down to the dual-process approach, which is the focus of this work.

In one of my previous books (Sun 1994), I put forth the following hypothesis (in which the word "knowledge" should be broadly interpreted):

> It is assumed in this work that cognitive processes are carried out in two distinct levels with qualitatively different processing mechanisms. Each level encodes a fairly complete set of knowledge for its processing, and the coverage of the two sets of knowledge encoded by the two levels overlaps substantially.

This idea is closely related to some well-known dichotomies in cognitive science, for example, the dichotomy of symbolic versus subsymbolic processing (Rumelhart and McClelland 1986), the dichotomy of conceptual versus subconceptual processing (Smolensky 1988), the dichotomy of explicit versus implicit learning (Reber 1989, Berry and Broadbent 1988, Lewicki et al. 1992), the dichotomy of controlled versus automatic processing (Shiffrin and Schneider 1977, Schneider and Oliver 1991), and the dichotomy of declarative versus procedural knowledge (Anderson 1983).

However, I went further here in positing separate and simultaneous existence of multiple levels (i.e., separate processors), each of which embodies one side of a dichotomy. In this work, the two sides of a dichotomy are not simply two ends of a spectrum, or two levels of analysis of the same underlying system. But they are two separate, although closely connected, systems.   The two levels encode similar and comparable content (or "knowledge" in a broad sense). But they encode their content in different ways, and one content is (mostly) derived from the other. Furthermore, they utilize different processing mechanisms. One works in a comportment-like way while the other in an explicit, symbolic, and conceptual way. Thus, they have qualitatively different flavors, although they function together.

As discussed before, the reason for having the two levels, or any other similar combination of components, is that these different levels potentially can work together *synergistically*, supplementing and complementing each other in a variety of different ways. For demonstrations of synergy, see chapters 3 and 5.

6.4   Computational Analysis of Everyday Activities

To probe deeper and further, we need to gain a better understanding of these ideas beyond mere philosophical speculation. I will sketch a brief picture of the mechanistic underpinning of this analysis, which CLARION helps to bring out.   Let me highlight a few basic ingredients. First of all, we start small, as in CLARION, assuming only minimum built-in initial structures in an agent. Some initial structures have to do with "pre-wired" reflexes, or predisposition for developing such reflexes, that is, genetic and biological pre-endowment. Some others have to do with learning capabilities, since most structures in cognition have to be constructed in an incremental fashion, during the course of individual ontogenesis. The development of structures is based on acting and learning in the world, that is, based on being-in-the-world, including both the physical world and the sociocultural world). Interaction prompts the formation of various low-level structures in behavior, which in turn lead to the emergence of high-level conceptual representation. As illustrated by CLARION, connectionist models can be utilized, in a properly generalized form, as the basic unifying medium of computational implementation, because of the many appealing properties of such models and because of the fact that they encompass both symbolic approaches and dynamical system approaches (Sun 1994, Port and van Gelder 1995).

6.4.1   Computational Processes of Comportment

First, let us examine computational processes of comportment.   I will emphasize the *development* of comportment in the "ontogenesis" of an individual agent, which is the essential means to acquire comportment (although innate structures might be formed evolutionarily, a priori, as mentioned before).

Generally speaking, in everyday activities (especially in direct comportment), an agent is under time pressure: Often, a mundane action "decision" has to be made in a fraction of a second; it falls outside of Allen Newell's "rational band" (i.e, cognitive processes that take minutes or hours to complete, which is what cognitive science and AI traditionally deal with). The agent is also severely limited in other resources, such as memory, so that memorizing and analyzing all the previous experience in detail is impossible (although some form of episodic memory obviously exists). The perceptual ability of the agent is limited in that only local perceptual information is available. Goals may not be explicit and a priori to an agent either. They may be implied in reinforcement received, and pursued as a side-effect of trying to maximize reinforcement.

Learning (or gradual formation) of comportment is an experiential, trial-and-error process; the agent develops its comportment, *tentatively*, on an on-going basis (because obviously it cannot wait until the end of its experience before making a decision and before starting to learn). As demonstrated by the work of Nosofsky et al. (1994) and Medin et al. (1987), human learning is mostly gradual, on-going, and concurrent, which is especially true in relation to comportment. The characteristics of the world, from the viewpoint of the learning agent, may not be stationary. It can be nonstationary ("drifting") in several ways: (1) The world can change over time; thus, the revision of comportment structures may be necessary. (2) Even when the world is stationary, it may still seem evolving to an agent learning to cope with the world, because different regions of the world may exhibit different characteristics and thus revisions over time may be required.[8] (3) Once a structure is revised, the agent has to view whatever it experienced before in new ways and thus experience may seem different and the world nonstationary. (4) A clear and steady criterion is lacking for learning comportment. Reinforcement may be received sporadically, and it is up to the agent to decide what to make of it. The agent has to assign credits/blames on the basis of existing structures, which are constantly changing. Because the learning criterion is a moving target, the learning process becomes nonstationary as well.

There are existing computational methods for accomplishing simple forms of such learning. Chief among them is the temporal difference

---

[8] In general, there is no preselected set of instances that provide a fixed view of the world.

method (Sutton 1988), a type of reinforcement learning that learns through exploiting the difference in evaluating actions in successive steps and thus handling sequences in an incremental fashion.   Another approach, evolutionary computation (e.g., Holland et al. 1986), may also be used to tackle this kind of task.   The first method is in fact one part of CLARION, the part that is specifically concerned with comportment (Sun 1997, Sun and Peterson 1998a, 1998b). Evidently, in this implementation of comportment, there is no elaborate explicit internal representation, and no internal connection between different entities representing different mental states. It is, therefore, a plausible way of implementing comportment.   In contrast, in some implementations of situated cognition, elaborate networks of pointers or other explicit mechanisms are devised that relate different internal states, in terms of their interrelations in action selection. Although starting out in the right direction, such schemes, unfortunately, fell right back into the representationalist trap, failing to capture the direct and unmediated nature of comportment.

Other existing computational implementations include the work of Agre (1988), Brooks (1991), Tyrell (1993), Beer (1996), Tani and Nolfi (1998), Scheier and Pfeifer (1998), and so on. They adopted different techniques, such as recurrent neural networks, evolutionary algorithms, dynamic systems, and hierarchical decision networks. Some of them, such as Agre (1988), Brooks (1991), and Chapman (1991), attempted to implement comportment without involving learning or ontogenetic development. For a technical comparison of these other methods, see chapter 9.

6.4.2   Computational Processes of Conceptual Processing

Now I will discuss computational implementations of agents' high-level conceptual processes, which necessarily involve (explicit) representation, and are in the service of agents' everyday activities.

Let us see how explicit representation is acquired computationally. In the machine learning literature, many symbolic learning algorithms are available for learning explicit rules (as a form of high-level explicit representation). However, the afore-identified characteristics of everyday activities render most of these existing rule learning algorithms inapplicable, because they require either preconstructed instance sets (Michalski 1983, Quinlan 1986), incrementally given consistent instances (Mitchell 1982,

Fisher 1987), or complex manipulations of learned symbolic structures when inconsistency is discovered (which is typically more complex than the limited time an agent may have in reactive activities) (Hirsh 1994). "Drifting", as analyzed before, is clearly more than noise and inconsistency considered by some learning algorithms, because it involves changes over time and may lead to radical changes in learned knowledge. Above all, most of the existing rule learning algorithms do not handle the learning of sequences, which is an essential form of agents' routines in everyday activities and necessarily involves temporal credit assignment.

Therefore, algorithms have to be developed specifically for the purpose of modeling the acquisition of explicit representation in agents (Sun and Peterson 1998a, 1998b). They should be bottom-up; that is, they utilize whatever is learned in the bottom level (the part of the model that implements comportment) and construct symbolic representation at the top level (the part that implements conceptual processes). We have discussed extensively the idea of bottom-up learning in the previous chapters. The RER (*Rule-Extraction-Revision*) algorithm in CLARION, described in detail in chapter 3, is exactly what we need. The RER algorithm grounds symbols and symbolic representation, through the process of bottom-up learning (knowledge extraction), in the comportment with the world.[9]

6.4.3   Concept Formation

While learning rules, CLARION forms concepts (Sun and Peterson 1998b). Although there are available distributed features in the bottom level for specifying rule conditions, a separate node is instead set up at the top level to represent the condition of a rule, which connects to the distributed features. So, along with induced rules, localist (i.e., symbolic) representation of concepts is formed.   Each localist node is linked to its corresponding distributed features in the bottom level, from which it was abstracted, through bottom-up activation (using a standard sigmoid activation function with uniform weights).

This kind of concept representation is basically a *prototype model* (Smith and Medin 1981, Rosch 1978). Localist nodes serve as identification and encoding of fuzzy features, in a bottom-up direction. They also serve

---

[9] Besides bottom-up processes, there are also top-down processes, as discussed before.

to trigger relevant fuzzy features, in a top-down direction, once a concept is brought into attention.[10]

Moreover, concepts formed in this way in CLARION are context-dependent and task-oriented, because they are formed with regard to the tasks at hand, while exploiting environmental regularities (Heidegger 1927a). Being emphasized in CLARION is the functional role of concepts and the importance of function in forming concepts. A concept is formed as part of a rule, which is learned to accomplish a task in a certain environment. Therefore, concepts acquired are functional. The task context and experience help an agent to determine which features in the environment need to be emphasized, what stimuli should be grouped together, and what constitutes a separate category (or concept). Thus, representation in an agent, for the most part, need not be determined a priori.[11] This approach may explain why human concepts are (mostly) concerned with existentially and biologically significant aspects of the world; they are not just "objective" partitioning of the world (Lakoff and Johnson 1980, Lave 1988).

This approach may have interesting implications for the frame problem in AI. The frame problem refers to the difficulty in keeping track of many propositions concerning a situation that may be in a constant flux. Any change in the situation may lead to the validation of many propositions and the invalidation of many others. This may lead to very high computational complexity in reasoning about the situation. This idea of "tracking" was envisaged in the symbolic representationalist framework of traditional AI, which makes such a process necessary. However, concepts being grounded, context-dependent, and task-oriented, as in CLARION, may alleviate the need for such "tracking". In this alternative approach, each situation is reacted to, first and foremost, by low-level comportment and then, through comportment, it triggers relevant concepts and propositions at the top level, which thus produces inferences that are tailored to the situation (Sun 1994). Purely logical reasoning concerning each and every proposition possible (as envisaged by traditional approaches) is computationally excessive and is rendered unnecessary by this approach (Sun 1994, 1995).

[10] They also facilitate "inheritance" reasoning based on distributed features, as discussed fully in Sun (1994, 1995).

[11] See Sun and Peterson (1998a, 1998b) for a more detailed analysis of concepts formed by agents during learning of specific tasks.

6.5   Representation and Intentionality

We now revisit the issue of representation based on the above analyses. I was critical of the traditionally dominant and currently lingering position on representation in cognitive science. However, rejecting representationalism does not necessarily mean rejecting (weak notions of) representation and symbols.

Let us examine CLARION. In the model, the top level indeed consists of representation in the sense implied by representationalism; this is because encoding used there is punctate (with each item being in an isolatable node) and also elaborate (with represented items forming a rather complete model of a domain, if CLARION is given enough time to learn). Moreover, the representation is symbolic, in the sense that a concept is assigned to an arbitrary node, without any intrinsic connection between a node and what it represents. Syntactic structures (i.e., concatenative compositional structures as defined by Fodor 1975) can be built on the basis of such representation. Syntactically sensitive symbolic processing can be performed on them. This level of the model is thus representational. However, the bottom level of CLARION is different. A connectionist model (i.e., backpropagation networks) is used; thus distributed feature encoding is involved. In such a scheme, there is no symbol, that is, no lexical item that can be assigned arbitrary meanings. Moreover, encoding is not a priori determined (beside certain pre-existing constraints). Encoding does not exist before an agent learns to interact with the world and thus develops; it is intrinsically tied to the experience of interaction between an agent and its environment. There is no syntactic structure in that level (in the sense of concatenative compositional structures of Fodor 1975). Thus, this level of CLARION is non-representational. Putting the two levels together, CLARION incorporates both representation and nonrepresentation. However, the model does not simply juxtapose the two qualitatively different parts, but combines them in an integral framework, so that the two parts of the model can interact.

What is the implication of the preceding discussion for the question of intentionality? Let us compare how the meanings of the contents of the bottom level and the top level are determined. To understand this issue, the notions of intrinsic intentionality and derived intentionality are pertinent and useful. According to Heidegger (1927b), any representation presupposes the more basic comportment with the world. Comportment carries with it a direct and unmediated relation to, and references of, things in the world; being-with-things is a fundamental part of being-in-the-world, a bridge to the existential context of an agent. Therefore, it provides an *intrinsic* intentionality (meanings), or in other words, a connection (to things in the world) that is intrinsic to an agent, given a particular existential context of the agent and its biological pre-endowment. In addition to intrinsic intentionality, there is also derived intentionality, which is, by definition, obtained through derivative means. In CLARION, intentionality can precisely be categorized into these two kinds: the bottom-level processes that capture direct comportment with the world and the top-level processes that are derived from the bottom-level processes (the result of extracting rules and concepts). The bottom-level processes acquire their internal encoding through learning from experience of direct interaction with the world, and thus meanings of the encoding lie in the intrinsicness of its weights and its wiring, which are determined by the process of unmediated interaction (through Q-learning and backpropagation in the model).[12] The top-level processes result from extraction, that is, derivation. Thus the meanings or intentionality of the representation can be traced to the derivation process. Through derivation/extraction, as well as through on-going connections to the bottom level (with both top-down and bottom-up connections), symbols at the top level are "grounded" in the bottom level and, through the bottom level, in the comportment with the world. Not only symbols themselves are derived from bottom-level processes but the meanings of these symbols are thus derived also from these processes.

Moreover, although Heidegger recognized the ontological precedence of intrinsic intentionality, it is important to further recognize, as in CLARION, that intrinsic intentionality is not only ontologically prior to derived intentionality, but also developmentally (ontogenetically) prior to it. As demonstrated by Inhelder and Piaget (1958), a child learns concepts and schemas only when the child learns to interact with objects in the world, and increasingly more complex concepts are developed through increasingly more complex interaction with objects. As suggested by Karmiloff-

---

[12] Such weights and wiring, unlike arbitrarily selected encoding at the top level, are intrinsically determined by inputs and outputs during interaction, as well as by their initial settings.

Smith (1992), the increasing mastery of concepts are accomplished, in part, through a "representational redescription" process: First, a child acquires an embodied performance ability, then through representational redescription, that is, through extracting explicit representation, the child learns explicit concepts and thereby further improves performance. CLARION, as described earlier, captures this developmental process (in a qualitative way).

6.6   Further Discussions

We can contrast the afore-outlined approach with some other approaches. One major difference that I see is that traditional thinking tends to overlook various external factors in cognition. David Hume (Hume 1938) believed that cognition can only be understood on the basis of sense data that an individual agent receives, based on which an agent forms associations that relate them, in order to make sense of them. In William James' *The Principles of Psychology* (James 1890), in a total of 28 chapters covering a wide ranging set of topics, cognition is construed as merely an internal process that works on data provided by external sources. In *Readings in Cognitive Science* edited by Collins and Smith (1988), a major collection of significant early work in cognitive science, the field of cognitive science was defined to be "the interdisciplinary study of the acquisition and use of knowledge". Despite the fact that knowledge is the result of agents' interaction with the world (individually and/or collectively), there is no treatment of such dynamic interaction in the book.

In contemporary cognitive science and AI, although ideas similar to some of those outlined here have started to seep into various segments of research communities (see, e.g., Damasio 1994, Sun 1994, Freeman 1995, Russell and Norvig 1995, Hutchins 1995, Agre 1997, Clancey 1997, Pfeifer and Scheier 1999), cognitive science/AI, as a whole, has not been particularly hospitable to these new ideas. See, for example, Vera and Simon (1993) and Hayes et al. (1994) for a glimpse of the oppositions to these ideas.

Another comparison is with regard to duality in cognition (i.e., dual processes or dual levels), which has long been speculated on. For example, the notion of the conscious versus the subconscious has captivated pop culture ever since Freud (Freud 1937). In mainstream academic psychology (especially cognitive psychology) and in mainstream academic philosophy, it is not quite readily accepted (although there are some notable exceptions such as Kitcher 1992). This distinction has been considered as belonging to the realm of pop psychology. The distinction of the conceptual versus the subconceptual was proposed, in the context of analyzing connectionist models (Smolensky 1988), as a sort of substitute for the distinction of the conscious versus the subconscious (to avoid the controversies surrounding the latter). The distinction of the conceptual versus the subconceptual has not been very popular either. In contrast, I take such dichotomies seriously and adopt them as the basis of CLARION.

The approach outlined here is consistent with situated cognition views, in the sense that coping with the world means acting in an environmentally driven fashion and dealing with moment-to-moment contingencies. My approach reflects such a view through a focus on reacting to the current state of the world. Also in line with situated cognition views, learning in the present approach is tied closely to specific situations as experienced (to reflect and exploit environmental contingencies and regularities). But there are some clear differences. Some situated cognition theorists sometimes claim that there should not be any elaborate model of the world or elaborate representation. However, instead of being completely antithetical to the representationalist view and hastily avoiding representation, I take a more inclusive approach: I show that explicit representation *can* be constructed on the basis of situated learning by situated agents, through a bottom-up process, thus unifying the two contradictory approaches.

6.7   Summary

This chapter shows how representation and representational content emerge from the interaction between agents and their environment. It hypothesizes the process that goes from unmediated comportment with the world to mediated cognition with symbolic, conceptual representation and the concomitant conceptual processing.

The framework outlined here reconciles representationalism and situated cognition interactivism. It does so through explicating the crucial role played by direct and unmediated comportment. Comportment bridges the gap between the world and the internal explicit representation in an agent. It makes explicit representation possible by giving rise to it through experience.

The key to this framework lies in recognizing the fact that experiences (everyday activities) come first and representation comes later and, based on that, demonstrating the computational feasibility of this process. Instead of Descartes' motto "I think, therefore I am" (or the revisionist version "I feel, therefore I am", as in Damasio 1994), I argue that it should be "I am, therefore I think". I believe that this reversal sets the priority right in studying the human mind.

Chapter 7

The Issue of Consciousness

> *The sheer functioning of consciousness, though it cannot possibly assure a worldly reality given to the senses and to reasons, confirms beyond doubt the reality of sensations and of reasoning.*
> — *Hannah Arendt: "The Human Condition".*

7.1 Introduction

In this chapter, I evaluate computational models of cognition, especially CLARION, in relation to the paramount issue of cognition—consciousness.

I will first critique various explanations of consciousness, especially those embodied by existing computational models. I will then explore the issue of the functional roles of consciousness and examine various views in this regard, in relation to the explanation of consciousness. In these examinations, I will argue in favor of the explanation based on the distinction between localist (symbolic) representation and distributed representation. I will also advance a proposal that encompasses various existing views concerning the functional roles of consciousness.

To begin with, let us examine some general approaches toward consciousness. A view held by William James (1890) is that consciousness is a kind of organ that is necessary for regulating the "blooming, buzzing" chaos of a plethora of stimuli and the behaviors associated with them.

Another view held by John Dewey (1958) saw consciousness as "that phase of a system of meanings which at a given time is undergoing re-direction, transitive transformation" (for example, when switching attention resulting from being alerted by a loud signal). Sigmund Freud suggested that consciousness and unconsciousness formed separate parts in the mind, and each had its intentions and competed to be manifested in behavior.

For many decades up until very recently, in experimental studies of the human mind, the notion of consciousness has been replaced with various operationalized notions. Many theories are clearly related to the issue of consciousness although under guises as theories for various operationalized notions. For instance, in cognitive psychology, there is the distinction of implicit memory versus explicit memory (Schacter 1990, Roedeger 1990). Based on the experimental dissociation of explicit and implicit memory tests, it has been suggested that implicit memory and explicit memory involve different memory systems (for example, the episodic memory system versus the semantic memory system, or the declarative memory versus the procedural memory; Bower 1996, Squire et al. 1993, Schacter 1990). Related to this, there is the distinction between implicit learning and explicit learning, as discussed amply before. The notion of automaticity (Shiffrin and Schneider 1977, Logan 1988) is also similar.[1] There is also the well-known distinction of procedural and declarative knowledge in cognitive psychology. Various models have been constructed along these lines.

Recently, in cognitive science there is a resurgence of interest in consciousness per se as a subject for experimental and theoretical studies. Various new philosophical views and computational models have been proposed, including consciousness as an emergent property (e.g., as in a connectionist model that settles into an attractor), consciousness as a system separate from the rest of the mind that works deliberately and serially, consciousness as a supervisory system, or consciousness as a dominant process in a pool of processes running in parallel, and so on.

In this chapter, I try to provide an overall examination of computational models of consciousness, on the basis of available psychological data, as well as existing philosophical accounts, and come

---

[1] Also relevant to this is the notion of attention (Posner and Petersen 1990): Controlled processing requires attention, while automatic processing requires no attention (Shiffrin and Schneider 1977, Kieras and Meyer 1997).

to some conclusions as to what a plausible computational account should be like, synthesizing various operationalized psychological notions of consciousness. In the next section, I first present various existing models and their explanations of the conscious/unconscious distinction. I then analyze the plausibility of each of these explanations, which leads to favoring one particular explanation, as embodied in CLARION, over all others. In section 3, I turn to analyzing the functional roles of consciousness and correspondingly how such roles can be captured in CLARION.

7.2   Explaining Consciousness

We generally assume the sufficiency and necessity of computational explanations of consciousness. By computational explanation, I mean any concrete physical processes, that is, computational processes in the broadest sense of the term *computational*. In terms of the *sufficiency* of such explanations, the following hypothesis serves as our working hypothesis (Jackendoff 1987):

> Hypothesis of computational sufficiency: every phenomenological distinction is caused by/supported by/projected from a corresponding computational distinction.

For the lack of a clearly better alternative, this hypothesis remains a viable working hypothesis, despite various criticisms of it.[2]   In general, "computation" is a broad term that can be used to denote any process that can be realized computationally, ranging from chaotic dynamics (Freeman 1995) and "Darwinian" competition (Edelman 1992), to quantum mechanics (Penrose 1994).

On the other hand, as to the *necessity* of computational explanations, it is obvious to anyone who is not a dualist that the foregoing specification of computational processes has to include the necessary condition for consciousness; for the physical basis of mental activities and phenomenal experience cannot be anything else but such computational processes (as defined broadly).

---

[2] These criticisms, for example, by Searle (1980) and Penrose (1994), generally failed to show that computation, in principle, could not account for the nature of consciousness, although they had some legitimate complaints about specific computational approaches and models.

We need an explanation of the computational basis of consciousness and its roles (or functions) in the human mind: What kind of mechanism leads to the conscious, and what kind of mechanism leads to the unconscious? What is the functional role of the conscious? What is the functional role of the unconscious?   Such questions are highly relevant as they lead to useful theoretical frameworks for empirical work.

7.2.1 Different Views

We can categorize existing explanations based on their different emphases, which may include emphases on: (1) differences in knowledge organization across two subsystems, (2) differences in knowledge content across two subsystems, (3) differences in knowledge representation across two subsystems, (4) differences in knowledge processing mechanisms across two subsystems, or (5) different processing modes underlying the same system. Let us discuss these categories of computational explanations.

First of all, some explanations are based on recognizing that there are two separate (sub)systems in the mind. The difference between the two systems can be explained in terms of differences in either processing mechanisms, knowledge organization, knowledge content, or knowledge representation. Some examples of such explanations are as follows.

The SN+PS view: Anderson (1983) proposed in the ACT* model that there are two types of knowledge: Declarative knowledge is represented by semantic networks, and it is consciously accessible; procedural knowledge is represented by production rules, and it is inaccessible. The difference lies in different ways of organizing knowledge: whether knowledge is organized in an action-centered way (procedural knowledge) or in an action-independent way (declarative knowledge). Both types of knowledge are represented symbolically, using either symbolic semantic networks or symbolic production rules. The semantic networks use spreading activation (Collins and Loftus 1975) to activate relevant nodes, and the production rules compete for control through parallel condition matching and firing. The ACT* model embodying this view has been used for modeling a variety of human skill learning tasks (see, e.g., Anderson 1983).

The PS+SN view: As suggested by Hunt and Lansman (1986), the "deliberate" process of production matching and firing, which is serial, can be assumed to be a conscious process, while the spreading activation

(Collins and Loftus 1975) in semantic networks, which is massively parallel, can be assumed to be an unconscious process. The model based on this view has been used to model controlled and automatic processing data in the attention-performance literature (Hunt and Lansman 1986).

This view is almost the exact opposite of the view advocated by Anderson (1983), in terms of the roles of the two mechanisms involved. However, the emphasis in this view is on the processing difference of the two mechanisms: serial versus parallel, not on knowledge organization.

The algorithm+instance view: As suggested by Logan (1988) and Stanley et al. (1989), instance retrieval and use should be considered unconscious (Stanley et al. 1989) or automatic (Logan 1988), while the use of "algorithms" involves conscious awareness, either during "algorithmic" processes (Logan 1988), or in their products—knowledge resulting from "algorithmic" processes (Stanley et al. 1989).[3] It was suggested that the use of an algorithm is under tight control and carried out in a serial, step-by-step way, while instances can be retrieved in parallel and effortlessly (Logan 1988). The emphasis here is, again, on the differences in processing mechanisms.

The instance+PS view: Proposed by Anderson (1993) in his ACT-R model, this is a variation on the declarative/procedural distinction in the ACT* model, in which explicit instances make up the declarative knowledge and production rules (learned from analogical use of instances) make up the procedural knowledge. Again, both types of knowledge are represented symbolically. The distinction is purely on the basis of the content difference between the two types of knowledge.

The episode+activation view: Bower (1996) suggests that unconscious processes are based on activation propagation through strengths or weights (e.g., in a connectionist fashion) between different nodes representing perceptual or conceptual primitives; conscious processes are based on explicit episodic memory of past episodes. What is emphasized is the rich spatial-temporal context of episodic memory—the plentiful ad hoc associations with contextual information, acquired on an one-shot basis, which is termed type-2 associations, as opposed to regular type-1 associations, which are based on semantic relatedness. This

---

[3] The term *algorithm* was not clearly defined in Logan (1988) and apparently referred to processes more complex than instance retrieval.

emphasis somewhat distinguishes this view from other views concerning instances/episodes, such as Neal and Hesketh (1997), Logan (1988), and Stanley et al. (1989).

The reliance on memory of specific events in this view bears some resemblance to some neurobiologically motivated views that rely on the interplay of various memory systems, such as those advocated by Taylor (1997) and McClelland et al. (1995).

The two-pathway view: There have been various proposals in neurobiology that there are different pathways in the human brain, some of which lead to conscious awareness, while others do not. For example, see Milner and Goodale (1995), Damasio (1994), and LeDoux (1992) for different versions of such a view.

The connection/disconnection view: As suggested by, for example, Schacter (1990) and Revonsuo (1993), in the human brain, multiple specialized processing modules co-exist, each of which performs specialized processing without incurring conscious awareness, with the exception of one unique module that is solely responsible for conscious awareness. Each of the specialized processing modules can send its output to the conscious module, thus making the output consciously accessible. There appears to be psychological and neurophysiological evidence supporting this claim (Schacter 1990).

The localist+distributed representation view: As proposed in Sun (1994, 1995, 1997, 1999), different representational forms in different subsystems may be used to explain the qualitative difference between the conscious and the unconscious. One type of representation is symbolic, or localist when implemented in connectionist models, in which one distinct entity (e.g., a node in a connectionist model) represents a concept. The other type of representation is distributed, in which a non-exclusive set of entities (e.g., a set of nodes in a connectionist model) are used for representing one concept and representations of different concepts overlap each other; in other words, in distributed representations, a concept is represented as a pattern of activations over a set of entities (e.g., a set of nodes).

Conceptual structures, for example, rules, can be implemented in the localist/symbolic subsystem in a straightforward way by various connections between relevant entities (see Sun 1994 for details). In distributed representations, such structures (including rules) are diffusely duplicated in a way consistent with the meanings of the structures (Sun 1994), which captures automatic, unconscious performance. There may be various connections between corresponding representations across the two subsystems.

In contrast to these two-(sub)system views, there are also views that insist on the unitary nature of the conscious and the unconscious. That is, they hold that the conscious and the unconscious are the different manifestations of the same underlying system or process (Dennett 1991). The difference is thus that of processing modes in the same system. The unitary views sometimes led to the outright dismissal of the notion of consciousness, or at least its significance in understanding cognition, as they tend to blur the distinction between conscious and unconscious beings (Dennett 1991). Let us look into some of these views.

The threshold view: As proposed by various researchers including Bowers et al. (1990), the difference between the conscious and the unconscious can be explained by the difference between activations of mental structures above a certain threshold and activations of such structures below the threshold. When activations reach the threshold level, an individual becomes aware of the content of the activated structures; otherwise, although the activated structures may influence behavior, they are not accessible consciously.

The chunking view: As described by Servan-Schreiber and Anderson (1987) and Rosenbloom et al. (1993), a chunk is considered a unitary representation and its internal working is oblique, despite the fact that its inputs/outputs are accessible. A chunk can be a (simple or complex) production rule, as in the SOAR model described in Rosenbloom et al. (1993), or a sequence of perceptual or motor elements, as in the model of Servan-Schreiber and Anderson (1987). Because of the lack of transparency of the internal working of a chunk, the formation and use of chunks are equated with implicit learning (Servan-Schreiber and Anderson 1987), or automaticity in skilled performance (Rosenbloom et al. 1993). Thus, according to this view, the difference between the conscious and the unconscious (e.g., in performing a particular task) is the difference between using multiple chunks, involving some consciousness, and using one (complex) chunk, involving no consciousness.

The coherence view: As suggested by Baars (1988), some sort of coherence in the activities of the mind (or the brain), for example, activation of a coherent pattern of representations, coherent firing of neurons, or a stable pattern of activation of a neural network, gives rise to consciousness. The emphasis here is on the role of internal consistency in the process of producing consciousness. The distinction of the conscious and the unconscious is reduced to the distinction between coherent and incoherent activities in the mind (or the brain).

The attractor view: As suggested by Mathis and Mozer (1996), being in a stable attractor of a dynamic system (a neural network in particular) leads to consciousness. The distinction between the conscious and the unconscious is hereby reduced to the distinction of being in a stable attractor versus being in a transient state. This is a case of the coherence view.

The synchronous firing view: As suggested by Crick and Koch (1990), synchronous firing of neurons in the human brain (at 35-75 Hz in particular) leads to conscious awareness of those objects represented by the neurons involved in synchronous firing. This is another case of the coherence view.

The reverberation view: As suggested by Damasio (1994) and Taylor (1997), consciousness is the result of reverberation of information flows across various cortical and sub-cortical areas. This is yet another case of the coherence view.

Note that some of the afore-discussed views are based on biological findings or concerned with biological mechanisms, processes or systems, such as the synchronous firing view, the reverberation view, and the two-pathway view, as discussed earlier.

Having enumerated these views, we shall now carry out a detailed analysis of them.

7.2.2   Analysis of Different Views

Below I show that the explanations in terms of knowledge content, knowledge organization, or knowledge processing are untenable. Thus, it leaves us with one possibility—knowledge representation.

Two important premises of subsequent discussions are *direct accessibility* of conscious processes and *direct inaccessibility* of unconscious processes. Conscious processes should be *directly* accessible, that is, directly verbally expressible, without involving intermediate interpretive or transformational steps, which is a requirement prescribed or accepted by many theoreticians (see, e.g., Clark 1993, Hadley 1995). Unconscious processes should be, in contrast, inaccessible directly (but may be accessed indirectly somehow, through some interpretive process), thus exhibiting different properties (see, e.g., Heidegger 1927a, Dreyfus and Dreyfus 1987, Reber 1989). The accessibility can be defined in terms of surface syntactic structures of the objects being accessed (at the level of outcomes or processes), not their semantic meanings. Thus, for example, a LISP expression is directly accessible, even though one may not fully understand its meaning. The internal working of a neural network may be inaccessible even though one may know what the network essentially does through an interpretive process.

First of all, let us examine these views that embrace a two-(sub)system perspective. Note that the following discussions are not meant to fully (or "fairly") characterize the position of each author mentioned, but instead are focused on the abstract positions per se, while drawing examples from different authors.

To begin with, the problem of the SN+PS view reviewed earlier (as in ACT* of Anderson 1983) is that both types of knowledge (declarative and procedural) are represented in an explicit, symbolic form (i.e., semantic networks and productions), and thus it did not explain the *qualitative* phenomenological differences in conscious accessibility between the two types of knowledge. Although the knowledge organization is apparently different between semantic networks and production rules (e.g., with different degrees of action-centeredness), the difference is inappropriate and irrelevant to account for the qualitative phenomenological difference in conscious accessibility, because both are symbolically represented and fundamentally the same. The difference in conscious accessibility is thus simply *assumed* instead of being *intrinsic* (in terms of something more fundamental). There is no theoretical reduction of accessibility/inaccessibility to any fundamental mechanistic (computational) notions.

Another way of looking at the difference between declarative knowledge and procedural knowledge is in terms of processing: One uses spreading activation (Collins and Loftus 1975) and the other uses rule matching and firing (Klahr et al. 1987). However, this difference cannot account for the conscious/unconscious difference, because there is no fundamental difference between symbolic spreading activation and symbolic rule matching and firing. Admittedly, rule matching and firing are often serial (e.g., as in Hunt and Lansman 1986, Logan 1988, Klahr et al. 1987, but not in Anderson 1983) and spreading activation is usually parallel (Collins and Loftus 1975), but there is no *fundamental* qualitative difference between the two mechanisms for accomplishing these two processes, both of which involve similar symbolic manipulation. Moreover, rule matching and firing can also be parallel, as demonstrated by, for example, Anderson (1983), Rosenbloom et al. (1993), and Sun (1995).

The problem with the instance+PS view (as in ACT-R of Anderson 1993), in which the difference is based on knowledge content, is similar: The difference between accessibility and inaccessibility is simply assumed, and there is no further explanation that can be offered by this view. This is because neither the difference between the symbolic representation of instances and the symbolic representation of production rules, nor the difference between the symbolic processing for instance use and the symbolic processing for production use, is relevant for accounting for the qualitative difference in conscious accessibility.

The PS+SN view (Hunt and Lansman 1986), in which serial production matching and firing are assumed to be a conscious process while parallel spreading activation in semantic networks is assumed to be a unconscious process, is almost the exact opposite of the SN+PS view (Anderson 1983). The problem with the view is also similar: There is no mechanistic difference that is sufficiently fundamental so as to be able to account for the qualitative phenomenological difference between the conscious and the unconscious, because both representations are symbolic and the two processing mechanisms (rules matching/firing and spreading activation) are highly similar.

The algorithm+instance view (see Logan 1988, Stanley et al. 1989) is actually similar to the PS+SN view of Hunt and Lansman (1986), except that "algorithms" (generalizations of production rule matching and firing) are used in place of production systems and "instances" are used in place of semantic networks. But the implication is the same: An algorithm, like a production system in the former view, is tightly controlled and carried out in a serial, step-by-step way, while instances, like semantic networks, get activated in parallel and "effortlessly". However, as in the PS+SN view, there is no substantial mechanistic (computational) difference that has sufficient explanatory power to account for the qualitative difference in conscious accessibility, because mechanistically, algorithms and instance matching may both require the same kind of symbolic manipulation.

The episode+activation view (Bower 1996) is also a manifestation of the approach that relies on the difference in terms of knowledge content, and in this case, it relies on the difference between having versus not having rich spatial-temporal associations. Although having rich spatial-temporal associations may be highly correlated with being conscious of something, it is neither a necessary nor a sufficient condition for consciousness. As it should be obvious to us, there are clearly cases in which we are conscious of something without rich spatial-temporal information coming to mind (see, e.g., later discussions of phenomenal consciousness). Thus viewing the distinction of the conscious and the unconscious as the distinction between episodes with spatio-temporal contexts and activation of pre-existing (semantic) knowledge, although intriguing, is not well founded.[4]

On the other hand, the problem with the *connection/disconnection* view is that there is no explanation of why there are two qualitatively different types of modules: one conscious and the other unconscious. There is nothing inherent in the view that can help to shed light on the difference between the conscious and the unconscious in terms of different mechanistic (computational) processes underlying them. Furthermore, although this view had some success in accounting for some implicit memory (dissociation) data, it has also had some difficulties in accounting for some others.

We can look at Schacter (1990)'s model as an example (see Figure 7.1). The model is based on neuropsychological findings of the dissociation of different types of knowledge (especially in brain damaged patients). It includes a number of "knowledge modules" that perform specialized and unconscious processing and may send their outcomes to a "conscious

---

[4] However, a variation of this view expressed in McClelland et al. (1995) relates the idea to the representational difference view and is thus more convincing.

awareness system", which gives rise to conscious awareness. Schacter's explanation of some neuropsychological disorders (e.g., hemisphereneglect, blindsight, aphasia, agnosia, and prosopagnosia) is that brain damages result in disconnection of some of the modules from the conscious awareness system, which causes their inaccessibility to consciousness. However, as has been pointed out by others, this explanation cannot account for many findings in implicit memory research (e.g., Roedeger 1990).[5]

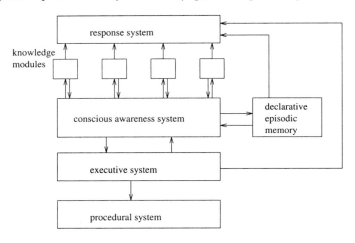

Figure 7.1. Schacter's model of consciousness

Similarly, the problem of the two-pathway view is that, although there is also ample biological evidence that indicates the existence of multiple pathways in the brain (in vision, language, and other modalities) and some are correlated with conscious awareness while some others are not (e.g., as described in Milner and Goodale 1995 and LeDoux 1992), there is no *explanation* of why some result in consciousness while others do not, beside the fact that they are involved with different neuropathways, which does not constitute an explanation. For example, LeDoux (1992) described one pathway as from stimuli to the thalamus to the cortex, which produced conscious thoughts, and another pathway as from stimuli to the thalamus then to the amygdala, which could lead directly to the brain stem and effect actions without any conscious process. Milner and Goodale (1995) similarly described two visual processing pathways: the ventral pathway

---

[5] Revonsuo (1993) also advocated this view, albeit from a philosophical viewpoint.

and the dorsal pathway. However, in either theories, although plausible neurobiological correlates of consciousness were identified, there was no mechanistic explanation of the processing difference of the two pathways involved. Much more biological research is needed to clarify this issue.

Having examined these two-system views, let us now turn to the unitary views (the single-system views). With the unitary views, no fundamentally different processes or mechanisms are needed to explain the difference between the conscious and the unconscious. Therefore, there seems to be an "elegant" parsimony of theoretical constructs, which is certainly appealing. The problem with the unitary views in general, however, is that there is the same lack of fundamental, qualitative difference, as with the aforementioned two-system views, between whatever is used to account for the conscious and whatever else is used to account for the unconscious, in contrast to the fundamental qualitative difference between the conscious and the unconscious. Whether it is coherence/consistency, or synchrony, or reverberation, or above-threshold activations, it is a leap of faith to believe that it can lead to conscious awareness, let alone the phenomenal experience of consciousness.

At this point, it may be helpful to examine a few instances of the unitary views in some details. We can first look into the coherence view. In Baars' (1988) model (see Figure 7.2), a large number of specialist processors performed unconscious processing and a global workspace coordinated their activities through selecting a coherent pattern of information and through global broadcasting of that information to ensure its consistency and availability. Consciousness was explained by the global consistency and global availability of information.

We can also examine Damasio's neuroanatomically motivated model (Damasio 1994), as an example of the reverberation view, a variation on the coherence theme. The model (see Figure 7.3) hypothesized the existence of many "sensory convergence zones" that integrated information from individual sensory modalities through forward and backward synaptic connections and the resulting reverberation of activations, without a central location for information storage and comparisons; it also hypothesized the global "multi-modal convergence zone", which integrated information across modalities through reverberation via recurrent connections.

It is my opinion that, in these coherence theories, the basis of the linkage between consistency/reverberation and consciousness is not clear, although these theories captured one (alleged) property of consciousness—consistency or coherence. Correlated with consistency in these models was global information availability; that is, once "broadcasting" or "reverberation" was achieved, all the information about an entity stored in difference places of the brain became available. This was believed to have explained the accessibility of consciousness. Quite to the contrary, however, we have reasons to believe that consciousness does not necessarily mean accessibility/availability of *all* the information about an entity, because otherwise, conscious inference, deliberate recollection, and other related processes would be unnecessary.

Similarly, Crick and Koch (1990) hypothesized that synchronous firing at 35-75 Hz in the cerebral cortex was the basis for consciousness: With such synchronous firing, pieces of information regarding different aspects of an entity were brought together, and thus consciousness emerged. Although consciousness has been experimentally observed to be somewhat correlated with synchronous firing at 35-75 Hz, there is no explanation of *why* this is the case and there is no explanation of any *qualitative* difference between 35-75 Hz synchronous firing and other firing patterns.

On the other hand, Mathis and Mozer (1996) proposed a model embodying the attractor view. In their model, a stable attractor was equated with conscious awareness, while transient states were considered inaccessible to consciousness due to short durations. However, there was no explanation of *why* settling in an attractor could lead to consciousness, beside the difference in duration (which did not seem relevant at all).

In the chunking view as embodied by SOAR (Rosenbloom et al. 1993), although the equation of the inaccessibility of the internal working of a chunk with the inaccessibility of the unconscious is appealing, the problem with the chunking view is that the assumption of inaccessibility of the inside of a chunk is not supported by any explanation of that inaccessibility in terms of the working of intra-chunk and inter-chunk mechanisms. It is *assumed*, rather than explained based on something that is more fundamental. As a result, there is no theoretical reduction being accomplished.

Shallice (1972) put forward a model, which embodied the threshold view. In the model, there were a number of "action systems" that

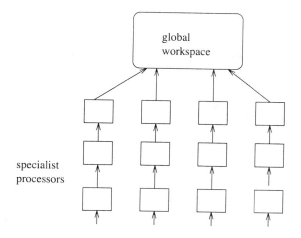

Figure 7.2. Baars' model of consciousness

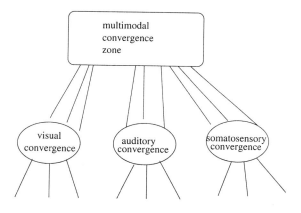

Figure 7.3. Damasio's model of consciousness

could be activated by "selector input", and the activated action systems corresponded to consciousness. However, there was no mechanistic (computational) explanation of the fundamental difference between conscious and unconscious processes being offered by this model.

Finally, the problem with the biologically motivated views in general is that the gap between phenomenology and physiology/biology is so great that something else is needed to bridge the gap. Otherwise, if we rush directly into complex neural physiological thickets, we may lose

sight of forests. Computation, in its broadest sense, can serve to bridge
the gap. It provides an intermediate level of explanation, in terms of
processes, mechanisms, and functions. It also helps to determine how
various aspects of the conscious and the unconscious figure into the
architecture of the mind, that is, to investigate the essential framework
of the mind rather than voluminous details many of which are certainly
irrelevant. In addition, being biological does not automatically constitute
explanatory sufficiency, although biological evidence does lend theories
more credibility in a subjective way. A middle level between phenomenology
and physiology/biology might be more apt at capturing fundamental
characteristics of consciousness.

Judging from the foregoing analysis, each of these views is
flawed in some way. In comparison, the representational difference
(localist+distributed) view has a distinct edge. Specifically, the advantage
of the view lies in the explanation of consciousness in terms of a mechanistic
(computational) distinction, reducing a set of vague notions needing
explanation to a set of notions that are better understood—the *reduction*
of the dichotomy of the conscious and the unconscious to the more
tangible dichotomy of localist (symbolic) representation and distributed
representation. This view will be examined in greater detail next.

7.2.3   Further Evidence and Arguments

I will present some plausible evidence and arguments for the duality, or
dichotomy, of the mind, which leads naturally to the representational
difference view and the related two-level models (e.g., Sun 1994, 1995, 1997,
1999). There have been various proposals, differing in emphasis, flavor,
and level of detail, that pertain to dichotomous structuring of the mind.
The disciplinary origins of these proposals include biology, psychology,
philosophy, and computer science (artificial intelligence).

First, let us look into some of the early ideas concerning dichotomies
of the mind that dated back before the inception of cognitive science.
For instance, Heidegger's distinction—the preontological versus the
ontological—is an abstract version of such a dichotomy. As a first
approximation, his view is that, because the essential way of being is
existence in the world, an agent always embodies an understanding of its
being through such existence. This embodied understanding is implicit

and embedded in skills, routines, and know-hows, without an explicit "ontology", and is thus *preontological*. On that basis, an agent may also achieve an explicit understanding, an *ontological* understanding, especially through making explicit the implicitly held understanding. In other words, the agent may turn preontological understanding into ontological understanding (Heidegger 1927a, Dreyfus 1992). Note that this dichotomy and the progression from the concrete to the abstract have been the basis of the CLARION model.

Also deserving mentioning is William James' (1890) distinction of "empirical thinking" and "true reasoning". Empirical thinking is associative, made up of sequences of "images" that are suggested by one another. It is "reproductive", because it always replicates in some way past experience, instead of producing novel ideas. Empirical thinking relies on overall comparisons of similarity among concrete situations and therefore may lose sight of critical information. On the other hand, "true reasoning" can be arrived at by abstracting particular attributes out of a situation. In so doing, an agent assumes a particular way of conceiving things; that is, it sees things as particular aspects of them. With a proper conception of a situation, an agent can reach a proper conclusion relatively easily. It is thus "productive", because it is capable of producing novel ideas through abstraction, in contrast to the holistic treatment in empirical thinking. It helps the agent in novel, unprecedented situations and thus serves an important function. "True reasoning" also serves to break up the direct link between thought and action and provides a means for articulately and theoretically reasoning about consequences of actions without actually performing them.

Dreyfus and Dreyfus (1987) more recently proposed the distinction of analytical and intuitive thinking, refining and revising Heidegger's distinction in a contemporary context. Their claim is that analytical thinking corresponds to what traditional (symbolic) AI models are aimed to capture: deliberate, sequential processing that follows rules and performs symbolic manipulation. According to them, when an agent first learns about a domain (for example, chess), it learns rules and follows them one-by-one. After gaining some experience with the domain, it starts to develop an overall understanding of a situation as a whole, that is, intuitive thinking, which has the characteristics of being situationally sensitive, non-rule-like, and "holographic". Contrasting these two types of thinking, there is clearly a dichotomy, although it is focused on the (reverse) progression from the abstract to the concrete.[6]

In addition, psychologists have proposed a host of empirical dichotomies, on the basis of experimental evidence in a variety of tasks. These dichotomies include implicit learning versus explicit learning, implicit memory versus explicit memory, automatic versus controlled processing, incidental versus intentional learning, and so on, as briefly reviewed earlier in this chapter. They are highly correlated with the notion of the conscious versus the unconscious, and in many cases, are special cases of the conscious/unconscious distinction. The support for these dichotomies lies in experimental data that reveal various dissociations and differences in performance under different conditions (see chapter 2 for some examples).

Although there is no consensus regarding the details of the dichotomies, there is a consensus on the *qualitative* difference between two different types of cognition. Moreover, most of the aforementioned authors believed in the necessity of incorporating both sides of the dichotomies, because each side serves a unique cognitive function and is thus indispensable. On the basis of the belief of the difference and the complementarity of the two sides, it is natural to hypothesize the existence of two separate subsystems, whereby each subsystem is responsible for one side of a dichotomy, for example, as has been variously proposed by Anderson (1993), Hunt and Lansman (1986), Logan (1988), Reber (1989), Schacter (1990), and Sun (1994, 1997).[7] Although the two subsystems were variously described as production systems versus semantic networks, as algorithmic processes versus instance retrieval, or as localist representation versus distributed representation, our analysis earlier did indicate that the best explanatory construct was in terms of representational difference: localist (symbolic) versus distributed representation, as advanced in connectionist theorizing. Reber (1989), Lewicki et al. (1992), and Squire et al. (1993) had similar views on the role of representational difference when interpreting their experimental data.

In recent years, inspired by some of the above theorizing, there have

---

[6] There are a few arguments from cognitive scientists, and connectionists in particular, that are relevant to this dichotomy, for example, Smolensky (1988) and Hinton (1990).

[7] Sigmund Freud's theories, by the way, also fit into this category.

been models based on the connectionist approach that support the two-system hypothesis and utilize representational difference. The success of these models is an indication of the plausibility of this sort of idea. For example, Hendler (1987) presented a hybrid system for planning. It utilized connectionist networks for priming relevant concepts through activation propagation, to pick out right action choices, in order to augment symbolic planning, which otherwise might have too many choices. The combination of the two types of mechanisms aided in the effectiveness of the system. CONSYDERR (Sun 1994) was another example, which consisted of two levels of connectionist networks: One level employed localist representation for modeling conceptual reasoning and the other level employed distributed representation for modeling subconceptual reasoning. Through the interaction of the two levels, many seemingly disparate and difficult patterns of commonsense reasoning were accounted for uniformly. See also Sun and Bookman (1994) for a number of other models adopting this view. The most relevant model, however, is CLARION, which accounts well for a variety of human data (see chapters 4 and 5).

Let us address the correspondence of consciousness and the two levels of CLARION. Rather than simply equating the top level with the conscious and the bottom level with the unconscious, the full picture is more complex. Of course, the top level, due to its explicitness, facilitates conscious awareness, and the bottom level, due to its implicitness, hinders such awareness (Clark and Karmiloff-Smith 1993). So there is a high degree of correlation between the two dichotomies. The two levels provide the representational correlates of the distinction between the conscious and the unconscious. However, the two-level structure alone does not completely explain the complexity of consciousness. First of all, because being accessible does not necessarily mean being accessed, whatever is going on at the top level is not necessarily conscious, but only potentially conscious; that is, it is conscious when it is *being* accessed. Being accessible is a necessary condition of consciousness, but not a sufficient condition. Second, the conscious access at the top level can be either with respect to the process, which is termed *reflective consciousness*, or with respect to the outcome, which is termed *access consciousness*. Third, when we say that the bottom level is not conscious, we mean that the processing detail at the bottom level is not directly accessible. However, indirect access can be obtained through the activation of corresponding explicit representations at the top level by the bottom level, which is an interpretive (or transformational) process that turns an implicit representation into an explicit one (Clark 1993, Hadley 1995, Sun 1995).

Next we turn to the discussion of functional roles of consciousness on the basis of this mechanistic explanation of consciousness.

7.3   Functional Roles of Consciousness

One philosophically well-established taxonomy of consciousness is dividing it into phenomenal consciousness, reflective consciousness, and access consciousness (Block 1994).   Consequently, I address the issue of the functional roles of consciousness in each of these three respects.

Let me first make clear the distinction among these three types of consciousness. In my definition, "access consciousness" refers to the direct availability of mental content for access (e.g., verbal report), while "reflective consciousness" refers to the direct availability of the *process* of mental activities for access.   That is, if access consciousness allows one to access the outcome of a reasoning process, reflective consciousness allows one to access the process, or steps, of the reasoning process.[8] However, beside the direct availability of mental content (processes or outcomes), there is also the issue of "phenomenal consciousness", that is, the phenomenal quality, the subjective feel, of mental content, as Thomas Nagel brought out in his famous article "What is it like to be a bat?" (Nagel 1974). Hence the tripartite structure of consciousness.

7.3.1   Access Consciousness

Concerning the functional role of access consciousness in the overall functioning of the mind, there have been various suggestions.

The veto view: As suggested by Libet (1985), the function of consciousness is to be able to veto unconsciously initiated actions. In his physiologically derived theory, an action is initiated unconsciously, and 250 ms after the unconscious initiation, there is a window of 100 ms in which consciousness can choose to veto the initiated action.

---

[8] Note that this definition is different from some existing definitions, such as that of Lloyd (1995), which is equivalent to the notion of self awareness.

The counterbalance view: As suggested by Kelley and Jacoby (1993), the function of consciousness is to counterbalance unconscious processes. Kelley and Jacoby (1993) showed in their experiments, through contrasting "aware" versus "unaware" conditions, that conscious awareness had a distinct causal role on behavior. The two different conditions produced different causal attributions by subjects, and in turn, different causal attributions led to different actions on the part of the subjects. This view of consciousness as providing a "counterbalance" to unconsciousness seems a generalization of Libet's view on the veto function of consciousness, which is a form of counterbalancing. Counterbalancing can take on other forms too: For example, in Jacoby et al. (1994), an inclusion and exclusion procedure was used through which the function of consciousness was manipulated with instructions. In the exclusion condition, subjects were told to respond to a stimulus if they did not have conscious recollection of it from a previous exposure. In the inclusion condition, subjects were told to respond to a stimulus regardless of whether they consciously remembered it or not. The two conditions led to different response patterns.

The situational difference view: As shown by Reber (1989), Stanley et al. (1989), and others, conscious and unconscious processes are suitable for different situations, especially for different learning situations, so that either a conscious or an unconscious process is applied to a situation depending on which is most suitable to the situation. In the psychological experiments they described, subjects tended to use explicit learning (with conscious awareness) if the situation was simple (e.g., a sequence in which the next position could be unambiguously predicted by the immediately preceding position), and to use implicit learning (without conscious awareness) if the situation was more complex.

The language/planning view: As suggested by Crick and Koch (1990), the function of consciousness is to enable the use of language and (explicit) planning, due to its explicitness. However, the questions remain: Why should we use language and planning in an explicit and conscious way? Why can't the function of language and planning be achieved without conscious awareness? We need a deeper explanation.

The synergy view: As suggested in Sun (1994, 1995, 1997, 1999), the function of the distinction between the conscious and the unconscious lies in the flexibility and synergy that this distinction affords. As shown in Sun

(1994, 1997), the interaction of the conscious and the unconscious (as two distinct processes) can, in many common circumstances, lead to a synergy in terms of learning and performance. Let us discuss in more detail this view.

As evidenced by the available psychological data (e.g., on implicit learning and implicit memory), conscious processes tend to be more crisp and focused (or selective), while unconscious processes tend to be more complex, broadly scoped (unselective), and context-sensitive.[9] Due to their vastly different and contrasting characteristics, it should not come as a surprise that the interaction of the conscious and the unconscious leads to synergistic results. In the statistical literature, it is well known that combining diversified processes (e.g., estimators) can improve performance. See, for example, Breiman (1996), Ueda and Nakano (1996), Wolpert (1992), and Efron and Morris (1973).[10]

There is some psychological evidence directly in support of the synergy view. We discussed in chapter 2 various findings that pointed to synergy between the conscious and the unconscious. Synergy has also been demonstrated computationally, in the domains of commonsense reasoning (Sun 1994, 1995) and skill learning (see chapters 3 and 5).

Furthermore, the synergy view encompasses all the aforementioned views regarding consciousness. According to the synergy view, consciousness can certainly veto or counterbalance unconsciousness, given the right circumstances when such veto or counterbalance improve the overall performance (that is, if they lead to synergy), or if explicit instructions dictate it (e.g., Jacoby et al. 1994). Likewise, the synergy view can explain the situational difference view, in that in some extreme cases, it may be advantageous to use only conscious or unconscious processes (although normally both types of processes are present due to their synergistic effect). The synergy view can also encompass the language/planning view, because it explains why one should use conscious language and planning processes, on top of ongoing unconscious processes: It is because of the possibility of improved performance through using both

---

[9] See Reber (1989), Berry and Broadbent (1988), and Seger (1994) regarding complexity; see Hayes and Broadbent (1988) regarding selectivity. Similar points have been made by, for example, Baars (1988), McClelland et al. (1995), and Sun (1997).
[10] However, it is clearly not *always* the case that combination leads to improved performance.

types of processes.

These synergy effects as revealed in psychological experiments vary with settings, which may be differentially benefitted from the interaction of conscious and unconscious processes. Special cases (and exceptions) abound in the psychological literature. Although different, these cases are nevertheless consistent with the synergy view of consciousness. For instance, purely *implicit learning* (without any detectable explicit or conscious knowledge, e.g., in Lewicki et al. 1987) occurs when a situation is so complex that no explicit/conscious learning processes can adequately handle it and thus no synergy can be expected from the interaction between the conscious and the unconscious. In such a situation, explicit (conscious) processes obviously need not be used. Thus, purely implicit learning results, which is not inconsistent with the synergy view.

Another particularly interesting situation is that of *automaticity*, in which the execution of actions (usually in perceptual-motor tasks) becomes (more or less) effortless. Shiffrin and Schneider (1977) suggested that, while controlled processes require attention, are usually serial, easily established and altered, and strongly dependent on load, automatic processes are well learned, difficult to alter, ignore, or suppress, mostly independent of attention, and almost unaffected by load. Automaticity has also been characterized based on limited resources (Navon and Gopher 1979). However, Logan (1988) has shown that attention, parallelism, load and resource limitations vary from task to task. What is common to all tasks is that while controlled processes involve explicit "algorithms" (as termed by Logan 1988), automatic processes involve only activating past memory. In such a situation, no conscious process is involved in the performance of a task per se, and unconscious processes take over. This is due to the fact that, when a task has been well learned and thus has become a routine (relying only on memory reactivation), there is no need for the synergy effect to improve either learning or performance. Implicit, unconscious processes suffice in such a situation. Therefore, explicit, conscious processes are not employed. This is the exception that proves the rule.

On the other hand, *implicit memory* (Schacter 1987, Roedeger 1990, Squire et al. 1993) refers to nonintentional retrieval of information from memory (while subjects are unaware of the retrieval). It is demonstrated through using "indirect" memory tests that show that an individual's performance in a given task improves due to prior information, as well as direct memory tests that show the lack of explicit conscious awareness of the information by the individual. Implicit memory occurs when too much or too complex information prevents the explicit retrieval of specific items. In such a situation, while explicit, conscious processes cannot successfully retrieve the information, implicit, unconscious processes are able to utilize the memory in some ways. Thus, there obviously cannot be a synergy between conscious and unconscious processes. This is clearly an extreme case, but it does not invalidate the synergy view in general.

Related to implicit memory, *unconscious perception* refers to the processing of perceptual information without conscious awareness (Merikle 1992). This phenomenon generally occurs when stimuli are too weak to be detected by conscious processes but nevertheless received, processed, and used by unconscious processes. Since only one type of process can possibly receive the information, there cannot be synergy.

Finally, *intuition* refers to unconscious processes of inference that lead to certain conclusions or decisions independent of conscious processes (e.g., Bowers et al. 1990, James 1890). The reason for intuition to take place, instead of having conscious reasoning processes accompanying unconscious processes or having conscious reasoning processes alone, can be complex and multifaceted. We have reason to believe that intuition, the unconscious reasoning process, is the product of implicit memory, implicit learning, unconscious perception, and automatization, all of which have been discussed above. When these processes lead to unconscious information being registered (Hasher and Zacks 1979, Stadler 1992), the information manifests itself and encourages unconscious inference processes. Since conscious processes have no access to such information, they cannot be involved (Nisbett and Wilson 1977). The result is intuition, reasoning without conscious awareness of how or what information has been used. In this case, no synergy between the conscious and the unconscious can be expected.

On top of all these phenomena, *attention* (Posner and Petersen 1990) is the regulation of the proportion of conscious and unconscious processing (as well as other aspects of cognition). It adjusts the amount of conscious processing assigned to a task (as a limited resource) based on, among other factors, task demands and complexity. There is no reason to believe that it is a separate mechanism, anything other than a phenomenon emerged as a by-product of the operation of conscious and unconscious processes.

As an example, the simulation results obtained from CLARION, a two-level model embodying the representational difference view of consciousness, clearly support the synergy view. Let me briefly review some particularly relevant results here. In the simulated minefield navigation task, as described earlier in chapter 3, in terms of learning speed, the superiority of the whole CLARION system over the bottom level alone was statistically significant. This indicated that incorporating both explicit and implicit (conscious and unconscious) processes helped to speed up learning. In terms of learned performance, CLARION outperformed the bottom level alone, with a statistically significant difference, indicating utilizing both processes helped to improve learned performance. Moreover, in transfer, CLARION outperformed the bottom level alone: The difference between the transfer performance of the bottom level alone and the transfer performance of the whole CLARION system was statistically significant. So again, incorporating both processes helped to facilitate transfer of learned skills. In all, CLARION was able to demonstrate the synergy effect between conscious and unconscious processes hypothesized above.

Another case is the capturing of the exclusion and inclusion procedure of Jacoby et al. (1994). In the exclusion condition, subjects were told to respond to a stimulus if they did not have conscious recollection of it from a previous exposure. In the inclusion condition, subjects were told to respond to a stimulus regardless of whether they consciously remembered it or not. The final result is synergistic of the two types of processes, in the sense that it is dependent on both types of processes and cannot be produced without the presence of either. CLARION allows the explicit manipulation of the combination function, through adjusting the parameters (see the discussion in chapter 3). Therefore, the phenomenon demonstrated by the exclusion/inclusion procedure can be accounted for by CLARION.

In addition to the synergy effect, CLARION can account for alternative situations discussed earlier, as follows. CLARION accounts for automaticity with a setting in the model in which only bottom-level modules are used for executing a task, leaving the top-level modules for other use, which happens when a task has been well learned and thus there is no more need for synergy. In relation to Logan's (1988) account of automaticity (that is, while controlled processes involve explicit "algorithmic" processes, automatic processes involve only reactivating past memory), we can equate reactivation of memory to the activations in the bottom level of CLARION, in which the weights formed from past experience constitute implicit memory of that experience, and equate "algorithmic" processes (as termed by Logan 1988) with the explicit processes at the top level of CLARION. When only memory reactivation is involved, unconscious, automatic processes dominate in CLARION.

Purely implicit learning (Reber 1989, Lewicki et al. 1992) occurs in CLARION when a situation is so complex that explicit learning processes at the top level cannot adequately handle it. The top level of CLARION does not lend itself easily to the learning of complex structures because of its crisp, individuated representations and rigid (hypothesis testing) learning processes. On the other hand, in the bottom level, distributed representations that incorporate gradedness and spatial-temporal contexts handle complex structures better (Sun 1997, Sun et al. 1998). This point can be easily seen upon examining the details of the two levels in the model (chapter 3). Our simulation of Lewicki et al. (1987), Stanley et al. (1989), Curran and Keele (1993), and Willingham et al. (1989) has also demonstrated this point (see chapter 5 as well as Sun 1999 and Sun et al. 2002).

Implicit memory can be explained by the two-level structure of CLARION. Knowledge in CLARION is separately represented in both the top level and the bottom level. While top-level information can quickly fade away due to crisp, individuated representations, especially when the information is weak and complex, bottom-level information is much more stable due to distributed representations across a large number of weights and slow change of weights (requiring multiple updating). Thus, while conscious processes may lose access to the explicitly represented information at the top level, unconscious processes retain access to the implicitly represented information at the bottom level. This leads to implicit memory phenomena. This account is essentially the same as conjectured by Bower (1996).

Unconscious perception (Merikle 1992) can be explained again based on the hypothesis in CLARION of two separate levels with localist and distributed representations respectively. While the top level fails to detect weak and complicated signals because of its crisp representations and rigid processing, the bottom level may register the information because of its distributed representations and flexible processing that accommodates complex or confusing signals due to the inherently similarity-based nature of its distributed representations.

In CLARION, the processes of implicit memory, implicit learning, unconscious perception, and automatization all lead to unconscious information being registered in the bottom level and consequently (necessarily) unconscious use of that information when circumstances require it. This leads to what is commonly referred to as intuition.

7.3.2   Reflective Consciousness

So far my view seems to fit the epiphenomenal view (Jackendoff 1987) with regard to the functional roles of consciousness.   This is because the synergy we are talking about results solely from the coexistence of the two different types of representations and consequently the two different types of processes operating on the two types of representations, respectively; only as a by-product, one of the two types of representations also gives rise to conscious awareness.   However, we have yet to address the function of reflective consciousness.

The function of reflective consciousness lies in explicit control and manipulation of mental processes, which involves meta-level processes on top of regular cognitive processes.   Such control and manipulation can include, for example, selecting a reasoning method, controlling the direction in which reasoning goes, enable/disable certain inferences, or evaluating the progress of reasoning.   When meta-level processes get assimilated into regular processes, further meta-level processes can be developed on top of them due to reflective consciousness.   Thus, potentially, we can have many levels of self-control and self-manipulation of mental processes.   Although I reject the claim that unconscious processes cannot be controlled and/or manipulated, they are clearly more difficult to be controlled or manipulated. Therefore, we see the difference between the conscious and the unconscious in terms of meta-level control and manipulation.

Relevant psychological work on meta-level processes includes cognitive studies on executive functions and meta-cognition (such as Nelson 1993, Metcalfe and Shimamura 1994, and Reder 1996), as well as behavioral studies on self control (such as Rachlin 1994).

To see how the two-level representational difference view of consciousness can account for reflective consciousness, we can examine reflective processes in CLARION. CLARION can allow many kinds of explicit control and manipulation at the top level with its use of crisp, discrete, and individuated encoding. Among these meta-level mechanisms are the following:

- Deciding reasoning methods: The reasoning methods that can be adopted include forward reasoning, backward reasoning, counterfactual reasoning (which especially requires meta-level control), and other verbally based reasoning methods.
- Altering reasoning processes: Reasoning processes at the top level can be altered by meta-level regulation such as blocking some nodes (i.e., blocking concepts represented by these nodes) by raising their thresholds, enabling some nodes by lowering their thresholds, and consequently directing reasoning processes into certain regions in certain directions.
- Controlling reasoning modes: We can change the threshold parameters globally, so that the overall readiness to reason changes accordingly, for example, from the credulous mode to the suspicious mode. Different levels of support for the conclusions to be drawn or the decisions to be made are required in these different modes.

The regulating processes operate on explicit representations at the top level of CLARION, although possibly a combination of top-level and bottom-level modules helps to carry out the control/manipulation processes on the top-level representations. Conceivably, these processes can also be performed on the bottom level, but the performance would be much more difficult and to a much more limited extent. This is because of the use of distributed representations that do not present crisp, individuated encoding of any entities, aspects, or events, which requires an interpretive or transformation process.

A related aspect is the allocation of a task to the top level, the bottom level, or a mixture of both. According to CLARION, the control is dynamic and emergent, determined by a host of factors, such as instructions, complexity of a task, and multiplicity of assigned tasks. For example, if a task is too complex for the top level to handle successfully, then the bottom level will be mainly responsible for it. If there is a dual task to be performed along with a primary task, the dual task interfere much more with the processing of the primary task at the top level than with that at the bottom level (Stadler 1995, Nissen and Bullemer 1987, Szymanski and MacLeod 1996). Thus, in such circumstances, the bottom level will dominate the processing. If the instructions given dictate that explicit reasoning at the top level be involved (e.g. by using reflection and verbalization), then the top level will be more involved in a task than usual, either to the detriment or to the benefit of the performance (see, e.g., Berry and Broadbent 1984, Willingham et al. 1989, Mathews et al. 2000, Sun et al. 2001). The interplay of these factors determines the allocation of a task to the two types of processes. An an example, the exclusion and inclusion procedure of Jacoby et al. (1994) as described earlier involves such meta-level allocation. In their experiments, the combination between the two types of processes is manipulated through verbal instructions, which corresponds to the external setting of the combination parameters in CLARION.

Putting together the discussion of access and reflective consciousness in CLARION, we see that the conscious processes at the top level of CLARION are characterized by explicit (localist/symbolic) representations, as well as explicit meta-level regulation (control and manipulation of processes operating on explicit representations). These two aspects together, according to the CLARION model, distinguish conscious processes from unconscious processes. The functional roles of access and reflective consciousness follow directly from these two aspects.

7.3.3 Phenomenal Consciousness

We may address the role of phenomenal consciousness in terms of the notion of qualia, which refers to the "phenomenal quality" of conscious experience (Nagel 1974, Chalmers 1993, Block 1994). Although access and reflective consciousness has a causal role in behavior as discussed earlier, qualia (phenomenal consciousness) are less clear in this regard (Block 1994).

The major problem with the notion of qualia lies in the difficulty this notion poses for functionalism, the currently popular view in philosophy of mind that the defining feature of any mental state is the set of causal relations it bears to other mental states, environmental input, and behavior of the body (see Churchland 1986).   There are a number of problems. What if the qualia that another person feels are different from what I feel, while the same functional organization (causal relationship) of mental states exists? What if there are no qualia at all in the other person, although the same functional organization of mental states is in place to generate appropriate behavior? These are the problem of inverted qualia (Kripke 1972) and the problem of absent qualia (Block 1980, Shoemaker 1982), which challenge the basic tenet of functionalism.

The key to the solution of this problem, I would suggest, lies in understanding the *multiple realizability* of behavioral capacities in functional organizations of mental states and in understanding the epiphenomenal nature of qualia. We see that it is clearly possible that there are many functionally equivalent organizations of mental states. Many of these functional organizations, although capable of generating certain behavioral patterns, do not lead to phenomenal experience, or at least not the right kind of phenomenal experience. That is,

> Hypothesis of the nonequivalence of functional organizations: The same set of behavioral capacities can be generated by multiple functional organizations of mental states, all of which are not the same in terms of leading up to phenomenal experience. There may be a unique functional organization (or a small set of them) that can produce the right kind of phenomenal experience.

Thus, with this hypothesis, many arguments leveled against functionalism are after all not so damaging to functionalism as to a narrowly conceived, strong form of functionalism in which a functional organization capable of generating behavior alone is a necessary and sufficient condition for consciousness (Newell and Simon 1976, Fodor 1975, 1983, Pollack 1989, Johnson-Laird 1983).

However, why should we be concerned with functional organizations of the mind, if it is not a necessary or sufficient condition of consciousness? The answer is that this is because the *right* functional organization, which is not only capable of generating behavioral capacities but also capable of generating some other, more intrinsic properties of the mind (Searle 1980) is a necessary and sufficient condition of consciousness, including qualia.

There have been many arguments in favor of such a weak-form functionalism. An especially relevant piece of work in favor of functionalism in relation to consciousness is Chalmers (1993), in which the "fading qualia" and "dancing qualia" arguments illustrate well the substitutability of any two systems with fine-grained functional isomorphism, in direct opposition to the "absent qualia" and "inverted qualia" arguments (Block 1980, Kripke 1972). Chalmers (1993) proposed the following hypothesis:

> The principle of organizational invariance: Any two systems with the same fine-grained functional organization will have qualitatively identical experience [or the lack of it].

What I would like to suggest is that, on the basis of the above principle of organizational invariance, we should distinguish different functional organizations capable of the same behavior, especially in terms of separating those that are capable of the behavior but not the more intrinsic properties of the mind from those that are capable of both the behavior and the more intrinsic properties of the mind. Thus, the search for consciousness can, after all, be the search for a functional organization—the *right* functional organization.

This proposal can avoid many arguments against a stronger form of functionalism, in that a functional organization capable of a certain range of behavior does not *necessarily* lead to consciousness. In other words, it may or may not have the requisite intrinsic intentionality that can lead to consciousness (Searle 1980). But, clearly, there is nothing that prevents *some* functional organizations (among those that are capable of the range of behavior) to have that intrinsic intentionality and conscious experience.

In addition to and on top of functionalism, we need to understand the *physical* nature of phenomenal consciousness. It is counterproductive to enshrine qualia in a sacred place, away from the physical world. (See Chalmers 1993 and Nagel 1974 for arguments against the physical nature of qualia and third-person explanations of them.) Rather, a mechanistic explanation should be attempted, despite the failure we have been seeing in such attempts so far. As has been noted by many, there are plenty of examples of dualistic "explanations" of difficult phenomena (such as life) having evaporated after further explorations that led to a better mechanistic account. However, it has been claimed by the proponents of the dualist view that the issue of consciousness is different, because we are not explaining a physical phenomenon (such as life), but subjective experience (Chalmers 1993). The fallacy of this argument is that it presupposed the nonphysical nature of subjective experience, which thus could only obstruct a constructive investigation into the physical nature of subjective experience, which might in turn lead to a mechanistic explanation of qualia.

A corollary is epiphenomenalism with regard to qualia: Because there are multiple, functionally equivalent organizations of mental states, some of which do not involve qualia, qualia are not necessary for accounting for behavioral capacities, and thus epiphenomenal in this sense.   However, qualia are not epiphenomenal if we look at functional organizations per se in which qualia play a role. If we contrast the condition in which an individual is consciously aware of something (with qualia) with the one in which the individual is not (without qualia). Qualia evidently entail high-intensity, qualitatively distinguishing states, demanding attention of the individual who is having them.

The foregoing discussions still leave open the question of what it is exactly that characterizes phenomenal consciousness mechanistically (computationally).   As has been pointed out by many (e.g., Chalmers 1993), there is indeed an "explanatory gap" in characterizing phenomenal consciousness. The best we can do for the time being is merely making some educated guesses and hoping that new advances will come along soon to precisely answer this question.

As a first approximation, qualia might be accounted for in CLARION by the totality of a multi-modal, multi-level, multi-module organization and its collective states, that is, the total-states.   These total-states are of extremely high complexity involving external perception (of many modalities), internal perception, routine decision making, explicit and implicit representations, etc.   This was termed the "manifold" by Van Gulick (1993), and the "superposed complexes" by Lloyd (1995).

In this approach, a particular kind of phenomenal quality may be accounted for by a particular region of a total-state space, involving the totality of all the aforementioned aspects, which gives rise to the sense of what something is like without explicit awareness of all the details (Nagel 1974). The reason for the lack of explicit awareness of details may include the integration of information of extremely high dimensionality and the high degree of heterogeneity of information.

Clearly, regions in a total-state space can only be formed on the basis of particular organizations of modules that support such a space of total-states. Qualia are thus (partially) the result of functional organizations, or architectures, of cognitive apparatuses. In CLARION, qualia are the result of the two-level organization, as well as intricate structures involved in various fine-grained modules (cf. Damasio 1994 and Bower 1996).

Dimensions	Bottom	Top
Cognitive phenomena	implicit learning implicit memory automatic processing intuition	explicit learning explicit memory controlled processing explicit reasoning
Source of knowledge	trial-and-error assimilation	external sources extraction
Representation	distributed features	localist conceptual units
Operation	similarity-based	symbol-based
Characteristics	more context sensitive fuzzier less selective more complex	less context sensitive more crisp more selective simpler

Figure 7.4. Comparisons of the two levels of the CLARION architecture

7.4 Summary

The importance of consciousness to cognitive science cannot be over-estimated. A central thesis of this chapter has in fact been the following (Lloyd 1995):

> [Consciousness] is a central question of cognition and human nature. Simply studying networks, or the brain, or both, will leave untouched the fundamental question of how we come to be conscious beings.

This chapter focused on the issue of the physical, mechanistic, and computational basis of consciousness, in the framework of a computational model, and consequently the issue of the functional roles of consciousness in this framework. Based on examining existing psychological evidence and philosophical theorizing, various existing models were compared and contrasted. A clear candidate for explaining the physical basis of consciousness and for explaining its functional roles emerged, based on the representational difference between the conscious and unconscious processes as in CLARION. Analyses and arguments showed that the difference between localist (symbolic) representations and distributed representations led to a plausible account of consciousness, and a plausible account of its functional roles as creating synergistic effects. See Figure 7.4 for a comparison of the two levels of CLARION, in relation to aspects of consciousness.

Much more work can and should be done along this direction. Such work may include further specifications and verifications of details of CLARION in relation to issues of consciousness, in particular the functioning of reflective consciousness in CLARION, as well as the exact nature of the functional organizations that give rise to qualia.

Chapter 8

Sociocultural Factors in Cognition

> *Learning as increasing participation in communities of practice concerns the whole person acting in the world.*
> — Jean Lave and Etienne Wenger: *"Situated Learning"*

Sociocultural issues should have significant bearing on cognitive science, if we ever want to understand cognition in the broad context of sociocultural environments in which cognitive agents exist. In this chapter, I examine the interplay among social sciences and cognitive science. I try to justify an integrated approach that incorporates different disciplinary perspectives. I show how CLARION can embody such an integrated approach through a combination of autonomous learning and assimilation of sociocultural milieu.

8.1 Introduction

Although a significant amount of work has been done in cognitive science studying individual cognition, sociocultural processes and their relations to cognition have never been a focus of cognitive research. In earlier days of cognitive science, there were even calls for cognitive scientists to ignore such aspects in studying cognition (e.g., Fodor 1980). As a result, sociocultural aspects of cognitive processes are less well understood (although there has been work on these aspects, especially in recent years, such as Suchman 1987, Lave 1988, Lave and Wenger 1991, Barkow et al. 1992, Hutchins 1995, Bruner 1995).

However, cognitive science has recently come to the conclusion that it needs to understand sociocultural processes. Cognitive science is in need of new theoretical frameworks and new technical tools for analyzing sociocultural aspects of cognition and cognitive processes involved in multi-agent interaction. It needs not only computational models for this purpose, but also deeper theories and broader conceptual frameworks that can, thus far, only be found in sociological, anthropological, and economic theorizing, which evidently has long and distinguished intellectual histories.

Conversely, to some degree, social and economic theories need cognitive science as well, because they clearly need better understanding and better models of individual cognition, only based on which better models of aggregate processes (i.e., multi-agent interaction) may be developed (cf. Ross 1973, Wilson 1975). Cognitive models may provide a more realistic basis for understanding social interaction, by embodying realistic constraints, capabilities, and tendencies of individual agents in their interaction with their environments, including both physical and social environments. This point has been made, for example, in the context of advocating cognitive realism of game theory (Kahan and Rapaport 1984, Camerer 1997, Sun 2001).

In studying cognition, we may identify two kinds of knowledge that an agent possesses, based on their origins: One kind comes from individual sources and the other from social sources. This dichotomy may be somewhat simplistic, but the contrast between the two kinds should prove to be important. The individual sources are made up of learning processes involving an agent's interaction with its environment (both sociocultural and physical) and the resulting (implicit or explicit) representations. The other kind of knowledge involves social sources, which results from concepts and conventions formed in broader contexts and is somehow imposed (or even "forced upon") individuals. This is an important kind of process in cognition, when mixed with individual processes. Without it, it would be hard to account for human cognition in its entirety. We need to consider not only individually acquired concepts but also collectively acquired concepts, not only self-generated knowledge but also socially formed knowledge, and overall, not only an agent in a world alone but also sociocultural processes among multiple agents and through social institutions.

In understanding this process, we need to gain much better

understanding of sociocultural dynamics. We need to draw on sociological theories and insights, which will not only help to understand sociocultural processes per se, but also help to study sociocultural processes in individual cognition.   We need to understand both macroscopic and microscopic processes.

8.2   Aspects of Sociality

Let us examine some sociocultural issues in the broad context of social sciences. Pierre Bourdieu, one of the best known contemporary sociologists, declared: "We must ...... seek the origins of reason not in human 'faculty', that is, a nature, but in the very history of these peculiar social microcosms in which agents struggle, in the name of the universal, and in the progressive institutionalization which owes its seemingly intrinsic properties to the social conditions of its genesis and of its utilization" (Bourdieu and Wacquant 1992).   Although the role of sociocultural processes has been apparently exaggerated here, it nevertheless accentuates the need to understand individual agents in their social contexts, their "peculiar social microcosms".   We need to have some understanding of societies, cultures, institutions, their genesis and structures, and their ramifications for individual cognition.

8.2.1   The Issue of Sociality

What counts as a sociocultural process? What is the difference between sociocultural and individual processes (for example, in action, in skill learning, or in concept acquisition)? These are the questions that we need to get a handle on.

Max Weber (1957) defined social action to be that "where the actor's behavior is meaningfully oriented to that of others. For example, a mere collision of two cyclists may be compared to a natural event. On the other hand, their attempts to avoid hitting each other, or whatever insults, blows, or friendly discussion that might follow the collision, would constitute social 'action'". Social processes begin when there are multiple autonomous agents each of which acts on its own while taking account of the actions of other agents.   When each agent tries to orient its behavior toward other agents, simultaneously and continuously, a complex dynamic process results. A culture is formed when certain conventions and conceptions are commonly assumed by a social group. Culture, in a profound way, shapes the dynamics of social interaction. Conversely, the process of social interaction shapes culture itself, through individual or collective actions (Hutchins 1995). Therefore, the whole nexus may be viewed as one single process: a sociocultural process above and beyond individual cognitive processes.

Sociology and anthropology, as well as other branches of social sciences, have been dealing with these issues for more than a century. Sociology aims to describe, understand, and explain social facts with clear, neutral, and abstract concepts.[1] Various schools of thought exist that are radically different from each other. The rivalry can be between collectivist sociology (see, e.g., Durkheim 1962 and Bourdieu and Wacquant 1992) and individualistic sociology (e.g., phenomenological and interpretive studies; see Geertz 1973 and Schutz 1967); or between functionalism, system theory, and symbolic interactivism; or between structuralism and anti-structuralism. Some schools of sociology are close to philosophy (especially phenomenological philosophy), while others seek to be quantitative and exact.[2] However, for our purposes, each of them provides some useful insight and a vocabulary, which we can utilize to further our understanding. Sociology constitutes the main intellectual source of perspectives on problems of culture, society, and civilization, which are inescapable in the study of both individual and collective cognition.

Let us discuss below, in some detail, major factors and aspects of society, in preparation for later discussions of these factors and aspects within cognition and in terms of cognition.

8.2.2　Social Structures

Social structures are the enduring, orderly, and patterned relationships among elements in a society. They are the results of both biological evolution and evolution of complex social interaction (Caporael 1997).

---

[1] It has deep intellectual roots in philosophy, history, and legal theories. Since the term "sociology" was coined by Auguste Comte in early 19th century, it has been developed vigorously, especially in the 19th century by Emile Durkheim in France, Max Weber in Germany, as well as many sociologists in America.

[2] For example, the majority of American sociology is aimed at being a quantitative science that influences the formation of public policy.

Simple group behavior, especially in lower species, may be the direct result of biological adaptation.[3] More complex kinds of social structures, such as those found in human societies, historically or currently, are the results of complex biological, social, cultural, and cognitive adaptation that goes beyond simple biological processes; in other words, they are extragenetic. The interplay of these factors (biological, sociocultural, and cognitive), acting through individual agents, gives rise to a variety of different forms of structures (Caporael 1997); these structures in turn act on individuals (Eggertsson 1990). Complex social structures are maintained through social control by a combination of various means (e.g., common values, coercion, and so on).

Social institutions, which themselves constitute a complex and important type of structure, reinforce and support existing social structures. They include kinship institutions, economic institutions, political institutions, stratification institutions, and cultural institutions. They are formed through certain social processes in which certain social practices become regular and continuous (i.e., "institutionalization"). Although social institutions are relatively stable (as they are means for maintaining stability of social structures), they are not immutable. Established social institutions can drift overtime and change drastically occasionally. The question is how they persist, function, and change, in relation to individual cognition.

8.2.3 Culture

Culture is a (structured) system of socially formed and transmissible patterns of behavioral and cognitive characteristics within a social group. It includes conventions, rules, social institutions, common symbols, common behavioral patterns, characteristic attitudes, shared values, shared skills, beliefs, knowledge, myths, rituals, and so on.

The notion of culture as a collective entity is akin to the notion of a *scientific paradigm* as proposed by Kuhn (1970): It is shared among the majority of participants; it is generally observed but not always followed; it is relatively stable but can undergo changes or even radical revisions

---

[3] For example, an ant colony is formed through genetically predetermined means (Wilson 1975, Deneubourg and Goss 1989), and it involves large-scale communication and coordination through simple biological means obtained evolutionarily.

sometimes; it is clear to those involved but may or may not be articulated in explicit ways (Caporael 1997).

With regard to the last point above, paradigms or culture may involve both explicit and implicit representations/processes. In this regard, Kuhn is clearly not in favor of the idea of a scientific paradigm as a set of explicit rules: "I have in mind a manner of knowing which is misconstrued if reconstructed in terms of rules that are first abstracted from exemplars and thereafter function in their stead" (Kuhn 1970). Culture, as a generalization of scientific paradigms, may largely consist of unarticulated (implicit, subconceptual) processes, as well as articulated (explicit, conceptual) processes.

This view is somewhat similar to the Jungian notions of collective consciousness and collective unconsciousness (minus any mysticism that may have come to be associated with them; Jung 1959). Bourdieu also adopts such a metaphor and sees the "socio-analysis" as a collective counterpart to Freudian psycho-analysis: It helps to unearth the social unconscious embedded into social institutions as well as lodged inside individual minds. However, we shall hold that the social unconscious is an emergent property rather than existent in and by itself.

With regard to the unity of scientific paradigms, Kuhn (1970) asked: "Why is the concrete scientific achievement ...... prior to the various concepts, laws, theories, and points of view that may be abstracted from it? In what sense is the shared paradigm a fundamental unit for the student of scientific development, a unit that cannot be fully reduced to logically atomic components which might function in its stead?" We can ask the same questions about culture in general. As has been observed by many, there seem to be a similar unity in culture as well. This in fact has also been the position of some important schools of sociologists. Emile Durkheim claimed that collective culture is not causally connected to "states of the consciousness of individuals but by the conditions in which the social group, in its totality, is placed." This leads to methodological holism, which bases its work on the premise that social systems have emergent properties that cannot be reduced to their constituting parts, so that the understanding of culture (and society in general) must start at the whole-system level. There are, however, alternatives to this view. Methodological individualism holds that culture and society are explicable purely based on cognitive processes of individual agents. Methodological "situationalism" seeks to transcend the difference between these two schools and takes instead the very properties emerged from situational social interaction as a starting point in understanding culture and society (Bourdieu and Wacquant 1992).

In summary, it might be useful to view culture as a collective entity, but we should always keep in mind that it is made up of actions, practices, as well as beliefs of individual agents. Hence, it involves both explicit and implicit processes, as in individual cognition.

8.2.4   Social Determinism?

Social determinism has been quite popular in some segments of social sciences. However, this position seems extreme in many ways, as in the following claim: "Collective representations, emotions, and tendencies are caused not by certain states of the consciousness of individuals but by the conditions in which the social group, in its totality, is placed. .... These individual natures are merely the indeterminate material that the social factor molds and transforms" (Durkheim 1962).   Pierre Bourdieu posited, as the determining factor, an individual agent's place in a "field" (a social environment that has a stable structure that places different agents in different positions; Bourdieu and Wacquant 1992); individual's cognition is determined through internalization of such an objective "reality". As he put it, "persons, at their most personal, are essentially the personification of exigencies actually or potentially inscribed in the structure of the field or, more precisely, in the position occupied [by the agent] within this field."

On the other hand, against the onslaught of social determinism, interpretive anthropology and sociology (especially the hermeneutic and the phenomenological varieties) try to ground the "objectivity" of social environments in individual minds. Phenomenological sociologists, such as Alfred Schutz (e.g., 1967), attempted to analyze, using the terminology of phenomenological philosophy, the construction of social reality, from the point of view of an individual agent (see also Putnam 1975). Geertz, and other ethnographers, tried to understand how people of different cultures comprehend and organize their world, through analyzing their explanations of their life experience (Geertz 1973). More recently, cognitive anthropology (see, e.g., D'Andrade 1989) generally holds that a society is fully determined by individuals and culture is composed of psychological structures by means of which individual agents guide their behavior. That is to say, a society's culture is made up entirely of rules in individuals' head, and therefore, as soon as we explicate all the rules, we can fully understand a society and its culture. This position has been accused of, rightfully I believe, extreme subjectivism (by, e.g., Bourdieu and Wacquant 1992). Much of the criticism against classical cognitivism (especially as discussed in Brooks 1991, Varela et al. 1993, Bickhard 1993, and Sun 1999) can be equally applied to this position as well.

In summary, to avoid extremity on either end, a proper balance between "objective" social reality and subjective cognitive processes is needed, in order to understand the true natures of sociocultural processes and cognition.

8.3   Sociocultural Processes and Cognition

We turn now to the very issue of how social processes influence cognition of individual agents and their individual and collective behaviors.

8.3.1   Inter-Agent Processes

Let us examine inter-agent processes within a small group. First, we note that many concepts are "social concepts", that is, concepts formed necessarily in a social context through interacting with other agents. As an extremely simple example, even in Agre's (1988) model of purely reactive agents, there are such social concepts; for example, the-block-that-I-can-use-to-kill-the-bee, the-bee-that-is-chasing-me, and so on are socially formed concepts (if we consider the "society" as consisting of the agent in question and the bee), since to form such concepts, there needs to be an antagonist bee around interacting with the agent. The same can be said of skills, routines, and other implicit cognitive processes in terms of their social characters (Wegner and Bargh 1998).

L.S. Vygotsky's description of the development of cognitive agents is illuminating. Vygotsky (1986) emphasized the *internalization* of social interaction as a major factor in the development of thinking in agents. One aspect of internalization is through the genesis of verbal (i.e., conceptual) thoughts. Speech develops before the development of internal verbal thinking. It starts at the single-word level, which merely serves the function of labeling (that is, linking signs/symbols to their meanings/denotations). Such labeling itself is sociocultural, because it is based on the established convention of a sociocultural and linguistic community (Steels 1998). However, when more complex speech develops, it directly serves a social function (e.g., to get someone to do something). When the speech loses its social functions (e.g., when nobody responds to a child's request, as discussed by Vygotsky 1962), it can be turned inward and thus become a request/command to oneself (in Vygotsky's term, an egocentric speech). Speech can thus be transformed from an interpersonal function to an intrapersonal function. Egocentric speech can be further turned inward and become internal verbal thoughts. Internal thinking relies on the internalized signs/symbols/concepts from social contexts, but can be accomplished without overt utterances or actions. According to Vygotsky, the development of thinking and behavior is the interweaving of biological processes (or "elementary processes"; Vygotsky 1986) and sociocultural processes (or "higher psychological functions"). What was not mentioned by Vygotsky but is equally important, I believe, is individual cognitive processes by an *autonomous* agent. More discussions of this point appear later.

A related issue in inter-agent interaction is communication. Communication can in part be accomplished through direct, unmediated comportment, in the same way as other everyday activities (Heidegger 1927a, Dreyfus 1992). The basis of this process is the shared world of the interacting agents and their shared understanding of the world. This shared background may not be explicitly represented, and may not be explicitly representable (Dreyfus 1972, 1992). We may thus see inter-agent interaction and communication essentially as comportment in the everyday world (Dreyfus 1992, Wegner and Bargh 1998), rather than being completely or mostly explicit.

Lave and Wenger's (1991) discussion of learning as increasing participation in communities of practice shared this view and addressed yet another aspect of inter-agent processes. To learn (e.g., to master a craft) is to participate in a community of practice, so as to share its routines, procedures, skills, beliefs (implicit or explicit), and values. Rather than detached, abstract learning processes that emphasize explicit knowledge, which are prevalent in the type of formal schooling found in contemporary societies, Lave and Wenger argued that increasing participation was a more natural and more essential way of learning. Thus, a due emphasis on comportment, routines, and implicit processes is justified in learning situations. This idea of gradually increasing participation in a social group, which is rather general and applicable to a broad range of social situations, may be viewed as an extension and an application of Vygotsky's idea of internalization of social interaction.

8.3.2 Social Processes

Beside direct inter-agent interaction, we shall also consider the impact of sociocultural processes, social structures, and social institutions on the cognitive process of an agent. Geertz (1973) proclaimed that "undirected by cultural patterns—organized systems of significant symbols—man's behavior would be virtually ungovernable, a mere chaos of pointless acts and exploding emotions, his experience virtually shapeless." Although the relationship between an individual agent and society is complex and goes in both ways, it has been recognized that, fundamentally, it is the influence from the society on individuals that matters more. This notion is best expressed as "power asymmetry" between individuals and societies (Geertz 1973, Turner et al. 1987). Individuals find themselves already "current in the community" (Heidegger 1927b). Their cognitive processes and thus their behaviors are shaped by their social environments. Such "shaping" may vary in degree, as some individuals are likely more engrossed in their particular sociocultural environments than others. The very existence of sociocultural shaping as a major determining factor in individual's cognition is undeniable.

In this regard, Bourdieu's notion of a "field" is illuminating. A social environment with a stable structure constitutes a "field" that places different social agents in different places playing different roles (in ways rather like a soccer field). An agent's place in a "field" is (partially) determined by the structure of the field and the rule of the game, which are external "objective" reality.[4] On top of a "field", for the sake of cognition, there is always a sociocultural system of signs/symbols. The

---

[4] Bourdieu (see, e.g., Bourdieu and Wacquant 1992) might take a more extreme position and claim that an individual agent's place in a "field" is *fully* determined by the structure of the field and the rule of the game.

system is not only an instrument of knowledge, but also an "instrument of domination". That is, it is an instrument for establishing and maintaining a "field"—a "pecking order" among agents. The stability of social structures is helped by "the orchestration of categories of perception of the social world which, being adjusted to the divisions of the established order ...., impose themselves with all appearances of objective necessity" (Bourdieu 1984).[5] Social structures determine to a large extent individual's cognition.

Perceiving social reality as mere aggregates of individuals—their volition, action, and cognition—misses the fact that the social structures are far more resilient than such a view would suggest and they *seem* to possess an objective and permanent character in their configurations rather than being instantaneously and arbitrarily constructed (Sowell 1996).

Although influences of societies on individuals is overwhelming, the influence in the other direction can nevertheless be discerned. As emphasized by phenomenological sociologists, social reality is an "ongoing accomplishment" actively constructed by agents through organized practice of everyday life. Social reality is, in some ways, an aggregate product of the actions, decisions, routines, and thoughts of individual agents each of which has a direct and meaningful interaction with its world.

The answer to this apparent dilemma is a proper integration of the two perspectives. As Bourdieu (1984) put it, "objectivism and subjectivism, mechanism and finalism, structural necessity and individual agency are false antinomies. Each term of these paired opposites reinforce the other; all collude in obfuscating the anthropological truth of human practice."

In an integrative perspective, a basic element at the microscopic (i.e., individual) level should be Heidegger's notion of *facticity*, that is, the way the sociocultural (and the natural) world appears to individuals as solid, taken for granted, and unalterable. In everyday existence, individuals can never get clear about their facticity, and therefore can never get rid of the facticity (Heidegger 1927a). The

---

[5] Examples of such sign/symbol systems abound. For example, nationalism of all sorts depends upon the social structure of a homogeneous ethnic and/or cultural group; it serves to maintain such a homogeneous group, its cohesion, and its territorial possession. Nationalistic sentiment is a socially patterned emotion that would not be there if not for being placed in a cohesive social "field" and up against opposing groups. Social stereotyping is another example of this. It works mainly within the structure of a "field". It serves to enforce and perpetuate the structure of the "field" and to put individuals in their supposed places.

existential experience of an agent is *partially* structured by sociocultural signs/symbols and concepts/categories, which are formed within particular social structures and thus reflect them.   The signs/symbols and concepts/categories internalized by agents determine the cognition of an agent from within (while external stimuli provide external constraints). Certainly, being autonomous, an agent may generate from within its own concepts/categories. But even internally generated representations of an agent may also reflect, to some degree (albeit a lesser degree), "objective" social reality, in the sense that these representations are influenced by given sociocultural signs/symbols and given social structures that have already been internalized.

Can we say the same about everyday routinized activities, or comportment of an agent, in a social world (which involve only subconceptual, or implicit, representations, as discussed by Heidegger 1927a)?   We can, if we recognize that such routine activities are (in part) constrained by internalized social reality and they are cultivated in a particular social environment with given social structures that the agent finds itself in.   The routines are thus in part sedimented social reality, and can be meaningful only within a particular sociocultural environment. Even the most immediate experience of agents cannot completely escape this predicament. This view of everyday routines is similar to the notion of *habitus* in Bourdieu's (1984) theory (but minus his social determinism). See also the discussions by Wertsch (1991, 1998), Sowell (1996), and Eggertsson (1990).

In the other direction, in terms of forming social structures ("fields") from the interaction of agents, there are some ideas from social and economic theories, for example, from game theory (Osborne and Rubinstein 1994), as well as recent work on multi-agent systems (e.g., Weiss and Sen 1996, Sandholm and Lesser 1997, Salustowicz et al. 1998, and Sun 2001). However, not enough emphasis has been placed on the *cognition* of individual agents in this process. Thus, existing models are largely simplistic and formalistic, or at the other extreme, conceptually vague and non-specific.

In terms of generating sociocultural signs/symbols and concepts/categories within given social structures from a cognitive standpoint, there is, however, a shortage of ideas and theories. We do not know clearly what processes are in the working and how we can best characterize them. We need better theories, especially computational models, in order to study such an issue.

8.4   Cognitive Modeling Incorporating Sociocultural Issues

Now I am ready to address the relation between the CLARION model and sociocultural processes. Theories of social sciences can benefit cognitive science through enhancing cognitive models by taking into account sociocultural processes in cognition, including the internalization of external sociocultural aspects. Below, I will first focus on the generation and the assimilation of symbolic structures in CLARION and then, in the next section, relate them to sociocultural cognition.

8.4.1   Autonomous Generation of Symbolic Structures

I will highlight a few possibilities for autonomous learning of symbolic, conceptual knowledge, as well as assimilation of socioculturally formed such knowledge, by individual agents, in the framework of CLARION. Let us first review some methods for autonomous learning, as has been discussed in chapter 3.

CLARION extracts symbolic rules at the top level to supplement neural networks at the bottom level. Rule extraction is based on observing the performance of bottom-level decision making, and extracted rules correspond to good decisions. Symbolic rule learning at the top level proves to be useful in enhancing reinforcement learning at the bottom level (see chapter 3).

Furthermore, CLARION can extract explicit plans at the top level that can be used in an open-loop fashion, from closed-loop policies resulting from reinforcement learning at the bottom level. A two-stage bottom-up process is employed, in which first reinforcement learning is applied to acquire a closed-loop policy and then explicit plans are extracted. The usefulness of results from reinforcement learning is enhanced by plan extraction. It improves the applicability of learned policies when environmental feedback is unavailable or unreliable.

Third, CLARION partitions a state space to form spatial regions that correspond to different categories for different modules to handle. Regions are partitioned using symbolic descriptions of categories. Partitioning regions reduces learning complexity, as well as simplifies individual modules (categories), thus facilitating overall learning.

Finally, yet another process involves learning to segment temporal action sequences to form subroutines. It creates hierarchies of subroutines, or temporal modules, to reduce temporal dependencies in order to facilitate learning.

8.4.2   Assimilation of External Symbolic Structures

Although CLARION can avoid relying on a priori or external knowledge, it can make use of such knowledge when it is available. Knowledge provided by other agents can guide the exploration of the receiving agent and speed up its learning. To deal with such instructed learning, in an agent, externally provided explicit knowledge, in the forms of symbolic structures such as rules, plans, subroutines, categories, and so on, are assimilated into reinforcement learning as well as combined with autonomously generated symbolic structures. That is, the agent performs internalization. Here is a review of some possibilities in this regard in CLARION.

When individual rules are given by other agents, these rules can be used at the top level to assist in action decision making as described before. In addition to that, supervised learning based on rules can be performed (with, e.g., backpropagation) for gradual assimilation of the rules into reinforcement learning at the bottom level. This process can be done between autonomous reinforcement learning. Alternatively, assimilation of symbolic knowledge can be done during reinforcement learning through the use of the symbolic knowledge in decision making, which influences reinforcement learning at the bottom level and leads to assimilation.

However, external instructions tend to be generic. Although helpful, generic knowledge alone is insufficient in achieving efficient performance of a task. An agent needs to develop more specific skills that can be more efficiently applied. This process may require operationalization, that is, turning instruction into a form compatible with the existing knowledge of an agent and directly usable. It may involve the recoding of the knowledge into an internal representation. It may also require a substantial general reasoning capability and a capability for interaction with other agents to progressively refine instructions.

Likewise, information concerning categories and concepts may be provided by other agents. Such information may be provided through a series of exemplars. The information can be assimilated through the aforementioned spatial partitioning method, which divides up the state space of reinforcement learning into regions that correspond to different categories. When information about a category is given, a separate module may be set up to handle the category specifically, and the module may be trained with the exemplars provided. Then (multi-module) reinforcement learning can continue as before.

Information concerning (sub)routines may be given by other agents as well. When such routines are detailed enough, the afore-mentioned temporal segmentation method may be used to assimilate the information. A sequential segment module can be set up specifically for a given routine and trained with information associated with the routine. Multi-module reinforcement learning can then continue as before.

When a skeletal plan (a sketch of a routine) is given by other agents, assimilation can be done the same way as rule assimilation. That is, the plan can be used at the top level to direct actions whenever they are applicable, and through the process, the reinforcement learning neural networks at the bottom level are trained (i.e., biased) by the externally provided plan.

8.5   Accounting for Sociocultural Cognition

How may this model capture sociocultural cognition we described in the earlier sections? First of all, the ideas reviewed in section 2 concerning sociocultural processes involving both comportment and conceptual processing correspond well with the dichotomy in the model (that is, the two levels of CLARION). In normal circumstances, an agent is almost wholly absorbed into a social role (e.g., as described by Bourdieu), "instinctively" following the rule of the game, through bottom-level implicit, subconceptual processes. In addition, explicit concepts and explicit conceptual processes, for dealing explicitly with sociocultural aspects, can be formed in the top level, in part based on externally given sociocultural concepts. This match should not come as a surprise, given all the preceding discussions on the learning of routines and the extraction of symbolic representations in the everyday world, because the sociocultural environment is part of that everyday world and thus the same two types of cognitive processes are involved as well.

Based on the earlier exposition, let us consider sociocultural processes in acquiring concepts. Vygotsky's notion of internalization is central to such processes. Internalization can be accomplished in CLARION through the top-down assimilation process described earlier, which matches well the phenomenological characterization of internalization. The direct acceptance of external rules, plans, and concepts in the top level of the model captures the initial stage of internalization. The assimilation into the bottom level as described earlier, however, captures a deeper process by which external symbolic structures are meshed with existing routines, reflexes, and behavioral propensities so that they can effectively affect an agent's comportment with the world. On the other hand, the implicit, subconceptual learning at the bottom level also captures the internalization of implicitly represented sociocultural aspects through interacting with them. Just as interacting with the physical world gives rise to our knowledge pertaining to the physical world, interacting with the sociocultural world gives rise to our knowledge pertaining to the sociocultural world.

Internalized sociocultural signs/symbols enable agents to develop richer representations, utilizing signs/symbols that are formed through sociocultural processes (Wertsch 1991). The internalized external signs/symbols are not innocuous: They carry with them particular sociocultural perspectives and biases. Through internalization, in CLARION, the behavior, and the thinking that directs the behavior, are *mediated* by externally given signs/symbols, as well as their associated perspectives and biases, matching phenomenological analyses.

I believe that several senses of *mediation* can be distinguished. The first one is mediation as think-in-terms-of. That is, with externally given concepts/categories, an agent accepts a particular division of the world into categories and thinks in terms of these categories, as opposed many other possible divisions. Another sense is mediation as perspective-taking: Along with accepting a particular division, the agent is forced to accept implicitly the perspective and the world view that are associated with it. The third sense is mediation as biases (whereby the notion of "bias" introduced in the machine learning literature is adopted). It basically means that a given representation may lead the agent to learn certain concepts more readily than others. Although these concepts may not be explicitly given, the agent is *biased* toward learning them (as opposed to their alternatives). All of these senses are applicable in CLARION, for describing the impact of sociocultural concepts/categories (and their corresponding symbols/signs) on cognition.

The kind of assimilation adopted in CLARION has been called *advice taking* or *learning by being told* in artificial intelligence (e.g., Michalski 1983). The other approach utilized in CLARION, *autonomous learning*, has been referred to as *learning by exploration*. While many models explored these two types of learning separately (Anderson 1983, Gelfand et al. 1989, Maclin and Shavlik 1994, Sun and Peterson 1998a, 1998b), CLARION emphasizes the integration of advice taking and autonomous learning (using both top-down and bottom-up learning processes). Through the combination of the two processes, an agent's conceptual system emerges while interacting with the world.

The issue of sociocultural concepts (acquired through assimilation) versus self-generated concepts (acquired through autonomous learning) has largely escaped the attention of L.V. Vygotsky. In the main, Vygotsky (e.g., 1962) viewed concepts as completely socioculturally generated. This is also the position taken by many sociologists, especially collectivists such as Durkheim. But CLARION reveals another side of the story. In CLARION, although concepts (symbolically represented in the top level) can be acquired from external sources, they can also be acquired internally through extraction from the bottom level (explication of implicit knowledge). In other words, there is clearly a self-generated component in cognition, according to CLARION. Of course, ultimately, self-generated concepts are based mostly on the external world (both the physical and the sociocultural world), because they are developed through the very process of interacting with the world, and affected by already assimilated sociocultural concepts/categories and signs/symbols. But they are not completely determined by the external world, in the sense that there are many alternative ways of describing the external world and thus by self-generating a particular set of concepts, an agent puts its own stamp on things and develops its own idiosyncrasy in its dealing with the world. This is generally advantageous, because self-generation contributes to the formation and the continuous revision of a rich, diverse, and useful set of concepts and beliefs shared by a society. CLARION illustrates how this is possible and how the two sources—external and internal—interact to accomplish individual cognition.

8.6 Representing Self and Others

I will discuss two additional aspects that can be incorporated into CLARION to better address sociocultural processes: that is, how an agent represents the notion of *self* and how it represents the notion(s) of *others* (Ashmore and Jussim 1997, Turner et al. 1987, Tajfel 1970). The reason why an agent needs to represent self and others is basically the same as that for representing individual physical objects: It is often advantageous to be able to distinguish different objects, so as to act or react appropriately (which, ironically, was often neglected in early work on autonomous agents). Moreover, it may also need to represent itself, so as to make appropriate inferences and decisions when "self" needs to be figured into decision making expressly.

8.6.1 Developing Self Representation

Self understanding is achieved primarily through comportment, direct and unmediated interaction (Heidegger 1927a), with the world and all of its aspects. This is because the primordial way is essential to the understanding of both the world and the self. This is in sharp contrast to a common approach in AI knowledge representation in which self and its desires, intentions, and beliefs are explicitly represented in some form of logic with which deliberate inference is conducted and is followed by purposive actions in relation to self-referential goals (Davis 1990).

However, although self understanding through transparent comportment is essential, it can result in misinterpretation, as pointed out by Heidegger (1927a), because the hidden and the distorted cannot be clarified due to a deep "involvement" of the agent with the world. One way in which this tendency can be counteracted is to establish an *explicit* self representation that can be explicitly manipulated, introspected, and adjusted, in accordance with proper criteria and using explicit reasoning.

Combining this explicit representation of self with the implicit (comportment) representation, we again have a two-level situation, in much the same way as other representations in CLARION. Self representation is thereby accommodated in the CLARION framework.

8.6.2   Developing Representation of Others

Similar to the representation of *self*, the representation of *others* can also be accomplished through a combination of the two types of representations.

First and foremost, *others* are accessible to an agent through their shared world and shared activities in the world, in the same way as *self* is understood, in a primordial (implicit and subconceptual) way. Thus, at the bottom level of CLARION, routines for interacting with different individuals or different types of individuals are developed. At the top level, an explicit representation may also be established for an individual or a type of individual, that is linked to relevant concepts regarding the characteristics of the individual(s) represented. According to Heidegger, such knowledge of others are disclosed through "concernful solicitude". In CLARION, top-level representations of others can be accomplished through either extraction from the bottom level or being given externally.

Representing agents (self or others) is more complex than representing physical objects. Associated with an agent representation, there is not only information about the identity of the agent, but also information about its state of mind, its behavioral propensity, its particular way of thinking (i.e., a "theory" of its mind), and so on. Each of these items can be handled by a combination of top-level explicit representations and bottom-level implicit representations. To capture such complexities, specialized modules can be developed in CLARION in the bottom level, each of which concerns specifically and exclusively one individual (or one type of individual), dealing with its state of mind, behavior propensity, and idiosyncrasy. Note that those and only those individuals (or types of individuals) that are highly relevant to the existential experience of an agent are given a specialized representation in a specialized module.

Representing others may have beneficial effects on co-learning in a social setting, while detrimental effects may occur if such representations are inaccurate in some critical respects (Sun and Qi 2000). For example, in the co-learning experiment using simple games involving two agents (Sun and Qi 2000), developing representations of the opponent by an agent often led to better learning curves, although the effect was not universal by any means. The simple left/right game is illustrated by Figure 8.1. The results are shown in Figures 8.2, 8.3, and 8.4. In these three figures, "level 0" indicates no representation of the opponent by agent 1 and "level 1" indicates the use of representation of the opponent by agent 1. Here "representation of the opponent" means that the agent treats its opponent as a rational being in its decision making, rather than as part of the (usually stochastic) environment. In case 1 and case 2, the representation of the opponent by agent 1 led to improved learning of agent 1, whereas in case 3, no significant difference was found.

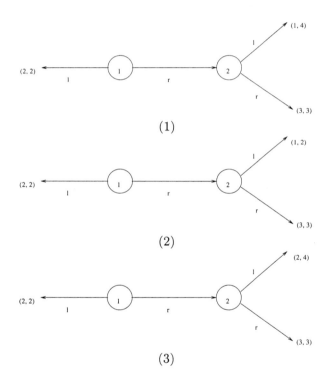

Figure 8.1. Three cases of the Left/Right game
The numbers in circles indicate agents. *l* and *r* are two possible actions. The pair of numbers in parentheses indicates payoffs (where the first number is the payoff for agent 1 and the second for agent 2).

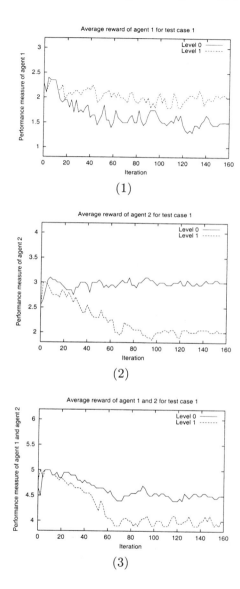

Figure 8.2. The learning performance in case 1 of the left/right game
(1) The payoff of agent 1. (2) The payoff of agent 2. (3) The total payoff. "Level
0" indicates no representation of the opponent by agent 1. "Level 1" indicates
the use of the representation of the opponent by agent 1.

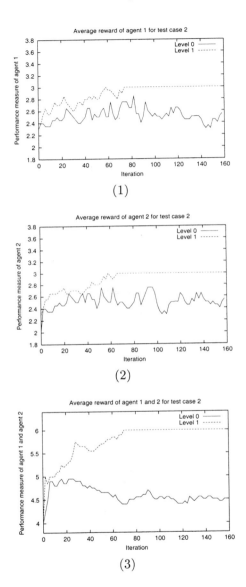

Figure 8.3. The learning performance in case 2 of the left/right game
(1) The payoff of agent 1. (2) The payoff of agent 2. (3) The total payoff. "Level
0" indicates no representation of the opponent by agent 1. "Level 1" indicates
the use of the representation of the opponent by agent 1.

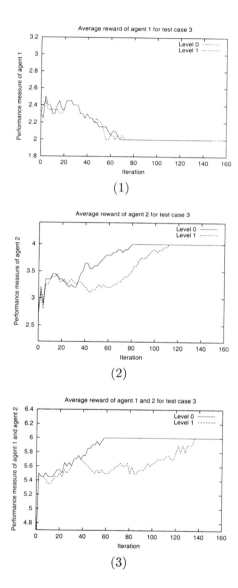

Figure 8.4. The learning performance in case 3 of the left/right game
(1) The payoff of agent 1. (2) The payoff of agent 2. (3) The total payoff. "Level
0" indicates no representation of the opponent by agent 1. "Level 1" indicates
the use of the representation of the opponent by agent 1.

8.7   Further Work

As future work, I will speculate on how computational cognitive models of agents, incorporating both autonomous learning and assimilation, can in turn help to better understand sociocultural processes themselves.

Computational studies have been undertaken to understand social issues. Statistical models have been used in sociological research, which, however, is of minimum relevance to a computational (mechanistic, process-based) understanding. Research on multi-agent systems has dealt with simplified versions of the problems of culture, social structures, and social institutions (Gilbert and Doran 1994). The formation of social structures is, in a way, similar to coalition formation in multi-agent systems (Kahan and Rapoport 1984, Weiss and Sen 1996), whereby continuous interaction in which each agent tries to maximize its own "gain" (defined in some way) leads to the formation of a coalition that maximizes the expected gain of each agent. Artificial Life (e.g., Levy 1992) is also relevant, in which the evolution of interacting simple organisms and the emergence of structures and regularities among them are considered. However, these areas assume only very simple agents, which are, by and large, not cognitively realistic (Kahan and Rapoport 1984). After all, social interaction is the result of individual cognition (which includes instincts, reflexes, and routines, as well as high-level conceptual processes). Therefore, details of individual cognition cannot be ignored in studying sociocultural processes. At least, the implications of such details should be understood first, before they are abstracted away (Camerer 1997). A detailed agent model that are sufficiently complex to capture essential features of individual cognitive processes, especially the combination of autonomous learning and assimilation, should be adopted. This is in contrast to simpler simulations that are constructed based on a set of abstract variables that do not translate well into mechanisms of individual cognition. In this regard, CLARION has a distinct advantage.

With a more realistic cognitive model, we should investigate how individual agents interact and give rise to emergent properties, and in turn, we should investigate how individual agents fare in the emerged structures (Gilbert and Doran 1994, Sun 2001). Moreover, we should investigate how the temporal course of such emerged structures and processes takes shape, and what their effects are on individual agents over their entire life courses.[6] Due to the complexity of these issues, computational modeling based on detailed cognitive models has a definitive role to play in this endeavor. Many important issues can be studied on the basis of CLARION.

There is also the issue of extragenetic versus genetic factors (Wilson 1975, Fetzer 1985). Society and culture, in general, are extragenetic. But it has come to light that deeper down, society and culture are also shaped by genetic factors determined through the evolutionary process (Cosmides and Tooby 1989), since they rely on cognitive agents, in a collective way, in their formation, maintenance, and change. There is, therefore, complex interaction between extragenetic factors on the one side and genetic and ontogenetic factors on the other side (Caporael 1997): Society and culture can affect ontogenetic development of individuals and affect the evolutionary process through natural selection, and conversely, genetic and ontogenetic processes of individual agents, collectively en masse, affect society and culture in various ways. These issues may be studied based on CLARION.

We may extend the CLARION framework to deal with additional aspects of sociocultural processes. Many existing theories in disciplines ranging from ethology and sociobiology to sociology can suggest important directions to be explored in computational modeling.

8.7.1 Simulating Social Processes

Suppose that we have a *set* of CLARION agents. These agents interact not only with the physical environment but also with other agents in order to survive (or to maximize some measure of its own gain). Given appropriate spatial proximity among agents (so that there can be interaction) and survival pressure (such as physical resource limitations), proper forms of cooperation will develop either in a biological way (through evolving specialized "instincts" phylogenetically; Wilson 1975, Cosmides and Tooby 1989), or in a cognitive way (through evolving a generic cognitive apparatus and through its development in individual ontogenetic courses).

---

[6] In other words, like Bourdieu (1984), we should investigate bidirectional interaction of "subjective" (i.e., individual) and "objective" (i.e., collective) structures, but we should not place one above the other methodologically (for instance, placing the "objective" over the "subjective" as Bourdieu did, or in the opposite way).

Forms of cooperation can develop into complex social structures that ensure effectiveness of cooperation. The CLARION agents in this system will develop not only behavioral routines and conceptual representations appropriate to the physical environment but also those appropriate to the social environment that consists of other agents (Caporael 1997).

New CLARION agents can also be assimilated into an established group (with its established social structures). This process can be studied to understand the implication of sociocultural systems on individuals, as well as, to a lesser degree, how individual beliefs and behaviors affect sociocultural systems and even social structures. That is, we can study how the "power asymmetry" works.

Let us now look into a few specific issues in particular.

8.7.2   Individual Beliefs and Sociocultural Beliefs

The question is how individual belief systems, which are formed as a mixture of sociocultural concepts/beliefs and individual self-generated concepts/beliefs, and the sociocultural belief system, which is the "average" (not the "sum total") of individual belief systems, interact. According to previous discussions, the influence is mutual: Individual beliefs affect sociocultural beliefs (which are constituted from individual beliefs); sociocultural beliefs in turn affect the formation, sustenance, and revision of individual beliefs. It is generally accepted that the influence overwhelmingly goes from established sociocultural beliefs to individual beliefs. We can study such influences computationally, based on the detailed cognitive model CLARION:

> What are the fundamental ways an individual can affect systems of sociocultural beliefs?   How do sociocultural beliefs change, computationally? As an entire system or by parts? How much "effort" is needed to make a change to a sociocultural belief, computationally? How much "power" does a sociocultural belief exert on individuals, computationally? When an individual belief conflicts with sociocultural beliefs, how is the conflict resolved?
>
> What is the relationship between explicit, conceptual representations and implicit, subconceptual representations, collectively as well as individually (Sun 1997, 1999)? What are their respective roles, computationally, in sociocultural belief systems?

8.7.3   Inter-Agent Interaction

We can also investigate, computationally, inter-agent interaction as has been described by, for example, Vygotsky (1962). With a set of CLARION agents, we can study many facets of this process (Resnick et al. 1991). For example,

> How does the collective behavior of a group of agents result from interaction, computationally (Mataric 1993)? How does interaction affect individual agents' behaviors? How does inter-agent communication develop in the process (Steels 1998, de Jong 2000)?
>
> How do concepts emerge, computationally, in inter-agent interaction? How much does this process depend on particular aspects of an agent model? Is the process best characterized by the internal properties within an agent or by the global emergent properties?
>
> How much is the outcome affected by the social structure of the group (Bourdieu and Wacquant 1992)? (See also the next subsection.)

8.7.4   Formation of Social Structures

We can investigate computationally how social structures are formed, enforced, and modified (either gradually or radically) through the interaction of individual agents, based on detailed models of agents. Although there are simplified models in sociobiology and economics (e.g., game theoretical models), there is not much done in understanding this issue through detailed cognitive models. CLARION can help with the investigation of the following issues:

> How can social structures be formed, dynamically in a distributed manner, without external intervention or central control (Hammond et al. 1995)? What are the different types of social structures that can be formed, in relation to various observed forms of human and animal societies (Wilson 1975)? What are the conditions for the formation of each type of social structure (Wilson 1975)? What are the conditions for the maintenance of each type of social structure? How do factors

such as population size, population density, means of production, technological sophistication, and so on affect the form of social structures (the scaling effects; Wilson 1975)?

How critical does a social structure (its formation, maintenance, and revision) depend on some particular mechanisms of cognition in individual agents (for example, a particular learning mechanism such as assimilation)? Do some particular aspects of social structures depend critically on evolutionarily developed specialized instincts (as captured in CLARION in the specialized modules in the bottom level), or on generic cognitive capabilities of agents?

8.7.5   Social Structures in Cognition

Social structures are imposed on individuals. Each social institution reinforces its views on agents through explicit and implicit means. CLARION provides a way for studying such an effect through computational experiments:

> How much and in what way do agents differ, from individual to individual, in their assimilation into social roles? How much social control is needed in order to get an individual agent into a social role? How much social control is needed in order to keep an individual agent in its role? What is a change of social role like? How much self initiative is needed for accomplishing a change? How much external control is necessary to force a change? What is the interaction of the two forces? How does an assigned social role affect an agent's behavior? In particular, how does it affect an agent's routine activities (in relation to the idea of habitus of Bourdieu and Wacquant 1992)? How does it affect an agent's conceptual representations?

In summary, CLARION provides a fertile ground for studying an extremely wide range of issues in sociocultural processes, not only those issues that have been examined before by social scientists, which CLARION can further clarify, but also those issues that have never come up before because of the lack of detailed computational models of individual agents, which CLARION can help to remedy.

8.8 Summary

In this chapter, I highlighted the following points: (1) Although existing cognitive models are mostly developed to study individual cognition in isolation, they can be enhanced to handle sociocultural aspects of cognition as well (through incorporating both autonomous learning and assimilation as in CLARION). (2) Such cognitive models can be integrated with models of multi-agent interaction. (3) The integration of the two strands enables us to investigate various forms of sociocultural processes under realistic assumptions about individual cognitive processes. (4) The integration also enables us to investigate contributions of various cognitive capacities on sociocultural processes. (5) The integration enables us to investigate the influence of sociocultural aspects on individuals as well.

Chapter 9

Comparisons

Comparisons do ofttime great grievance.
— John Lydgate: *"Bochas"*

Now that we have explored the implication of our approach to a significant extent, it is time for broadening the scope by comparing our approach, and especially our model, to a broad spectrum of existing cognitive models and theories. This comparison not only serves to show the differences and similarities between our model and other models, but also to highlight important points that have been advocated. These points include autonomous learning, bottom-up learning, duality in cognition and the structuring of two levels of processes, consciousness and the two-level structuring, and the two-level structuring as cognitive architectures.

In this discussion, no attempt is made to fully characterize the positions of any individuals, especially because researchers may change views over time and may sometimes embrace multiple views inconsistent with each other. I only contrast highly abstracted ideas that epitomize different approaches, not the nuances of each approach or the common grounds shared by multiple approaches. The comparison is rather technical in places.

9.1   Cognitive Models Involving Implicit Learning

Let us look into models that involve the distinction of implicit and explicit processes.

9.1.1   Process Differences of the Two Levels

It is worth noting, first of all, that the process difference in the two levels of CLARION resembles, to some extent, those in some other psychological models of learning. For instance, it resembles (1) the difference between the strategies of look-ahead versus table look-up as proposed by Broadbent et al. (1986) for explaining the difference between explicit and implicit learning; (2) the difference between algorithms versus instance retrieval as proposed by Logan (1988) for accounting for the difference between initial trials and later skilled performance in the course of skill learning; (3) the difference between mental models/theories versus experiences as proposed by Stanley et al. (1989) in relation to the difference between explicit verbalization and implicit skills; (4) the difference between central processing versus spreading activation proposed by Posner and Snyder (1975) to handle conscious and unconscious memory processes (see also Hunt and Lansman 1986 for a similar view); (5) the difference between type-2 associations and type-1 associations proposed by Bower (1996) for explaining dissociated memory measures. The former type in each dichotomy is more deliberate and more crisp, while the latter is more automatic and more fuzzy.

It appears that such a mechanistic difference may be applicable to modeling a variety of cognitive processes. It has been applied in CONSYDERR (Sun 1994), a two-level model for everyday commonsense reasoning using a combination of rule-based and similarity-based processes. Another model applying the two-level dual-representation framework was CONSPIRE (Sun 1993), which was designed to investigate introspective reasoning through the interaction of two levels via a variety of top-down and bottom-up connections. CLARION is a further extension of these models.

9.1.2   Connectionist Modeling of the Simulated Skill Learning Tasks

Let us discuss some existing models concerning, or related to, the data sets and the cognitive phenomena that are dealt with by CLARION. For instance, Ling and Marinov (1994) simulated the data from Lewicki et al. (1987), using a decision tree learning algorithm. Their model produced data on quadrant prediction accuracy and, based on the data, they succeeded in matching the human reaction time data, using a transformation that included a power function (for capturing unspecific learning). However, they did not attempt the match without such a power function (as we did in chapter 5). They did not deal with those other tasks that we examined here. (See chapter 5 for a detailed comparison.)

Cleeremans and McClelland (1991) simulated an SRT task of their own design, which was an extension of the usual SRT tasks (e.g., Willingham et al. 1989) by using nondeterministic grammars, which were more difficult. They employed a recurrent backpropagation network that saw one position at a time but developed an internal context representation over time that helped to predict next positions. The model succeeded in matching human data in terms of degrees of dependency on preceding segments in a sequence (i.e., conditional probabilities). However, their success was obtained through introducing additional mechanisms for several types of priming (e.g., short-term weight changes and accumulating activations). They did not deal with capturing directly the reaction time data of their subjects as we did (see chapter 5).

Dienes (1992) compared connectionist networks[1] and a number of memory-array (instance-based) models (e.g., Hintzman 1986) for capturing human data in learning artificial grammar tasks. He tried to match each of the models with human data on a number of measures, including percent correct, rank ordering of string difficulty, percentage of strings on which an error was made on all the presentations, and percentage of strings on which an error was made only on some of the presentations. His models were specifically designed for artificial grammar learning tasks and did not extend into other tasks that we examined before.

A major shortcoming in these models, which are most pertinent to the present work, is that most of these models focused only on implicit learning, and they ignored (1) the role of explicit learning in these tasks, (2) the interaction between the explicit and the implicit in learning and performing the tasks, and (3) the possibility of bottom-up learning. The only exception to this is Cleeremans (1994). However, Cleeremans (1994) used a simple buffer network to capture the effect of explicit knowledge, which was inadequate for tasks in which the interaction of explicit and

---

[1] These networks are either partially or fully recurrent, either using Delta learning rule, which was similar to backpropagation, or Hebb rule, which focused on direct associations.

implicit knowledge occurred in more complex ways or more complex forms of explicit knowledge were involved.

9.1.3   Connectionist Modeling of Other Tasks

There were some computational models that tried to take into account the interaction of implicit and explicit processes. But they were concerned with different types of tasks (usually memory tasks), quite distinct from the learning tasks that we focused on. For example, McClelland et al. (1995) proposed a model involving two complementary memory (sub)systems, to address the issue of catastrophic forgetting (exhibited by simple connectionist models such as backpropagation networks). They suggested that one first stored explicit traces in an explicit short-term memory and then gradually assimilated them into an implicit long-term memory. Thus, their model embodied only a very simple type of interaction between explicit and implicit processes: top-down learning, in which explicit knowledge was assimilated into implicit knowledge (see more discussions of this type of model later). Bower (1996) discussed a model for addressing implicit memory tasks (especially dissociations in priming), in which links of two distinct types were utilized. One type (type-2) was explicit while the other (type-1) was implicit. Thus the model can conceivably account for some interactions, although none was addressed.

On the other hand, Schneider and Oliver (1991) were concerned with automatization.[2] Their model implemented top-down learning, in which explicit knowledge was assimilated into implicit skills. A deliberate (explicit) calculation was performed first but later, through repeated trials, an automatized (implicit) process took over. Both processes were implemented in neural networks. J.Cohen et al. (1990) and Mehwort et al. (1992) also addressed attention and automatization. They showed how the data on mutual interference of two separate tasks could be accounted for by a backpropagation model, without involving explicit processes, which nevertheless relied on an additional mechanism of gating connections (for modulating the hidden units of the backpropagation network, based on task specifications). As the authors themselves pointed out, explicit processes (such as captured in CLARION) might be needed in order to capture other

---

[2] Automatization refers to skill learning that goes from explicit processes to implicit processes, which is the exact opposite of bottom-up learning that we focus on.

data and phenomena. The model cannot be easily extended to the learning tasks and the phenomena that we captured in this work.

There were also a large array of connectionist models of memory and categorization that bore some resemblance to the present work. But they usually did not make the distinction between implicit and explicit processes, and they focused on tasks (memory or categorization tasks) that were different from the learning tasks that we dealt with. Thus these models cannot be directly compared to CLARION. For a review of such connectionist models, see, for example, Hintzman (1990) and Brown et al. (1995).

9.1.4   Nonconnectionist Modeling of Skill Learning Tasks

Among non-connectionist models of skill learning (that involved implicit learning), Servan-Shreiber and Anderson (1987) presented a model using only a simple mechanism, "chunking", which was successful in accounting for artificial grammar learning data.[3] However, the model was incapable of accounting for the interaction of the two types of knowledge and those phenomena that we simulated. There was also no straightforward way of extending it to address tasks other than artificial grammar learning.

Logan (1988) proposed a model that accomplished skill learning (automatization) through the storage of specific instances encountered during practice (see also Stanley et al. 1989). For example, in a lexical decision task, repeated exposure of a letter string led to progressively faster responses. During the initial exposures to the letter strings, general knowledge was used to classify them. These instances were stored. On later exposures to the strings, stored instances were retrieved and used to perform classification, competing with the general knowledge. Thus, on average, reaction time was reduced as a result. Eventually, mostly instances were used to control the responses. This is a case of top-down learning, different from bottom-up learning that we focused on.

Dienes and Fahey (1995) developed an instance-based model for a process control task. Their model was based on acquiring successful instances from trials (as in Logan 1988 and Hintzman 1986), supplemented

---

[3] Chunking here consists of merging fragments into larger ones if these fragments appear together often enough.

by a set of a priori rules to start with.[4]   However, it is not clear how the model can account for gradual explication of implicit knowledge, for example, as reported in Stanley et al. (1989) and Willingham et al. (1989). Dienes and Fahey (1995) also examined an alternative model, which focused instead on testing rules (without using instances), accomplished through competitions among rules. They found that neither model fitted the data completely: While the instance model fitted better the nonsalient version of the task, the rule model fitted better the salient version of the task. This suggests that it may be advantageous to include both types of learning in one unified model (as in CLARION) in which the effect of the difference in saliency emerges from the interaction of the two learning processes.

Lebiere et al. (1998) simulated the Dienes and Fahey (1995) data using ACT-R (see discussions on ACT-R later). The simulation was based on a combination of instance-based learning implemented in ACT-R and a set of hand-coded (a priori) rules similar to those used in Dienes and Fahey's model. Although a fit with data was found, a fundamental shortcoming of the model was that there was no principled distinction between implicit knowledge and explicit knowledge, due to the representational framework of ACT-R (to be discussed later). It was not clear either how the model can account for gradual explication of implicit knowledge (Stanley et al. 1989, Willingham et al. 1989, Sun et al. 1998, 2001).

Somewhat similar to the above model, Vandierendonck (1995) developed a model for category learning that involved both rule learning and instance learning. The model stored instances acquired through trials and attempted to generalize these instances by combining similar ones (cf. Anderson 1983). It resembles CLARION because of its use of two representation and learning subsystems. However, in CLARION, generalization (and specialization) of a rule is based on an information gain measure that determines whether the change is beneficial or not in terms of improving the performance (e.g., accuracy) of the rule. Moreover, Vandierendonck's (1995) model cannot be extended to deal with sequential tasks because of its lack of temporal credit assignment mechanisms. Erickson and Kruschke (1998) essentially presented a connectionist version

---

[4] The use of these rules were justified based on the observation of the initial set of moves made by the subjects (which presumably reflected the a priori knowledge of the subjects).

of the model. Ashby et al. (1996) proposed a similar model motivated by neuropsychological considerations. In machine learning, Domingos (1996) also proposed a rule-and-instance learning model using essentially the same generalization method as Vandierendonck (1995).

9.2   Top-down versus Bottom-up Models

Although a number of theories of cognition assumed the distinction between implicit knowledge and explicit knowledge, most of them involved only top-down learning. For example, Anderson (1983, 1993) put forth two similar models: ACT* and ACT-R. ACT* is made up of a semantic network (for declarative knowledge) and a production system (for procedural knowledge). Productions are formed through "proceduralization" of declarative knowledge, modified through use by generalization and discrimination (i.e., specialization), and have strengths associated with them, which are used for firing. ACT-R is a descendant of ACT*, in which procedural learning is limited to production formation through mimicking, and production firing is based on log odds of success.

Hunt and Lansman (1986) hypothesized another top-down learning process for explaining automatization data, which top-down learning models fit most naturally. They used a production system for capturing controlled processes, and a semantic network for capturing automatic processes. They hypothesized that, through practice, production rules were assimilated into the semantic network, thus resulting in automatic processes. The production system in Hunt and Lansman's model clearly resembles the top level in CLARION, in that explicit rules are used in much the same way. Likewise, the spreading activation in the semantic network in Hunt and Lansman's model resembles spreading activation in the bottom level of CLARION. However, while the learning in CLARION is mostly bottom-up (but capable of being top-down), the learning in their model is completely top-down. Logan (1988), which was also meant to capture automatization data (as reviewed earlier), was similar in this regard. Schneider and Oliver (1991) employed essentially the same idea (also reviewed earlier). Similarly, Gelfand et al. (1989) proposed a skill learning model in which, through practice, externally given symbolic knowledge of a task was assimilated into a neural network (using backpropagation). In the end, the network was able to capture the skill for performing the task in an implicit form. The model was also top-down.

There are also other theories and models that hypothesize, more generally, that learning consists of specializing general knowledge. For example, Rosenbloom et al. (1993) contains a collection of work along this line using the SOAR architecture, which utilizes explanation-based learning, a way of specialization. A large amount of initial (a priori) knowledge (about states and operators) is required in the model. Hence its learning process can also be characterized as being top-down.

However, as reviewed before, top-down approaches were contradicted by much evidence, such as Schraagen (1993), Owen and Sweller (1985), Rabinowitz and Goldberg (1995), Reber and Lewis (1977), and Willingham et al. (1989). Evidently, human learning is not exclusively top-down. A distinct feature of CLARION is its ability of going the other way around, capturing bottom-up learning, which makes it unique and complementary to the afore-reviewed models.

9.3   Generic Cognitive Architectures

CLARION can be compared to other cognitive architectures. In CLARION, as in many of these other architectures, different modules are incorporated, different representations are used, and elaborate mechanisms are developed. Somewhat different from these architectures is the fact that CLARION utilizes a combination of reinforcement-backpropagation learning and rule induction, and exploits synergy of the two. In addition, in CLARION, representations (both explicit and implicit ones) are mostly acquired through autonomous exploration by an agent, instead of being externally given.

Let us compare CLARION with a few architectures in detail. Although each of these architectures has advantages that our approach is not designed to capture, I only focus on their limitations here. First, ACT* and ACT-R (Anderson 1983, 1993) both utilize the distinction between procedural and declarative knowledge. CLARION succeeds in explaining two issues that ACT does not address. First, whereas ACT relies mostly on top-down learning, CLARION can proceed completely bottom-up; CLARION is able to learn on its own without an external teacher providing correct exemplars or instructions of any form. Second, in ACT, both declarative and procedural knowledge are represented in an explicit, symbolic form (i.e., semantic networks plus productions), and thus it does not explain, from a representational viewpoint, the differences in accessibility between the two types of knowledge. CLARION accounts for this difference based on the use of two different forms of representations. The top level of CLARION is symbolic/localist and thus naturally accessible/explicit, while the bottom level contains knowledge embedded in a network with distributed representations and is thus inaccessible/implicit. Thus, this distinction in CLARION is intrinsic instead of assumed.[5]

The SOAR (Rosenbloom et al. 1993) architecture is based on the ideas of problem spaces, states, and operators. When there is an outstanding goal on the stack, different productions propose different operators and operator preferences for accomplishing the goal. Learning consists of *chunking*— the creation of a new production that summarizes the process leading to achieving a subgoal, so as to avoid impasses subsequently, which is a form of explanation-based learning. SOAR does not distinguish the two types of knowledge; chunking is used to account for performance improvement. In terms of the difference in conscious accessibility, it assumes the inaccessibility of the internal working of individual productions, so as to distinguish deliberate and automatized processing with the difference of multiple productions versus a single production. In addition, as mentioned earlier, SOAR requires a large amount of initial (a priori) knowledge about operators and their preferences to begin with; hence its process of learning is not bottom-up.

EPIC (Meyer and Kieras 1997) is also different from CLARION, because it makes no implicit/explicit distinction either. However, the novel part is that it incorporates elaborate motor and perceptual processes as part of a cognitive architecture.

Drescher (1991) developed an architecture that attempted to implement the Piagetian constructivist view of child development. The learning mechanism is based on statistics collected during interaction with the world. New schemas (i.e., rules) are created and their conditions identified and tuned through statistical means based on relevance (Jones and VanLehn 1994). It can also build abstractions out of primitive actions.

---

[5] The newer versions of the ACT models (Anderson 1993) posited a dichotomy of exemplars versus rules (cf. Logan 1988, Hintzman 1986). However, in these models, exemplars are assumed to be explicit and production rules implicit, which is the opposite of CLARION.

However, the model does not make the dichotomous distinction of the two types of knowledge and thus does not account for the distinction of implicit versus explicit learning. The model deals only with low-level procedural learning (for motor interaction).

9.4   Models of Consciousness

Let us now turn to models of consciousness. In chapter 7, I attempted to explain issues surrounding consciousness, based essentially on the difference between localist (symbolic) and distributed representations. It is worthwhile to point out that, much earlier, Reber (1989) hypothesized that the primary difference between the conscious and unconscious processes lies in the forms of their representations. Lewicki et al. (1992) and Squire et al. (1993) had similar views in interpreting their data. My view is an extension of these previous conjectures. The advantage of the representational difference (localist+distributed) explanation of consciousness is that it provides a mechanistic (computational) distinction that explains the phenomenological distinction between the conscious and the unconscious, thus grounding a set of vague notions needing explanation in another set of notions that are more tangible (i.e., physical and computational) and more fundamental. Thus, it plausibly accounts for the physical basis of consciousness.

Let us look into a few other models of consciousness in detail. Bower's (1996) model can be viewed as a special case, or an instantiation, of CLARION in the context of modeling implicit memory phenomena. The type-1 and type-2 connections, hypothesized by Bower (1996) as the main explanatory constructs, can be equated roughly to top-level representations and bottom-level representations in CLARION, respectively. In addition to making the distinction between type-1 and type-2 connections, Bower (1996) also endeavored into specifying multiple pathways of spreading activation in the bottom level. These pathways are phonological, orthographical, semantic, and other connections that store long-term implicit knowledge as weights on links that connect relevant nodes involved. On the other hand, associated with type-2 connections (in the top level), rich contextual information was stored. These details of Bower's model complement the specification of CLARION and can thus be incorporated into the latter model.

We can also compare CLARION with Schacter's (1990) model, which is based on neuropsychological findings of dissociation of different types of knowledge. It is similar to CLARION, in that it includes a number of "knowledge modules" that perform specialized and unconscious processing (analogous to the bottom-level modules in CLARION) and send their outcomes to a "conscious awareness system" (analogous to the top level in CLARION), which gives rise to conscious awareness. However, Schacter's model did not explain the qualitative distinction between the conscious and the unconscious in that the "conscious awareness system" lacks any qualitative physical difference from the unconscious systems.

Similarly, in Baars' (1988) model, a large number of "specialist processors" perform unconscious processing and a global workspace coordinates their activities through global broadcasting to achieve consistency and thus conscious experience. The model bears some resemblance to CLARION, in that unconscious specialist processors in that model can be roughly equated to modules in the bottom level of CLARION, and the global workspace may be roughly captured by the top level, which "synthesizes" bottom-level modules and is essential to conscious processing. Global broadcasting in Baars' model can be viewed as the interaction of the two levels of representations (involving multiple modules in the bottom-level) in CLARION, which does produce somewhat consistent outcomes. One difference is that CLARION does not emphasize as much internal consistency, which is believed to be a by-product of consciousness. A shortcoming of Baars' model is that there is no reduction of the phenomenological distinction of the conscious and the unconscious to more fundamental physical distinctions.

Damasio's neuroanatomically motivated model (Damasio 1994) hypothesized the existence of many "sensory convergence zones" that integrated information from individual sensory modalities through forward and backward synaptic connections and the resulting reverberation of activations. It also hypothesized the global "multi-modal convergence zone", which integrated information across modalities also through reverberation via recurrent connections. In relation to CLARION, different sensory convergence zones may be roughly captured by bottom-level modules of CLARION, each of which takes care of sensory inputs of one modality, and the role of the global multi-modal convergence zone (similar to the "global workspace" in a way) may be played by the top level of CLARION, which has the ultimate responsibility for explicitly representing information of all types. The process of reverberation (Damasio 1994) may be captured in CLARION through recurrent connections within modules and through top-down and bottom-up information flows across the two levels, which lead to some degree of unity of consciousness that involves the synthesis of all information present (Marcel 1983, Baars 1988).

9.5   Objections and Responses

Let us look into several categories of possible objections to our approach. I will respond to these objections one by one.

9.5.1   One Level or Two?

A possible argument against CLARION is that, if a simpler model, an one-level model, can account for the data, then there is no need for the second level. I would argue that this simplicity argument is, by all measures, the wrong way to look at models. Intuitively and commonsensically, there is the distinction between explicit and implicit thinking (or conscious and unconscious processes). This is well established. The "simplest" explanation (or computational account) for this distinction is a system that has two corresponding components, which is exactly what we have in CLARION. On top of that, there are also numerous philosophical arguments and existing psychological data that support the point that the distinction of two levels is a minimal structure necessary (see chapter 2). More remotely relevant, there is also the biological evidence that points out that the brain has multiple pathways each of which has different characteristics.

If we look at each experimental condition that CLARION simulated alone, of course we can capture the data with a one-level model. But we need to capture a wide range of data together and take into considerations of all sources of evidence (including existing psychological theories and philosophical arguments that we reviewed in chapter 2), because only in this way do we have any chance of arriving at a generic and principled cognitive model. In particular, the synergy effect as a whole (Mathews et al. 1989, Sun and Peterson 1998a, 1998b, and Sun et al. 2001) cannot be easily generated without (at least) two components. There is no known easy way of explaining away the synergy effect without resorting to two or more components. Thus, the model, in an abstract way, appears to be the minimum model that we can have to explain this type of data.

In addition, it is not completely clear that one-level models are inherently simpler than two-level models. It depends on the nature of parameters, manipulations, and internal structural complexity that are needed to get the one-level model to perform the same tasks as the two-level model did. Consequently, if there are two different types of knowledge that need to be captured, then a two-level model may be an inherently simpler way to capture them than having to construct a complex one-level model to handle both types of knowledge.

In summary, with regard to the issue of one level versus two levels, there exists a fundamental—philosophical and methodological—difference of opinions. Compared with the opposing views, my position is relatively well supported.

9.5.2   Need for Symbolic Representation

Whether symbolic representations, as classically conceived, are needed or not is not a settled matter. However, there is no dispute that some form of symbolic representations, in connectionist or classical sense, is needed to account for high-level cognition. Some connectionists believe that symbols may emerge from dynamic interactions in networks (Smolensky 1988, Bechtel and Abrahamson 1991). Others believe that symbols may be encoded in connectionist networks, in much the same way as in symbolic models (Sun 1992, 1995). I do not make any claim as to in what form symbols should be, only that there should be some. Only for matters of convenience, did I use localist encoding of symbols in the model (Sun 1992). Psychological and linguistic data overwhelmingly point to the existence of symbolic representations in human cognition, especially in language, reasoning, and concept formation (Chomsky 1980, Hadley 1990, Smith et al. 1992, Nosofsky et al. 1994, Sun 1995). For these reasons, symbolic representations, in the form of localist encoding, are included in CLARION.

9.5.3   Hybridization

Some have criticized "wholesale mixing" of what they perceive to be irreconcilably different types of models—connectionist and symbolic models, and of the two "schools of thought" behind them. They believe that such mixing leads only to incoherent models. However, in criticizing "wholesale mixing", they might have assumed that connectionist and symbolic models were totally incompatible. Although there are differing opinions on how to approach this issue, there is a growing trend that views the two "schools of thought" as highly compatible, and even fundamentally the same, with only minor differences in emphasis. This current, more mature understanding needs to be taken into account, which is quite different from the early days of connectionism during which overstated claims and counter-claims abounded. Judged in this light, CLARION is not "incoherent" as a result of its making simultaneous use of the two paradigms.

I should point out that it is the modeling of human performance that prompted us to consider such an option and that there is a growing body of data from human experiments that suggests that models that make use of both connectionist and symbolic structures are well suited for this purpose (Mathews et al. 1989, Schneider and Oliver 1991, Sun 1995, 1997, 1999). What we have done is not an ad hoc addition of components. Rather, what we offer is a well-justified architecture that is a response to the overwhelming empirical data and theoretical concerns, which demand the adoption of a multiple-principles account of cognition.

It is true that there are psychological models that rely exclusively on distributed representations (e.g., Rumelhart et al. 1986), but these models typically do not capture explicit processes and explicit knowledge. There have been suggestions, even in such work, that more than distributed representations may be needed for modeling explicit processes (see, e.g., Cleeremans and McClelland 1991).

Beside the fact that there can be multiple explanations in an area where there is no consensus, in this case, our hybrid model is broader and accounts for a broader range of data. Thus it is justified to be somewhat more complex, on an empirical basis (based on the data that it accounts for) as well as on a theoretical basis (as discussed in chapter 2). Finally, as pointed out earlier, a two-level hybrid model could be a more parsimonious explanation. It naturally accounts for the dichotomy of the explicit and the implicit whereas alternative accounts may not have such an intuitively (and theoretically) appealing explanatory parsimony.

9.5.4 Free Parameters?

Some may object to the model based on the (false) observation that the model has many parameters all of which affect performance and thus matching human data is a trivial matter. I disagree with this view. Values of all the parameters, of course, affect the performance. But most of them were not changed throughout various experimental conditions, and therefore these parameters should be treated as part of the fixed model specification. In this sense, they are not free parameters. Put it another way, they do not contribute to the degree of freedom that we have in the model to match the change of performance across different experimental conditions for human subjects. See, for example, McClelland et al. (1995) for a similar point.

9.5.5 Verification of Explicit Knowledge

We considered verifying knowledge at the top level through comparing it with explicit knowledge elicited from human subjects, as might be suggested by some. However, we came to the conclusion that "protocol analysis" is not directly applicable for the purpose of verifying the top-level knowledge, for the following reasons: (1) Verbalization does not necessarily cover only the content of the top level (although mostly so). This is because the bottom-level content, through some interpretive and transformational processes, may show up in verbalization. (2) Verbalization does not necessarily exhaustively cover the content of the top level. This is because what is verbalizable is not necessarily verbalized. (3) Verbalization has a certain post hoc character to it. This case is very well argued for in the literature (see, e.g., Nisbett and Wilson 1977). Although protocol analysis appears to be successful in high-level cognitive skill domains, it is much less applicable to lower-level domains prevalent in everyday activities, because in such domains, more implicit learning is involved and it becomes much more difficult to verbalize.

Generally speaking, it is not always possible to verify all parts of a complex model directly with human data. For example, as a comparison, ACT* (Anderson 1993) and SOAR (Rosenbloom et al 1993) are well known models and neither could verify all their components with human data. Such a shortcoming is inevitable at the present time, but should be addressed in the future.

9.5.6 Neurobiological Evidence

My view on representations may at times seem at odds with existing neurobiological knowledge. For example, it is believed that the ventral visual pathway is responsible for explicit visual awareness while it is understood that the area employs rather "distributed" representations (Milner and Goodale 1995). The answer to such apparent paradoxes is two-fold: (1) The localist/distributed distinction applies only at certain levels of abstraction, not necessarily at all possible levels of description. For example, at the molecular level, all the representations have to be "distributed". (2) Localist representation has many variations, as discussed by Feldman and Ballard (1982), some of which may seem to resemble distributed representation to some extent, for example, when *replicated* localist nodes are distributed spatially. However, such seemingly "distributed" representations are actually localist.[6] Thus a dogmatic view on localist representation is unwarranted.

Let me address, more generally, the relationship between the abstract distinction of localist and distributed representations (posited in CLARION) and the biological brain mechanisms (as they are known currently). First of all, currently, both psychological and biological understanding of the human mind is rudimentary (although brain sciences are making rapid progress). We thus need ideas from other disciplines, including computational modeling, in order to make better progress in understanding important issues such as consciousness. Moreover, given the preliminary nature of present-day biological understanding and biology-based theorizing, it is helpful to go beyond them when we search for ideas and explanations, even when such ideas and explanations may appear at odds with some current biological theorizing (Dror and Gallogly 1999). This is because biology has only explored a small part of the vast space of possible biological

---

[6] That is, spatial characteristics are not determining factors of representation as the term is used here. See Feldman and Ballard (1982) for a full characterization.

mechanisms and processes, and its understanding of even that small part may not be complete or clear enough to reveal all the intricacies. At this time, it is, in general, not prudent to dismiss any model or theory based on current, limited biological understanding. We need different approaches that serve complementary roles. Computational modeling on the basis of psychological data, whether or not mapped to biology, is important, in that it broadens the scope of exploration, and thus it may provide useful ideas and insight, or may even constrain and guide biological studies in the future. The distinction of localist and distributed representations may be useful in this sense.

9.6   Computational Issues

I will now attend to computational issues involved in CLARION. Specifically, I will compare various aspects of CLARION with other related models in existence. The comparison is divided into the following aspects: reinforcement learning, rule learning, planning, spatial partitioning, and temporal partitioning. This section is more technical than the previous ones.

9.6.1   Models of Reinforcement Learning

Reinforcement learning has many variations (Sutton 1990, Bertsekas and Tsitsiklis 1996). *Q-learning* (Watkins 1989) is but one variation. Much existing work shows that Q-learning is as good as any other reinforcement learning method, if not better (Sutton 1990, Lin 1992, Mahadevan and Connell 1992, Zhang and Dietterich 1995).

Reinforcement learning (including Q-learning) is problematic when the input space is large, in which case reinforcement learning using table lookup is not applicable and neural network implementations are not guaranteed successful learning (Lin 1992, Tesauro 1992). Our experiments suggested that CLARION helped in this regard, because rules complemented function approximators (neural networks) by correcting over-generalization (see Sun and Peterson 1998a for analyses) and because modular methods were used to simplify learning.

There have been a variety of techniques for speeding up or otherwise helping Q-learning. Such techniques include reuse of previous experience, gradual expansion of state spaces, hierarchical learning, and construction and use of high-level features. Some of these were adopted in CLARION (see later subsections). Some others cannot be used in CLARION, because they require a large amount of a priori knowledge which CLARION does not assume or because they are designed to deal with issues that are not the goal of CLARION.

Let us also examine some alternatives to reinforcement learning methods. There are some alternatives from the neural network literature, such as recurrent backpropagation networks. Such networks use hidden nodes as a memory, which represent a condensed record of past states. The hidden nodes are connected recurrently so that the previous states are taken into account in the present. The problem with such networks is that they generally require supervised learning. There are techniques that get around the problem of requiring teacher input (supervision), but they are generally slower. They also suffer from other problems, including the lack of a proper (discriminating) temporal credit assignment mechanism, and the imprecision of hidden unit representations.

Yet another alternative is genetic algorithm (e.g., Grefenstette 1992, Meeden 1996, Beer 1996). GA is a weak method for knowledge-lean heuristic search. It updates its knowledge based mostly on experience of an entire generation, each member of which goes through many trials, at the end of all their trials, not on individual experience of a step or a trial. Therefore learning time required by the algorithm is expected to be much longer than CLARION.

9.6.2   Models of Rule Learning

Let us compare CLARION with connectionist rule extraction algorithms. Fu (1991) proposed an exhaustive search algorithm to extract conjunctive rules from backpropagation networks. To find rules, the algorithm first searches for all the combinations of positive conditions that can lead to a conclusion; then, in the second phase, with a previously found combination of positive conditions, the algorithm searches for negative conditions that should be added to guarantee the conclusion. In the case of three-layered networks, the algorithm extracts two separate sets of rules, one for each layer, and then integrates them by substitution.

Towell and Shavlik (1993) used rules of an alternative form, the *N-of-M* form: *If N of the M conditions, a_1, a_2, ..., a_M, is true, then the conclusion b is true.* It was believed that some rules could be better expressed in such a form, which more closely resembled weighted-sum computation in neural networks, in order to avoid the combinatorial explosion. A four-step procedure was used to extract such rules, by first grouping similarly weighted links, eliminating insignificant groups, and then forming rules from the remaining groups through an exhaustive search.

However, these rule extraction algorithms are meant to be applied at the end of the training of a network. Once extracted, the rules are fixed; there is no modification on the fly, unless the rules are re-extracted after further training of the network. On the other hand, in CLARION, an agent can extract and modify rules dynamically. Connectionist reinforcement learning and rule learning work together simultaneously; thus the synergy of the two algorithms can be utilized to improve learning. Extracting and modifying rules dynamically is computationally less expensive because it minimizes search necessary, although CLARION incurs slightly more cost each step during learning.[7] Furthermore, CLARION avoids examining the details of the network from which rules are extracted. Instead, it focuses on the *behavior* of the network and acquires rules on that basis. Our approach also helps agents to adapt to changing environments by allowing the addition and removal of rules at any time.

Now let us turn to rule learning methods in symbolic AI. Though CLARION learns rules, CLARION tackles tasks different from what is usually dealt with by traditional AI rule learning algorithms. Most of the supervised concept/rule learning algorithms (such as AQ and ID3; Michalski 1983, Quinlan 1986) require consistent data and pre-classification, which are not available to CLARION. Furthermore, as "batch" algorithms, they require an agent to obtain all data before learning starts, which means higher space complexity, slow start in learning, and no "drifting" (without extra mechanisms). They cannot be applied directly to sequential tasks because they do not perform temporal credit assignment. There is also the incremental variety of supervised learning (e.g., the version space algorithm of Mitchell 1982). Although incremental, they require pre-

---

[7] In CLARION, to reduce cost, one can stop neural network learning early and obtain a reasonably good (but not necessarily optimal) rule set. In Fu (1991) and Towell and Shavlik (1993), one may also shorten neural network learning, but one cannot shorten the exponential-time search process for rule extraction.

classified, complete, and consistent descriptions of instances, which are not available to CLARION. They do not handle sequences either.

Unsupervised rule/concept learning algorithms, such as Fisher (1987) and Stepp and Michalski (1986), are also unsuitable, in that (1) in our tasks, there is feedback available (i.e., reinforcement), although there is no direct supervision; such feedback must be taken into consideration in order to achieve goals; (2) temporal credit assignment is necessary; (3) a complete description of instances on which an agent can base its decisions is usually not available. For example, for CLARION, a state (input) may be a partial description of an actual situation, and typically contains only limited amount of information about the actual situation. The consequence of a state-action pair may not be known for a long time, but is nevertheless part of the information about an instance that a learning agent needs; when finally a payoff occurs, it is up to the temporal credit assignment mechanism to decide which step that has been experienced deserves the credit.

One might argue that the problem of sequences can be avoided by evaluating the values of states and/or actions statically (in isolation). However, static evaluation typically relies on a great deal of a priori knowledge about a task. In contrast, we assume minimum a priori knowledge in an agent.

In explanation-based learning, an agent tries to extract specific rules concerning a situation by examining inferences regarding the situation and identifying relevant conditions in the inferences. There has been work on combining explanation-based learning and reinforcement learning. Such models bear some remote resemblance to CLARION. However, they rely on a priori, externally given knowledge which CLARION does not require.

9.6.3 Models of Planning and Plan Learning

Let us compare plan extraction in CLARION with probabilistic planning, such as Kushmerick et al. (1995), Dearden and Boutilier (1997), and Draper et al. (1994). Specifically, Kushmerick et al. (1995) performed probabilistic planning by searching for actions that established preconditions for some other actions (the probabilistic equivalent of backward chaining). The planning process was based on given domain-specific rules. On the other hand, Dearden and Boutilier (1997) used given representations of a domain, simplified them through the use of domain knowledge, and transformed them into a Markov decision process. Dynamic programming was then applied to obtain an optimal policy for the MDP. These models were different from CLARION in that they used much a priori domain-specific knowledge to begin with. Therefore, they did not capture autonomous learning of planning.

The key underlying plan extraction in CLARION is the relation between Q values and probabilities of reaching goals. Although this connection has been noted before (Sutton 1988), we used it to derive an algorithm for plan extraction. By utilizing the probabilities of reaching goals from current states as well as the probabilities of being in the current states (which can be obtained from the traversed paths), we derive an algorithm similar to the A* algorithm in the sense that it utilizes two "cost" estimates: the "cost" incurred thus far (the probability of reaching a current state) and the estimated future "cost" (the probability of reaching goals from the current state). However, instead of an additive combination of the two "costs", we use an essentially multiplicative combination.[8] While A* uses best-first search, we use beam search, due to the need to consider multiple outcomes in deciding plan steps in order to avoid backtracking.

Temporal projection was used in plan extraction, which was different from the use of similar processes in existing planning models. Kushmerick et al. (1995), as well as Draper et al. (1994), used temporal projection for planning through exhaustive search. Our method can be more efficient: It first learns implicitly through using reinforcement learning algorithms, the cost of which is comparable to, or less than, the cost of collecting statistics (for estimating transition probabilities) needed in Kushmerick et al. (1995). Instead of collecting statistics only, we acquire Q values as well with the use of reinforcement learning that facilitates the process. Then, limited beam search is conducted to extract explicit plans. A Q function provides estimates of success probabilities. Using the guidance provided by the Q function, we can narrow down the search (focusing only on the most promising paths) and avoid exhaustive search of the entire space of all possible paths. When optimal plans are not required, such a limitation

---

[8] One way to reconcile our method with A* is to view "costs" as the logarithms of probabilities: $c_1(s) = \ln p_1(s)$ and $c_2(s) = \ln p_2(s)$, where s is a state, p_1 is the probability of the path traversed and p_2 is the probability of reaching goals in the future, so that we can relate multiplicative combinations with additive combinations: $c_1(s) + c_2(s) = \ln p_1(s) + \ln p_2(s) = \ln(p_1(s) * p_2(s))$.

on the beam width is often feasible, although there is no guarantee that this will always be the case.

Drummond and Bresina (1990) also performed beam search in temporal projection to find the most likely path to achieve the goal. However, because their method was based only on state transition probabilities, without accurate estimates of future success probabilities (such as Q values), it needed to heuristically estimate future probabilities in order to decide which action to select.   Dean et al. (1993) used temporal projection in the search for an adequate set of states to be considered for planning. They iteratively expanded the set of states (termed an "envelop") using temporal projection, on the basis of an elaborate mathematical formulation that decided how big a state set to use (based on the expectation with regard to improvement in performance). It differs from our approach in that their model extracts a set of states before each run, while our approach extracts a set of states and state transitions (i.e., explicit plans) after reinforcement learning.[9]

In terms of learning from experience of planning, Kambhampati et al. (1996) and others dealt with modifying existing plans based on failure. However, these algorithms were complex, specifically designed methods for plan modification, treating learning initial plans and subsequent modification as separate processes. Our approach provides a unified means for both plan learning and modification by learning continuously. DeJong and Bennett (1997) used learning to adjust planners' biases in response to failure and thus conditioned planners to actions that tended to work. Different from our approach, these approaches required much a priori domain-specific knowledge to begin with.

9.6.4   Models of Spatial Partitioning

The region-splitting method in CLARION has some relative advantages compared with other partitioning methods in reinforcement learning. For instance, our approach does not require a priori partitioning of an input space such as in Singh (1994) and Humphrys (1996).[10]   Our approach

---

[9] Our model runs with the entire state space because of the use of function approximation and/or state aggregation. See Sun (1997b) for further details.

[10] For example, Humphrys (1996) used prewired, differential input features and reward functions for different agents. Singh (1994) used separate training for different agents.

does not require a priori division of a task into subtasks as in, for example, Dietterich (1997), which is one way of simplifying learning but requires a priori decisions that determine preset subgoals or predetermined subsequences and is very different from our approach of autonomous learning. Our approach is not limited to selecting a module for an entire subsequence, as in Dayan and Hinton (1992). Our approach of incrementally creating regions through splitting appears to be better justified algorithmically than more ad hoc methods such as Humphrys (1996). Our approach also differs from feature selection approaches, such as McCallum (1996), which uses decision trees to select features to create useful states on which reinforcement learning is based, because such work does not divide up a space into regions for *different* modules to handle to make learning easier.

Our approach differs from radial-basis functions (such as in Blanzieri and Katenkamp 1996), in that (1) we use hypercubes (and possibly other region types), different from spherical regions used by RBF and (2) more importantly, instead of a Gaussian function as in the RBF approach, we use a more powerful approximator in each region, which is capable of arbitrary functional mappings and thus eliminates the need for overlapping regions.[11] Our approach also differs from CMAC (Sutton 1996), in that we use a more powerful approximator in each region, thus avoiding highly overlapping placement of regions. The same comparison applies to fuzzy logic based methods as well (see, e.g., Takagi and Sugeno 1985).

Our approach is more suitable for incremental learning that involves changes over time, unlike some of the existing work that predetermines partitioning and thus makes it hard or impossible to undergo changes. It is especially suitable for situations in which the world changes in a minor way continuously. In such a case, the changes can be quickly accommodated due to the use of localized regions, which make each individual mapping to be learned by an approximator (a neural network) simpler and thus make the overall learning easier. Furthermore, localized regions tend to group together inputs that have similar value distributions (with regard to actions) and are easier to adjust. When major changes occur, our approach

---

[11] Individual radial basis functions are not capable of arbitrary mappings, and thus overlapping placement of such functions throughout the input/state space is necessary in order to approximate arbitrary functions.

can also accommodate them by creating corresponding drastic changes in the allocations of regions and modules. However, such changes are costly.

Our approach is similar to the concurrently developed work of Tani and Nolfi (1998), in terms of partitioning the perception-action space to give rise to distinct concepts on the basis of both perception and action (see chapter 6). The difference is that their model is based on recurrent backpropagation networks, and subject to all the shortcomings of such models (see the earlier discussion), while our model is based on reinforcement learning.

9.6.5 Models of Temporal Partitioning

The need for hierarchical learning that can produce (sub)sequences of actions, corresponding to differing scales of events in the world, has been demonstrated by Dayan and Hinton (1992), Kaelbling (1993), Parr and Russell (1997), and many others. However, shortcomings of structurally pre-determined hierarchies, whereby structures are derived from a priori domain knowledge and remain fixed, are evident. The problems include cost (because it is costly to obtain a priori domain knowledge to form hierarchies), inflexibility (because the characteristics of the domain for which fixed hierarchies are built can change over time), and lack of generality (because domain-specific hierarchies most likely vary from domain to domain). Even when limited learning is used to fine tune structurally pre-determined hierarchies of sequences, some of these problems persist.

There are a number of existing reinforcement learning models that assume a fixed domain-specific hierarchy of sequences in place before learning starts. For example, Mahadevan and Connell (1992) used a hand-coded ("subsumption") hierarchy in which each module was predestined for a particular subtask by receiving a separate special reward. In the models of Dayan and Hinton (1992), Parr and Russell (1997), and Dietterich (1997), although learning was involved, domain-specific hierarchical structures were pre-constructed from a priori knowledge. Wiering and Schmidhuber (1998) applied a fixed structure that chained modules, although the modules themselves were adapted.

Our approach is learning hierarchies of sequences automatically by learning at multiple levels simultaneously. Our approach does not use separate rewards for different modules, separate training for different modules, or pre-segmentation into elemental tasks. Our approach also does not involve explicit use of global measures (and the optimization of such measures).

We use one and only one principle in automatically forming hierarchies, that is, the maximization of expected reinforcement, which is used in learning action policies, learning control policies, and learning abstract control policies. This is in contrast with work that uses additional, auxiliary principles in forming hierarchies, for example, the principle of description length minimization, secondary error terms, or entropy measures (see Sun and Sessions 1999a for further discussions).

Hierarchical reinforcement learning is related to hierarchical planning (Sacerdoti 1974), which has been prominent in the planning literature. In hierarchical planning, an abstract plan consisting of abstract operators is proposed first and is subsequently reduced to more primitive operators before it is executed. Pfleger and Hayes-Roth (1996) proposed the idea of plans as "intention". Plans that represent intention are expressed as constraints rather than abstract actions. This approach does not require a priori specification of refinements of abstract operators, so as to allow an agent to exploit, during execution in accordance with the plan, knowledge acquired separately as well as particular characteristics of environments that were encountered. In comparison, our hierarchical method is neither fixed reduction of operators, nor mere expression of constraints. It is learned stochastic "reduction" of stochastic procedures, which is not a priori specified, and thus it is more flexible than operator reduction, in the sense that there is no pre-determined steps, goals, or subroutines, but more structured than constraint specifications.

Chapter 10

Conclusions

> *No man can be wise, out of which love for wisdom, or philosophy, was born.*
> — *Socrates*

10.1 Major Theses

Starting with fundamental methodological questions in cognitive science and artificial intelligence led directly to the basic tenet of my approach, which put clear emphases on (1) the existential context of a cognitive agent, instead of purely on either internal representations or external environments, and (2) the coexistence, codevelopment, and interaction of implicit and explicit processes, instead of only on one of them or on the two processes separately. An integrative approach toward cognitive science was developed in this way.

A major point advanced in this book is that cognition is not just internal explicit representations, symbol manipulations, and conceptual structures on the one hand (as advocated by traditional approaches to cognitive science), and embodiment, situated cognition, and sociocultural cognition on the other hand, but a proper integration of all of the above (and more), in a properly configured cognitive architecture. A particular cognitive architecture, CLARION, is developed to illustrate and synthesize these ideas. What is important, however, is not the architecture per se but the points that are illustrated by the architecture. The architecture has been used in empirical work of modeling cognitive processes, especially in learning skills and routines. So the theoretical discussions in this book are empirically grounded.

In all, I advocated the following four *theses* in this work:

- *The existentiality thesis.* Being-in-the-world, on top of biological/genetic pre-endowment, is fundamental to cognition. Especially important is comportment with the world, in an immediate, nondeliberative way, which serves as the basis of conceptual thinking, symbolic processes, and consciousness.

- *The whole-structure thesis.* The temporal and spatial structure that links various external situations with various actions/reactions, on the basis of their shared participation in an agent's everyday activities, determines the essential characteristics of cognition in an agent.

- *The dual representation thesis.* There are fundamentally two types of cognitive processes, either immediate and reflexive, or conceptual and reflective; that is, either implicit or explicit. Cognition is carried out by these two distinct levels together.

- *The dual origin thesis.* There are fundamentally two sources of knowledge: sociocultural and individual.

In this work, I attempt to synthesize various schools of thoughts on cognition. In a sense, I undertake a recontextualization process of existing work in cognitive science and artificial intelligence.

Although this approach is integrative, I believe that it is not a mere eclectic mixture of existing ideas, a compromise of some sort. Instead, I attempt to highlight the issues and the implications of *integrating* these important ideas, not just these ideas per se, and to emphasize the synergy resulting from the integration.

10.2 Methodological Issues

It has been pointed out by many that cognitive science has been plagued by stagnation and fragmentation in recent years. Research programs in cognitive science have in general settled into one position or another: either classical computationalism (Newell and Simon 1976, Fodor and Pylyshyn 1988), or connectionism (Rumelhart et al. 1986, Smolensky 1988, Clark

1993). Both of the two positions tend to pay little attention to, and indeed relegate to the fringe, certain issues such as everyday activities, sociocultural cognition, consciousness, affect, and so on, which some researchers have now come to consider to be of fundamental importance. There are some ominous signs. Recently, one conference call-for-papers boldly declared that "cognitive science is in crisis", and consequently proposed a "close reexamination" of the foundation of the field. A number of monographs denounced traditional approaches to cognitive science and declared their futility, although each in a different way. The books by Wertsch (1991), Damasio (1994), Freeman (1995), and Bruner (1995) all belong to this category. Judging from all the signs, it seems that a reexamination of the foundation of cognitive science is in order (Von Eckardt 1992).

The problem that is plaguing cognitive science may be attributed to the following tension: Although cognitive science in the main gained its initial identity and momentum through taking a computational stance, it is now being limited, fragmented, and impeded by this stance. Although there is nothing in that stance that is inherently damaging, it is the perspectives that are most frequently derived from that stance that can prevent one from seeing things beyond them, especially some equally (or even more) important factors in cognition some of which were enumerated earlier (including situated action, consciousness, biological constraints, and sociocultural factors). If cognitive science is to become an all-encompassing science of the mind, as most of us would like it to be, we need to open up our horizons and be much more accommodating.

In order to take into account all of these different issues and aspects mentioned here, first and foremost, we need to bring together sociological, psychological, computational, biological, and other perspectives, and incorporate their respective methodologies, theories, data, and models. This is because the totality of existential experience, composed of all the aspects of agents' existence in physical, social, and cultural worlds is what matters.

In this work, through integration, I intend to avoid some (intrinsic or probable) pitfalls of each of the original ideas that have contributed to this approach. For example, I attempted to alleviate Vygotsky's apparent external determinism by incorporating traditional AI and cognitive science methods of concept formation based on individual experience.   I tried also to counterbalance Heidegger's persistent downplay of higher mental functions (conceptual thinking with symbolic processes) by illustrating how such functions could emerge out of low-level behavior and in turn complement low-level behavior. Above all, I tried to dispel the theoretical confusions over implicit and explicit processes and argue for the coexistence of both types.

Second, it is admittedly highly desirable to develop a single, completely unified theoretical language, as a means of expressing fundamental theories of the mind and its various manifestations, components, and phenomena. In place of the classical formalism—symbolic computation, we would certainly like to see a new logico-mathematical formalism that is (1) more analyzable (e.g., in the form of mathematical entities, as opposed to computer programs, which are notoriously difficult to analyze), (2) more inclusive (for example, being able to include both symbols and numeric values, and both serial and parallel processing), and (3) properly constrained (that is, being able to express exactly what needs to be expressed). However, thus far, there is no such a single unified formalism in sight.

In fact, I believe that there are plenty of theoretical reasons why we *cannot* find such a formalism, based on the hypothesis of the two cognitive levels. Given this fact, short of a completely unified logico-mathematical formalism, we may strive for a formalism that contains several different components but is structurally integrated nevertheless, to partially satisfy the afore-identified desiderata. I believe in such a "hybrid" formalism, and have been attempting to develop one throughout this work.

Consequently, what is important for cognitive science is the understanding and development of cognitive *architectures*. That is, we need to answer the following questions: How do different processes interact and how do different subtasks fit together, instead being mere collections of small and limited models? The study of architectural issues helps us to gain new insight, to narrow down possibilities, and to delineate processes. Although we are still far away from being sufficiently clear about the brain, in this way we can advance the understanding of the mind. This is what I believe to be needed for an integrative cognitive science that seeks (1) to instantiate its theories and (2) to fit various pieces together to form a coherent whole.

Given the broad scope of this approach, its emphasis cannot be on *extremely* fine-grained modeling of tasks involved. Models are coarser by necessity, inevitable given the nature of this approach. Nevertheless, I believe that a high-level synthesis and a broad-stroke coverage of a wide range of data are not only useful but essential to understanding the *general* principles of human cognition, which is the ultimate goal of cognitive science.

10.3 Cognitive Implications

The framework advanced in this work connects with, and encompasses, various existing theoretical constructs in cognitive science. Let us look into some of these constructs.

New interpretations of old ideas. Compared with existing theories, approaches, and perspectives concerning human cognition, CLARION is distinct in its emphasis — learning through the interaction of implicit and explicit processes, and in a mostly bottom-up (implicit-to-explicit) direction. Due to this emphasis, it offers a new perspective in interpreting old issues and ideas, as well as a new direction for theorizing about, and experimenting with, human cognition.

Let me clarify the relationship between the implicit/explicit distinction and the procedural/declarative distinction. In Anderson (1983, 1993), procedural knowledge is encoded in an action-oriented way (with production rules that can only be used in one direction—from conditions to actions), and declarative knowledge in a non-action-oriented way (with knowledge chunks that can be used in any possible direction). The difference in action-orientedness is the main factor in distinguishing the two types, while explicit accessibility is a secondary factor. On the other hand, much explicit knowledge in CLARION is action-oriented, and thus it is not declarative in the above sense of declarative knowledge. But it *is* declarative, if we define declarativeness in terms of accessibility. As demonstrated in CLARION, action-orientedness does not necessarily go with inaccessibility (Sun et al. 2001), and non-action-orientedness does not necessarily go with accessibility either (as in priming and implicit memory; see, e.g., Schacter 1987). The two dichotomies overlap to a large extent and can be reconciled if we adopt the latter definition. I believe that the former definition unnecessarily confounds two issues: action-orientedness and accessibility, and can be made clearer through separating the two.[1]

The notion of automaticity (automatic versus controlled processes) is also relevant to CLARION. The notion has been variously associated with (1) the absence of competition for limited resources (attention) and thus the lack of performance degradation in multi-task settings (Navon and Gopher 1979), (2) the absence of conscious control/intervention in processes (J.Cohen et al. 1990), (3) the general inaccessibility of processes (Logan 1988), (4) the general speedup of skilled performance (Hunt and Lansman 1986). CLARION is compatible with these senses. The top level can account for controlled processes (the opposite of these above properties), and the bottom level has the potential of accounting for all the afore-mentioned properties of automatic processes. We have in fact separately covered these issues in this work: the speedup of skilled performance, the inaccessibility of processes in the bottom level, including their ability of running without conscious intervention, and the lack of resource competition (due to the existence of multiple bottom-level modules that can run in parallel). Thus, automaticity may serve as an umbrella term that describes a set of phenomena occurring in the bottom level of CLARION.

The issue of accessibility (and the way in which it is accounted for) should be of major importance to theories of cognition, considering its inextricable relationships with various fundamental dichotomies in cognition. In most existing theories, the difference between accessible and inaccessible representations is simply assumed, without grounding in representational forms. Thus the difference in their theories is not intrinsic. CLARION on the other hand accounts for this difference based on the use of two different forms of representations. Thus, this distinction in CLARION is *intrinsic* instead of *assumed*. I would suggest that this is a more principled way of accounting for the accessibility difference. This explanation extends into accounting for consciousness as discussed in chapter 8.

A new look at old paradigms. In relation to the above notions, let us also look into the controversy of connectionist models versus symbolic models (Fodor and Pylyshyn 1988, Smolensky 1988). First of all, there was the question of which paradigm was more suitable for cognitive modeling

---

[1] My view on this issue is close to Hunt and Lansman's (1986), because they separated two types of processes (controlled versus automatic) also based on representational forms instead of on action-orientedness. In fact, both types of knowledge in their model were action-oriented.

in the 1980s and 1990s. This has been an issue of great controversy among theoretically minded cognitive scientists. However, CLARION sidesteps this stalemate by incorporating both paradigms, in a principled way. We showed that the two could be combined to create synergy, which in turn suggested the general advantage of this combination. CLARION is one of many so-called hybrid models that emerged in the late 1980s, which have received increasing attention recently (see Sun 1994, Sun and Bookman 1994, Sun and Alexandre 1997, and Wermter and Sun 2000).

In relation to this issue, there is also the more specific issue of the ability (or the inability) of one modeling paradigm or the other in accounting for implicit learning. It has been claimed, on the connectionist side, that a vast majority of human activities (i.e., implicit processes), including "perception, motor behavior, fluent linguistic behavior, intuition in problem solving and game playing—in short, practically all skilled performance", can only be modeled by subsymbolic computation (connectionist models), and symbolic models can give only an imprecise and approximate explanation to these processes (Smolensky 1988). It has also been claimed, on the symbolicist side, that "one and the same algorithm can be responsible for conscious and nonconscious processes alike", or even that implicit learning "should be better modeled by symbolic rule learning programs" (Ling and Marinov 1994; see also Fodor and Pylyshyn 1988). I believe that this issue is a red herring: Being able to simulate some data of implicit learning amounts to very little, in that any Turing equivalent computational process, that is, any generic computational model, should be able to simulate these data. Thus, simulation of data by itself does not prove whether a particular model is a suitable one or not (Cleeremans 1997). Other considerations need to be brought in to justify a model. I would suggest that one such issue is the accessibility issue discussed above. While symbolic models of implicit learning lead to explicit symbolic representation of implicit knowledge (e.g., Anderson 1993, Ling and Marinov 1994, Lebiere et al. 1998) that is evidently accessible (without using any add-on auxiliary assumptions), connectionist models of implicit learning lead to implicit (subsymbolic) representation of knowledge that is inherently inaccessible (such as in the bottom level of CLARION). Thus, connectionist models have a clear advantage: Being able to match human implicit learning data (at least) as well as symbolic models, they also account for the inaccessibility of implicit knowledge better and more naturally than symbolic models. In this sense, they are better models. On the other hand, it is generally agreed upon that symbolic/localist models have their roles to play too: They are better at capturing explicit processes. This contrast lends support to the belief that, because connectionist models are good for implicit processes and symbolic models for explicit processes, the combination of the two types should be adopted in modeling cognition (Smolensky 1988, Sun 1994, 1995, 1997).

The relationship between CLARION and instance-based models (e.g., Logan 1988, Dienes and Fahey 1995) can also be explicated. Logan (1988) showed that skill learning (automatization of skills) could be captured by the acquisition of a domain-specific knowledge base that was composed of experienced instances represented in individuated forms (Hintzman 1986). Shanks and St.John (1994) developed a theoretical perspective in which implicit learning was viewed as nothing more than learning instances, although this perspective has been criticized for various failings. Stanley et al. (1989) also described implicit learning/performance as mainly the result of relying on memory of past instances, which were utilized by being compared to a current situation and transformed into a response to the current situation. At first glance, these models may seem at odds with CLARION. However, upon closer examination, we see that connectionist networks used in the bottom level of CLARION can be either exemplar-based (essentially storing instances; Kruschke 1992) or prototype-based (summarizing instances; Rumelhart et al. 1986). The instance-based models, however, generally do not handle the learning of explicit knowledge, especially not bottom-up learning.

Finally, as a result of its distinct emphasis, CLARION is also clearly distinguishable from existing unified theories/architectures of cognition, such as SOAR, ACT, and EPIC. The differences have been discussed at length in chapter 9.

10.4   A Final Summary

We cannot overstate the importance of understanding the human mind, because this understanding is fundamental to, and intrinsically tied with, a variety of the most important issues in the modern world. At the beginning of the new millennium, it appears appropriate to redouble our effort to achieve a better understanding of the human mind. The present work might be viewed in this context.

Most importantly, this work highlights the duality of the human mind: implicit versus explicit processes, individual versus sociocultural origins, innate versus acquired capacities, conscious versus unconscious cognition, and so on. The technical contribution of this work lies in capturing a wide range of human data through the interaction of the two types of processes, thus demonstrating psychological plausibility of the interaction, and also in showing computational feasibility of capturing such interaction. Furthermore, this work also demonstrates computational feasibility and psychological plausibility of bottom-up learning, that is, autonomous learning with little or no a priori knowledge to begin with that goes from implicit skills to explicit knowledge, which complements extensive existing treatments of top-down learning in the literatures. It fills a significant gap.

Moreover, beyond narrow technical issues, through utilizing the duality of the mind, we can tackle broader subject matters, including providing a reasonably cogent account of an array of theoretically important issues. Such issues include the nature of consciousness, intentionality (symbol grounding), and sociocultural processes. They have been among the most prominent and the most controversial issues of philosophy of mind in the past, and in all likelihood, will continue to draw tremendous interest and effort in the new millennium. I hope that this work has something interesting to contribute to the on-going dialogue on these fundamental issues.

References

[1] P. Ackerman, (1988). Determinants of individual differences during skill acquisition: cognitive abilities and information processing. *Journal of Experimental Psychology: General*, 1117 (3), 288-318.

[2] P. Agre, (1988). The dynamic structure of everyday life. Technical report, MIT AI Lab, MIT, Cambridge, MA.

[3] P. Agre, (1997). *Computation and Human Experience.* Cambridge University Press, New York.

[4] P. Agre and D. Chapman, (1987). Pengi: An implementation of a theory of activity. *Proceedings of the 6th National Conference on Artificial Intelligence.* Morgan Kaufmann, San Mateo, CA.

[5] P. Agre and I. Horswill, (1997). Lifeworld analysis. *Journal of Artificial Intelligence Research*, 6, 111-145.

[6] M. Ahlum-Heath and F. DiVesta, (1986). The effect of conscious controlled verbalization of a cognitive strategy on transfer in problem solving. *Memory and Cognition*, 14, 281-285.

[7] W. Ahn and D. Medin, (1992). A two-stage model of category construction. *Cognitive Science*, 16, 81-121.

[8] J. R. Anderson, (1983). *The Architecture of Cognition.* Harvard University Press, Cambridge, MA

[9] J. R. Anderson, (1985). *Cognitive Psychology and Its Implications.* W. H. Freeman, New York.

[10] J. R. Anderson, (1990). *The Adaptive Character of Thoughts.* Lawrence Erlbaum Associates, Hillsdale, NJ.

[11] J. R. Anderson, (1993). *Rules of the Mind.* Lawrence Erlbaum Associates. Hillsdale, NJ.

[12] J. Anderson and E. Rosenfeld (eds.), (1988). *Neurocomputing.* MIT Press, Cambridge, MA.

[13] F. Ashby, L. Alfonso-Reese, and U. Turken, (1996). A formal neuropsychological theory of multiple systems in category learning. Technical report, University of California, Santa Barbara.

[14] R. Ashmore and L. Jussim (eds.), (1997). *Self and Identity: Fundamental Issues*. Oxford University Press, New York.

[15] B. Baars, (1988). *A Cognitive Theory of Consciousness*. Cambridge University Press, New York.

[16] D. Ballard, (1991). Animate vision. *Artificial Intelligence*, 48, 57-86.

[17] R. Bapi and K. Doya, (2001). Multiple forward model architecture for sequence learning. In: R. Sun and L. Giles (eds.), *Sequence Learning: Paradigms, Algorithms, and Applications*. Springer-Verlag, Heidelberg, Germany.

[18] J. Barkow, L. Cosmides and J. Tooby, (1992). *The Adapted Mind: Evolutionary Psychology and the Generation of Culture*. Oxford University Press. New York.

[19] L. Barsalou, (1989). Intraconcept similarity and its implications. In: S. Vosniadou and A. Ortony (eds.), *Similarity and Analogical Reasoning*. Cambridge University Press, New York.

[20] L. Barsalou, (1999). Perceptual symbol systems. *Behavioral and Brain Sciences*, 22, 577-609.

[21] A. Barto, S. Bradtke, and S. Singh, (1996). Learning to act using real-time dynamic programming. *Artificial Intelligence*, 72 (1), 81-138

[22] A. Barto, R. Sutton, and P. Brouwer, (1981). Associative search networks: A reinforcement learning associative memory. *Biological Cybernetics*, 40, 201-211.

[23] W. Bechtel, (1988). *Philosophy of Mind: An Overview for Cognitive Science*. Lawrence Erlbaum Associates, Hillsdale, NJ.

[24] W. Bechtel and A. Abrahamsen, (1991). *Connectionism and the Mind*. Basil Blackwell, Oxford, UK.

[25] R. Beer, (1996). Toward the evolution of dynamic neural networks for minimally cognitive behavior. *Proceedings of the 4th International Conference on Simulation of Adaptive Behavior*, 421-429. MIT Press, Cambridge, MA.

[26] H. Ben-Zur, (1998). Dimensions and patterns in decision-making models and the controlled/automatic distinction in human information processing. *The European Journal of Cognitive Psychology*, 10 (2), 171-189.

[27] D. Berry, (1983). Metacognitive experience and transfer of logical reasoning. *Quarterly Journal of Experimental Psychology*, 35A, 39-49.

[28] D. Berry, (1991). The role of action in implicit learning. *Quarterly Journal of Experimental Psychology*, 43A, 881-906.

[29] D. Berry and D. Broadbent, (1984). On the relationship between task performance and associated verbalizable knowledge. *Quarterly Journal of Experimental Psychology*, 36A, 209-231.

[30] D. Berry and D. Broadbent, (1988). Interactive tasks and the implicit-explicit distinction. *British Journal of Psychology*, 79, 251-272.

[31] D. Bertsekas and J. Tsitsiklis, (1996). *Neuro-Dynamic Programming*. Athena Scientific, Belmont, MA.

[32] M. Bickhard, (1993). Representational content in humans and machines. *Journal of Experimental and Theoretical Artificial Intelligence*, 285-333.

[33] I. Biederman and M. Shiffrar, (1987). Sexing day-old chicks: A case study and expert systems analysis of a difficult perceptual-learning task. *Journal of Experimental Psychology: Learning, Memory, and Cognition*, 15, 517-526.

[34] E. Blanzieri and P. Katenkamp, (1996). Learning radial basis function networks on-line. *Proceedings of International Conference on Machine Learning*, 37-45. Morgan Kaufmann, San Francisco, CA.

[35] N. Block, (1980). Are absent qualia impossible? *Philosophical Review*, 89, 257-274.

[36] N. Block, (1994). on a confusion about a function of consciousness. *Brain and Behavioral Sciences*, 18 (2), 227-287.

[37] P. Bourdieu, (1984). *Distinction: A Social Critique of the Judgement of Taste*. Harvard University Press, Cambridge, MA.

[38] P. Bourdieu and L. Wacquant, (1992). *An Invitation to Reflexive Sociology*. University of Chicago Press, Chicago.

[39] A. Bower and W. King, (1967). The effect of number of irrelevant stimulus dimensions, verbalization, and sex on learning biconditional classification rules. *Psychonomic Science*, 8 (10), 453-454.

[40] G. Bower, (1996). Reactivating a reactivation theory of implicit memory. *Consciousness and Cognition*, 5 (1/2), 27-72.

[41] K. Bowers, G. Regehr, C. Balthazard, and K. Parker, (1990). Intuition in the context of discovery. *Cognitive Psychology*, 22. 72-110.

[42] L. Breiman, (1996). Bagging predictors. *Machine Learning*, 24 (2), 123-140.

[43] L. Breiman, L. Friedman, and P. Stone, (1984). *Classification and Regression*. Wadsworth, Belmont, CA.

[44] D. Broadbent, P. Fitsgerald, and M. Broadbent, (1986). Implicit and explicit knowledge in the control of complex systems. *British Journal of Psychology*, 77, 33-50.

[45] R. Brooks, (1991). Intelligence without representation. *Artificial Intelligence*, 47, 139-159.

[46] R. Brooks and L. Stein, (1994). Building brains for bodies. *Autonomous Robots*, 1 (1), 7-26.

[47] G. Brown, P. Dalloz, and C. Hulme, (1995). Mathematical and connectionist models of human memory: A comparison. *Memory*, 3 (2), 113-145.

[48] J. Bruner, (1995). *Acts of Meaning*. Harvard University Press, Cambridge, MA.

[49] J. Bruner, J. Goodnow, and J. Austin, (1956). *A Study of Thinking*. John Wiley and Sons, New York.

[50] T. Burge. (1979). Individualism and the mental. In: *Midwest Studies in Philosophy*, Vol.IV. University of Minnesota Press, Minneapolis, MN.

[51] J. Busemyer and I. Myung, (1992). An adaptive approach to human decision making: Learning theory, decision theory, and human performance. *Journal of Experimental Psychology: General*, 121 (2), 177-194.

[52] C. Camerer, (1997). Progress in behavioral game theory. *Journal of Economic Perspectives*, 11, 4. 167-188.

[53] L. Caporael, (1997). The evolution of truly social cognition: The core configuration model. *Personality and Social Psychology Review*, 1 (4), 276-298.

[54] R. Carnap, (1969). *The Logic Structure of the World*. University of California Press, Berkeley, CA.

[55] B. Challis, B. Velichkovski, F. Craik, (1996). Level-of-processing effects on a variety of memory tasks. *Consciousness and Cognition*, 5 (1/2), 142-164.

[56] D. Chalmers, (1990). Why Fodor and Pylyshyn were wrong: The simplest refutation. *Proceeding of the Cognitive Science Conference*. Lawrence Erlbaum Associates, Hillsdale, NJ.

[57] D. Chalmers, (1993). *Towards a Theory of Consciousness*. Ph.D. thesis, Indiana University, Bloomington, IN.

[58] C. Chan, (1992). *Implicit Cognitive Processes: Theoretical Issues and Applications in Computer Systems Design*. Doctoral dissertation, University of Oxford, Oxford, UK.

[59] D. Chapman, (1991). *Vision, Instruction, and Action*. MIT Press, Cambridge, MA.

[60] M. Chi, M. Bassok, and M. Lewis, P. Reimann, and P. Glaser, (1989). Self-explanation: How students study and use examples in learning to solve problems. *Cognitive Science*, 13, 145-182.

[61] N. Chomsky, (1980). *Rules and Representation*. Columbia University Press, New York.

[62] P. Churchland, (1986). *Neurophilosophy: Toward a Unified Science of the Mind-Brain.* MIT Press, Cambridge, MA.

[63] W. Clancey, (1993). Situated action: A neuropsychological interpretation. *Cognitive Science,* 17 (1), 87-116.

[64] W. Clancey, (1997). *Situated Cognition: On Human Knowledge and Computer Representations.* Cambridge University Press, Cambridge, U.K.

[65] W. Clancey, (2000). *Conceptual Coordination.* Lawrence Erlbaum Associates, Mahwah, NJ.

[66] A. Clark, (1989). *Microcognition: Philosophy, Cognitive Science, and Parallel Distributed Processing.* MIT Press, Cambridge, MA.

[67] A. Clark, (1993). *Associative Engines: Connectionism, Concepts, and Representational Change.* MIT Press, Cambridge, MA.

[68] A. Clark, (1997). *Being There.* MIT Press, Cambridge, MA.

[69] A. Clark and A. Karmiloff-Smith, (1993). The cognizer's innards: A psychological and philosophical perspective on the development of thought. *Mind and Language,* 8 (4), 487-519.

[70] A. Cleeremans, (1994). Attention and awareness in sequence learning. *Proceedings of the Annual Conference of Cognitive Science Society,* 330-335.

[71] A. Cleeremans, (1997). Principles for implicit learning. In: D. Berry (ed.), *How implicit is implicit learning?,* 195-234. Oxford University Press, Oxford, England.

[72] A. Cleeremans and J. McClelland, (1991). Learning the structure of event sequences. *Journal of Experimental Psychology: General,* 120, 235-253.

[73] J. Cohen, K. Dunbar, and J. McClelland, (1990). On the control of automatic processes: A parallel distributed processing account of the Stroop effect. *Psychological Review,* 97 (3), 332-361.

[74] A. Collins and J. Loftus, (1975). Spreading activation theory of semantic processing. *Psychological Review,* 82, 407-428.

[75] A. Collins and E. Smith, (1988). *Readings in Cognitive Science.* MIT Press, Cambridge, MA.

[76] L. Cosmides and J. Tooby, (1989). Evolutionary psychology and the generation of culture II. *Ethology and Sociobiology,* 10, 51-97.

[77] L. Cosmides and J. Tooby, (1994). Beyond intuition and instinct blindness: Toward an evolutionarily rigorous cognitive science. *Cognition,* 50, 41-77.

[78] F. Craik and R. Lockhart, (1972). Level of processing: A framework for memory research. *Journal of Verbal Learning and Verbal Behavior,* 11, 671-684.

[79] F. Crick and C. Koch, (1990). Toward a neurobiological theory of consciousness. *Seminars in the Neuroscience*, 2, 263-275.

[80] T. Curran and S. Keele, (1993). Attention and structure in sequence learning. *Journal of Experimental Psychology: Learning, Memory, and Cognition*, 19, 189-202.

[81] A. Damasio, (1994). *Decartes' Error: Emotion, Reason, and the Human Brain*. Grosset/Putnam, New York.

[82] R. D'Andrade, (1989). Cultural cognition. In: M. Posner (ed.), *Foundations of Cognitive Science*. MIT Press, Cambridge, MA.

[83] E. Davis, (1990). *Representations of Commonsense Knowledge*. Morgan Kaufman, San Mateo, CA.

[84] P. Dayan and G. Hinton, (1992). Feudal reinforcement learning. In: *Advances in Neural Information Processing Systems 5*, 271-278. MIT Press, Cambridge, MA.

[85] T. Dean, L. Kaelbling, J. Kirman, and A. Nicholson, (1993). Planning under time constraints in stochastic domains. *Proceedings of AAAI'93*, 574-579. Morgan Kaufman, San Mateo, CA.

[86] R. Dearden and C. Boutilier, (1997). Abstraction and approximate decision theoretic planning. *Artificial Intelligence*, 89, 219-283.

[87] E. de Jong, (2000). *Autonomous Formation of Concepts and Communication*. Ph.D. thesis, Artificial Intelligence Laboratory, Vrije Universiteit Brussels, Brussels, Belgium.

[88] G. DeJong and S. Bennett, (1997). Permissive planning: Extending classical planning to uncertain task domains. *Artificial Intelligence*, 89, 173-217.

[89] J. Deneubourg and S. Goss, (1989). Collective patterns and decision making. *Ethology, Ecology, and Evolution*, 1, 295-311.

[90] D. Dennett, (1991). *Consciousness Explained*. Little, Brown and Company, Boston.

[91] D. Dennett, (1993). Review of John Searle's "The Rediscovery of the Mind". *The Journal of Philosophy*, 193-205.

[92] R. DeShon and R. Alexander, (1996). Goal setting effects on implicit and explicit learning of complex tasks. *Organizational Behavior and Human Decision Processes*, 65 (1), 18-36.

[93] J. Dewey, (1958). *Experience and Nature*. Dover, New York.

[94] Z. Dienes, (1992). Connectionist and memory-array models of artificial grammar learning. *Cognitive Science*, 16. 41-79.

[95] Z. Dienes and D. Berry, (1997). Implicit synthesis. *Psychonomic Bulletin and Review*, 4, 68-72.

[96] Z. Dienes and D. Berry, (1997). Implicit learning: Below the subjective threshold. *Psychonomic Bulletin and Review*, 4, 3-23.

[97] Z. Dienes and R. Fahey, (1995). Role of specific instances in controlling a dynamic system. *Journal of Experimental Psychology: Learning, Memory and Cognition*, 21 (4), 848-862.

[98] T. Dietterich, (1997). Hierarchical reinforcement learning with MAXQ value function decomposition. http://www.engr.orst.edu/~tgd/cv/pubs.html.

[99] P. Domingos, (1996). Unifying instance-based and rule-based induction. *Machine Learning*, 24, 141-168.

[100] R. Dominowski, (1972). How do people discover concepts? In: R. L. Solso (Ed.), *Theories in Cognitive Psychology: The Loyola Symposium*, 257-288. Lawrence Erlbaum Associates, Potomac, MD.

[101] R. Dominowski and N. Wetherick, (1976). Inference processes in conceptual rule learning. *Journal of Experimental Psychology: Human Learning and Memory*, 2 (1), 1-10.

[102] M. Dorigo and L. Gambardella, (1995). Ant-Q: A reinforcement learning approach to combinatorial optimization. Technical report 95-01. Universite Libre de Bruxelles, Belgium.

[103] J. Doyle, (1983). What is rational psychology? *AI Magazine*, 4 (3), 50-53.

[104] D. Draper, S. Hanks, and D. Weld, (1994). Probabilistic planning with information gathering and contingent execution. *Proceedings of AIPS-94*. AAAI Press, Menlo Park, CA.

[105] G. Drescher, (1991). *Made-Up Minds*. MIT Press, Cambridge, MA.

[106] F. Dretske, (1981). *Knowledge and the Flow of Information*. MIT Press, Cambridge, MA.

[107] H. Dreyfus, (1972). *What Computers Can't Do*. Harper and Row. New York.

[108] H. Dreyfus, (1982). *Husserl, Intentionality, and Cognitive Science*. MIT Press, Cambridge, MA.

[109] H. Dreyfus, (1992). *Being-In-the-World*. MIT Press, Cambridge, MA.

[110] H. Dreyfus and S. Dreyfus, (1987). *Mind Over Machine: The Power of Human Intuition*. The Free Press, Glencoe, IL.

[111] I. Dror and D. Gallogly, (1999). Computational analyses in cognitive neuroscience: In defense of biological implausibility. *Psychonomic Bulletin and Review*, 6 (2), 173-182.

[112] M. Drummond and J. Bresina, (1990). Any time synthetic projection. *Proceedings of AAAI'90*, 138-144. Morgan Kaufmann, San Mateo, CA.

[113] W. Durkheim, (1895/1962). *The Rules of the Sociological Method*. The Free Press, Glencoe, IL.

[114] D. Dulaney, R. Carlson, and G. Dewey, (1984). A case of syntactic learning and judgment: How conscious and how abstract. *Journal of Experimental Psychology: General*, 113, 541-555.

[115] G. Edelman, (1992). *Bright Air, Brilliant Fire*. Basic Books, New York.

[116] T. Eggertsson, (1990). *Economic Behavior and Institutions*. Cambridge University Press, Cambridge, UK.

[117] J. Elman, (1990). Finding structure in time. *Cognitive Science*, 14, 179-212.

[118] S. Epstein, (1994). For the right reasons, the FORR architecture for learning in a skill domain. *Cognitive Science*, 18, 479-511.

[119] M. Erickson and J. Kruschke, (1998). Rules and exemplars in category learning. *Journal of Experimental Psychology: General*, 127, 107-140.

[120] W. Estes, (1986). Memory storage and retrieval processes in category learning. *Journal of Experimental Psychology: General*, 115, 155-174.

[121] O. Etzioni, (1991). Embedding decision-analytic control in a learning architecture. *Artificial Intelligence*, 49, 129-159.

[122] J. Feldman and D. Ballard, (1982). Connectionist models and their properties. *Cognitive Science*, 205-254.

[123] J. Fetzer, (1985). *Sociobiology and Epistemology*. Reidel Publishing, Dordrecht, Netherlands.

[124] D. Fisher, (1987). Knowledge acquisition via incremental conceptual clustering. *Machine Learning*, 2, 139-172.

[125] P. Fitts and M. Posner, (1967). *Human Performance*. Brooks/Cole, Monterey, CA.

[126] J. Fodor, (1975). *The Language of Thought*. Crowell, New York.

[127] J. Fodor, (1980). Methodological solipsism considered as a research strategy in cognitive psychology. *Behavioral and Brain Sciences*, 3, 417-424.

[128] J. Fodor, (1983). *The Modularity of Mind*. MIT Press, Cambridge, MA.

[129] J. Fodor and Z. Pylyshyn, (1988). Connectionism and cognitive architecture: A critical analysis. In: S. Pinker and D. Mehler (eds.), *Connections and Symbols*. MIT Press, Cambridge, MA.

[130] W. Freeman, (1995). *Societies of Brains: A Study in the Neuroscience of Love and Hate*. Lawrence Erlbaum Associates, Hillsdale, NJ.

[131] S. Freud, (1937). *A General Selection from the Works of Sigmund Freud*. Hogarth Press, London.

[132] L.M. Fu, (1991). Rule learning by searching on adapted nets. *Proceedings of AAAI'91*, 590-595. Morgan Kaufmann, San Francisco, CA.

[133] R. Gagne and E. Smith, (1962). A study of the effects of verbalization on problem solving. *Journal of Experimental Psychology*, 63, 12-18.

[134] W. Gardner and B. Rogoff, (1990). Children's deliberateness of planning according to task circumstances. *Developmental Psychology*, 26 (3), 480-487.

[135] C. Geertz, (1973). *The Interpretation of Culture*. Basic Books, New York.

[136] J. Gelfand, D. Handelman and S. Lane, (1989). Integrating knowledge-based systems and neural networks for robotic skill acquisition. *Proceedings of IJCAI*, 193-198. Morgan Kaufmann, San Mateo, CA.

[137] J. Gibson, (1950). *The Perception of the Visual World*. Houghton Mifflin, Boston, MA.

[138] J. Gibson, (1979). *The Ecological Approach to Visual Perception*. Houghton Mifflin, Boston, MA.

[139] F. Gibson, M. Fichman, and D. Plaut, (1997). Learning in dynamic decision tasks: Computational model and empirical evidence. *Organizational Behavior and Human Decision Processes*, 71 (1), 1-35.

[140] M. Gick and K. Holyoak, (1980). Analogical problem solving. *Cognitive Psychology*, 12, 306-355.

[141] N. Gilbert and J. Doran, (1994). *Simulating Societies: The Computer Simulation of Social Phenomena*. UCL Press, London, UK.

[142] L. Giles and M. Gori, (1998). *Adaptive Processing of Sequences and Data Structures*. Springer-Verlag, Berlin.

[143] L. Giles, B. Horne, and T. Lin, (1995). Learning a class of large finite state machines with a recurrent neural network. *Neural Networks*, 8 (9), 1359-1365.

[144] A. Glenberg, (1997). What memory is for. *Brain and Behavioral Sciences*, 20 (1), 1-55.

[145] M. Gluck and G. Bower, (1988). From conditioning to category learning. *Journal of Experimental Psychology: General*, 117 (3), 227-247.

[146] D. Gordon, A. Schultz, J. Grefenstette, J. Ballas, and M. Perez, (1994). *User's Guide to the Navigation and Collision Avoidance Task*. Naval Research Laboratory, Washington, DC.

[147] D. Gordon and D. Subramanian, (1993). A multistrategy learning scheme for agent knowledge acquisition. *Informatica*, 17, 331-346.

[148] J. Grefenstette, (1992). The evolution of strategies for multiagent environments. *Adaptive Behavior*, 1 (1), 65-90.

[149] R. Hadley, (1990). Connectionism, rule following, and symbolic manipulation. *Proceedings of AAAI'90*, 579-586. Morgan Kaufmann, San Mateo, CA.

[150] R. Hadley, (1995). The explicit-implicit distinction. *Minds and Machines*, 5, 219-242.

[151] K. Hammond, T. Converse, and J. Grass, (1995). The stabilization of environments. *Artificial Intelligence*, 72, 305-328.

[152] S. Harnad, (1990). The symbol grounding problem. *Physica D*, 42, 335-346.

[153] J. Hasher and J. Zacks, (1979). Automatic and effortful processes in memory. *Journal of Experimental Psychology: General*, 108, 356-358.

[154] N. Hayes and D. Broadbent, (1988). Two modes of learning for interactive tasks. *Cognition*, 28 (3), 249-276.

[155] P. Hayes, K. Ford, and N. Agnew, (1994). On babies and bathwater: A cautionary tale. *AI Magazine*, 15 (4), 14-26.

[156] R. Haygood and L. Bourne, (1965). Attribute and rule learning aspects of conceptual behavior. *Psychological Review*, 72 (3), 175-195.

[157] M. Heidegger, (1927a). *Being and Time.* English translation published by Harper and Row, New York, 1962.

[158] M. Heidegger, (1927b). *The Basic Problem of Phenomenology.* Harper and Row, New York.

[159] J. Hendler, (1987). Marker passing and microfeature. *Proceedings of the 10th IJCAI*, 151-154. Morgan Kaufmann, San Mateo, CA.

[160] G. Hinton, J. McClelland, and D. Rumelhart, (1986). Distributed representations. In: D. Rumelhart, J. McClelland, and the PDP Research Group (eds.), *Parallel Distributed Processing I.* MIT Press, Cambridge, MA.

[161] D. Hintzman, (1986). Schema abstraction in a multiple-trace memory model. *Psychological Review*, 93, 528-551.

[162] D. Hintzman, (1990). Human learning and memory: Connections and dissociations. *Annual Review of Psychology*, 41, 109-139.

[163] G. Hinton, (1990). Mapping part-whole hierarchies into connectionist networks. *Artificial Intelligence*, 46, 47-76.

[164] L. Hirschfield and S. Gelman (eds.), (1994). *Mapping the Mind: Domain Specificity in Cognition and Culture.* Cambridge University Press, Cambridge, UK.

[165] H. Hirsh, (1994). Generalizing version spaces. *Machine Learning*, 17, 5-46.

[166] J. Holland, N. Nisbitt, T. Thagard and J. Holyoak, (1986). *Induction: A Theory of Learning and Development.* MIT Press, Cambridge, MA.

[167] J. Houk, J. Adams, and A. Barto, (1995). A model of how the basal ganglia generate and use neural signals that predict reinforcement. In: J. Houk, J. Davis, and D. Beiser (eds.), *Models of Information Processing in the Basal Ganglia.* MIT Press, Cambridge, MA.

[168] J. Howard and J. Ballas, (1980). Syntactic and semantic factors in classification of nonspeech transient patterns. *Perception and Psychophysics*, 28, 431-439.

[169] D. Hume, (1938). *An Abstract of A Treatise of Human Nature.* Cambridge University Press, Cambridge, UK.

[170] M. Humphrys, (1996). W-learning: A simple RL-based society of mind. Technical report 362, Computer Laboratory, University of Cambridge, Cambridge, UK.

[171] E. Hunt and M. Lansman, (1986). Unified model of attention and problem solving. *Psychological Review*, 93 (4), 446-461.

[172] E. Husserl, (1970). *Logical Investigation*. Routledge and Kegan Paul, London.

[173] E. Hutchins, (1995). How a cockpit remembers its speeds. *Cognitive Science*, 19, 265-288.

[174] B. Inhelder and J. Piaget, (1958). *The Growth of Logical Thinking from Childhood to Adolescence*. Routledge & Kegan Paul, London, England.

[175] R. Jacobs, (1990). *Task Decomposition Through Competition in a Modular Connectionist Architecture*. Ph.D. thesis, University of Massachusetts, Amherst, MA.

[176] R. Jacobs, M. Jordan, S. Nowlan, and G. Hinton, (1991). Adaptive mixtures of local experts. *Neural Computation*, 3, 79-87.

[177] L. Jacoby, J. Toth, A. Yonelinas, and J. Debner, (1994). The relation between conscious and unconscious influence: Independence or redundancy? *Journal of Experimental Psychology: General*, 123 (2), 216-219.

[178] R. Jackendoff, (1987). *Consciousness and the Computational Mind*. MIT Press, Cambridge, MA.

[179] W. James, (1890). *The Principles of Psychology*. Dover, New York.

[180] M. Johnson, (1987). *The Body in the Mind: The Bodily Basis of Meaning, Imagination, and Reason*. University of Chicago Press, Chicago.

[181] P. Johnson-Laird, (1983). A computational analysis of consciousness. *Cognition and Brain Theory*, 6, 499-508.

[182] R. Jones and K. VanLehn, (1994). Acquisition of children's addition strategies: A model of impasse-free knowledge-level learning. *Machine Learning*, 16, 11-36.

[183] M. Jordan and R. Jacobs, (1994). Hierarchical mixtures of experts and the EM algorithm. *Neural Computation*, 6, 181-214.

[184] C. G. Jung, (1959). *The Archetypes and the Collective Unconscious*. Pantheon Books, New York.

[185] L. Kaelbling, (1987). An architecture for intelligent reactive systems. In: *Reasoning About Actions and Plans: Proceedings of the 1986 Workshop*. Morgan Kaufmann, Los Altos, CA.

[186] L. Kaelbling, (1993). *Learning in Embedded Systems*. MIT Press. Cambridge, MA.

[187] J. Kahan and A. Rapoport, (1984). *Theories of Coalition Formation*. Lawrence Erlbaum Associates, Mahwah, NJ.

[188] D. Kahneman and A. Treisman, (1984). Changing views of attention and automaticity. In: R. Parasuraman and D. Davies (eds.), *Varieties of Attention*. Academic Press, New York.

[189] S. Kambhampati, S. Katukam, and Y. Qu, (1996). Failure driven dynamic search control for partial order planners: an explanation based approach. *Artificial Intelligence*, 87, 253-315.

[190] A. Karmiloff-Smith, (1986). From meta-processes to conscious access: Evidence from children's metalinguistic and repair data. *Cognition*, 23, 95-147.

[191] A. Karmiloff-Smith, (1992). *Beyond Modularity: A Developmental Perspective on Cognitive Science*. MIT Press, Cambridge, MA.

[192] S. Keele, R. Ivry, E. Hazeltine, U. Mayr, and H. Heuer, (1998). The cognitive and neural architecture of sequence representation. Technical report No.98-03, Institute of Cognitive and Decision Sciences. University of Oregon, Eugene, OR.

[193] F. Keil, (1989). *Concepts, Kinds, and Cognitive Development*. MIT Press, Cambridge, MA.

[194] C. Kelley and L. Jacoby, (1993). The construction of subjective experience: Memory attribution. In: M. Davies and G. Humphreys (eds.), *Consciousness*. Blackwell, Oxford, UK.

[195] A. Kersten and D. Billman, (1992). The role of correlational structure in learning event categories. *Proceedings of the 14th Annual Meeting of Cognitive Science Society*, 432-437. Lawrence Erlbaum Associates, Mahwah, NJ.

[196] P. Kitcher, (1992). *Freud's Dream*. MIT Press, Cambridge, MA.

[197] D. Klahr, P. Langley, and R. Neches (eds.), (1987). *Production System Models of Learning and Development*. MIT Press, Cambridge, MA.

[198] C. Knoblock, J. Tenenberg, and Q. Yang, (1994). Characterizing abstraction hierarchies for planning. *Proceedings of AAAI'94*, 692-697. Morgan Kaufmann, San Mateo, CA.

[199] S. Kripke, (1972). *Naming and Necessity*. Harvard University Press, Cambridge, MA.

[200] J. Kruschke, (1992). ALCOVE: An examples-based connectionist model of category learning. *Psychological Review*, 99, 22-44.

[201] T. Kuhn, (1970). *Structure of Scientific Revolutions*. University of Chicago Press, Chicago.

[202] N. Kushmerick, S. Hanks and D. Weld, (1995). An algorithm for probabilistic planning. *Artificial Intelligence*, 76 (1/2), 239-286.

[203] G. Lakoff, (1986). *Women, Fire and Dangerous Things*. MIT Press, Cambridge, MA.

[204] G. Lakoff and M. Johnson, (1980). The metaphoric structure of human conceptual system. *Cognitive Science*, 4, 193-208.

[205] J. Lave, (1988). *Cognition in Practice*. Cambridge University Press, Cambridge, England.

[206] J. Lave and E. Wenger, (1991). *Situated Learning: Legitimate Peripheral Participation*. Cambridge University Press, Cambridge, UK.

[207] N. Lavrac and S. Dzeroski, (1994). *Inductive Logic Programming*. Ellis Horword, New York.

[208] C. Lebiere, D. Wallach, and N. Taatgen, (1998). Implicit and explicit learning in ACT-R. *Proceedings of the European Conference on Cognitive Modeling*, 183-189. Nottingham University Press, Nottingham, UK.

[209] J. LeDoux, (1992). Brain mechanisms of emotion and emotional learning. *Current Opinion in Neurobiology*, 2 (2), 191-197.

[210] Y. S. Lee, (1995). Effects of learning contexts on implicit and explicit learning. *Memory and Cognition*, 23, 723-744.

[211] S. Levy, (1992). *Artificial Life*. Jonathan Cape, London.

[212] P. Lewicki, (1986). Processing information about covariations that cannot be articulated. *Journal of Experimental Psychology: Learning, Memory, and Cognition*, 12, 135-146.

[213] P. Lewicki, M. Czyzewska, and H. Hoffman, (1987). Unconscious acquisition of complex procedural knowledge. *Journal of Experimental Psychology: Learning, Memory and Cognition*, 13 (4), 523-530.

[214] P. Lewicki, T. Hill, and M. Czyzewska, (1992). Nonconscious acquisition of information. *American Psychologist*, 47, 796-801.

[215] J. Lewis, (1970). Semantic processing of unattended messages using dichotic listening. *Journal of Experimental Psychology*, 85, 220-227.

[216] B. Libet, (1985). Unconscious cerebral initiative and the role of conscious will in voluntary action. *Behavioral and Brain Sciences*, 8, 529-566.

[217] L. Lin, (1992). Self-improving reactive agents based on reinforcement learning, planning and teaching. *Machine Learning*, 8, 293-321.

[218] L. Lin, (1993). *Reinforcement Learning for Robots Using Neural Networks*. Ph.D. thesis, Carnegie-Mellon University, Pittsburgh, PA.

[219] C. X. Ling and M. Marinov, (1994). A symbolic model of the nonconscious acquisition of information. *Cognitive Science*, 18(4), 595-621.

[220] D. Lloyd, (1995). Consciousness: A connectionist manifesto. *Minds and Machines*, 5, 161-185.

[221] G. Logan, (1988). Toward an instance theory of automatization. *Psychological Review*, 95 (4), 492-527.

[222] G. Luger, (1994). *Cognitive Science: The Science of Intelligent Systems*. Academic Press, San Diego, CA.

[223] R. Maclin and J. Shavlik, (1994). Incorporating advice into agents that learn from reinforcements. *Proceedings of AAAI-94*, 694-699. Morgan Kaufmann, San Mateo, CA.

[224] G. Madison, (1981). *The Phenomenology of Merleau-Ponty*. Ohio University Press, Athens, Ohio.

[225] E. Maguire, N. Burgess, J. Donnett, R. Frackowiak, C. Frith, and J. O'Keefe, (1998). Knowing where and getting there: A human navigation network. *Science*, 280, 921-924.

[226] S. Mahadevan and J. Connell (1992). Automatic programming of behavior-based robots with reinforcement learning. *Artificial Intelligence*, 55, 311-365.

[227] J. Mandler, (1992). How to build a baby. *Psychological Review*, 99, 4, 587-604.

[228] A. Marcel, (1983). Conscious and unconscious perception: An approach to the relations between phenomenal experience and perceptual processes. *Cognitive Psychology*, 15, 238-300.

[229] A. Marcel, (1988). Phenomenal experience and functionalism. In: A. Marcel and E. Bisiach (eds.), *Consciousness in Contemporary Science*. Oxford University Press, Oxford, England.

[230] A. Markman and E. Dietrich, (1998). In defense of representation as mediation. *Psycoloquy*, 9 (48).

[231] D. Marr, (1980). *Vision*. MIT Press, Cambridge, MA.

[232] M. Mataric, (1993). Kin recognition, similarity, and group behavior. *Proceedings of the Annual Conference of Cognitive Science Society*, 705-710. Lawrence Erlbaum Associates, Mahwah, NJ.

[233] R. Mathews, R. Buss, W. Stanley, F. Blanchard-Fields, J. Cho, and B. Druhan, (1989). Role of implicit and explicit processes in learning from examples: A synergistic effect. *Journal of Experimental Psychology: Learning, Memory and Cognition*, 15, 1083-1100.

[234] D. Mathis and M. Mozer, (1996). Conscious and unconscious perception: A computational theory. *Proceedings of the 18th Annual Conference of Cognitive Science Society*, 324-328. Lawrence Erlbaum Associates, Hillsdale, NJ.

[235] A. McCallum, (1996). Learning to use selective attention and short-term memory in sequential tasks. *Proceedings of the Conference on Simulation of Adaptive Behavior*, 315-324. MIT Press, Cambridge, MA.

[236] J. McCarthy, (1968). Programs with common sense. In: M. Minsky (ed.), *Semantic Information Processing*. MIT Press, Cambridge, MA.

[237] J. McCarthy, (1980). Circumscription—a form of non-monotonic reasoning. *Artificial Intelligence*, 13, 27-39.

[238] J. McClelland, B. McNaughton and R. O'Reilly, (1995). Why there are complementary learning systems in the hippocampus and neocortex: Insights from the successes and failures of connectionist models of learning and memory. *Psychological Review*, 102 (3), 419-457.

[239] W. McCulloch and W. Pitts, (1943). A logical calculus of the ideas immanent in nervous activity. *Bulletin of Mathematical Biophysiology*, 5, 115-133.

[240] D. McDermott and J. Doyle, (1980). Non-monotonic Logic I. *Artificial Intelligence*, 13 (1/2), 41-72

[241] L. Meeden, (1996). An incremental approach to developing intelligent neural network controllers for robots. *IEEE Transactions on Systems, Man, and Cybernetics, Part B: Cybernetics*, 26 (3), 474-485.

[242] D. Medin, W. Wattenmaker, and R. Michalski, (1987). Constraints and preferences in inductive learning: An experimental study of human and machine performance. *Cognitive Science*, 11, 299-339.

[243] D. Mehwort, J. Braun, and A. Heathcote, (1992). Response time distributions and the Stroop task: A test of the Cohen, Dunbar and McClelland (1990) model. *Journal of Experimental Psychology: Human Perception and Performance*, 18 (3), 872-887.

[244] P. Merikle, (1992). Perception without awareness: Critical issues. *American Psychologists*, 47, 792-795.

[245] M. Merleau-Ponty, (1962). *Phenomenology of Perception*. Routledge and Kegan Paul, London.

[246] M. Merleau-Ponty, (1963). *The Structure of Behavior*. Beacon Press, Boston.

[247] J. Metcalfe and A. Shimamura (eds.), (1994). *Metacognition: Knowing About Knowing*. MIT Press, Cambridge, MA.

[248] D. Meyer and D. Kieras, (1997). A computational theory of executive cognitive processes and human multiple-task performance: Part 1, basic mechanisms. *Psychological Review*, 104 (1), 3-65.

[249] R. Michalski, (1983). A theory and methodology of inductive learning. *Artificial Intelligence*, 20, 111-161.

[250] D. Milner and N. Goodale, (1995). *The Visual Brain in Action*. Oxford University Press, New York.

[251] P. Milner, (1999). *The Autonomous Brain*. Lawrence Erlbaum Associates, Mahwah, NJ.

[252] M. Minsky, (1981). A framework for representing knowledge. In: J. Haugeland (ed.), *Mind Design*, 95-128. MIT Press, Cambridge, MA.

[253] M. Mishkin, B. Malamut, and J. Bachevalier, (1984). Memories and habits: Two neural systems. In: *Neurobiology of Human Learning and Memory*. Guilford Press, New York.

[254] T. Mitchell, (1982). Generalization as search. *Artificial Intelligence*, 18, 203-226.

[255] T. Mitchell, (1998). *Machine Learning*. McGraw-Hill, New York.

[256] P. Montague, P. Dayan, and T. Sejnowski, (1997). A framework for mesencephalic dopamine systems based on predictive Hebbian learning. *Journal of Neuroscience*, 16 (5), 1936-1947.

[257] M. Moscovitch and C. Umilta, (1991). Conscious and unconscious aspects of memory. In: *Perspectives on Cognitive Neuroscience*. Oxford University Press, New York.

[258] G. Murphy and D. Medin, (1985). The role of theories in conceptual coherence. *Psychological Review*, 92, 289-316.

[259] T. Nagel, (1974). What is it like to be a bat? *Philosophical Review*, 4, 435-450.

[260] H. Nakahara, K. Doya, L. Hikosaka, and S. Nagano, (1997). Reinforcement learning with multiple representations in the basal ganglia loops for sequential motor control. *Proceedings of the International Joint Conference on Neural Networks*, 1553-1558.

[261] K. Nakamura, K. Sakai, and O. Hikosaka, (1998). Neuronal activity in medial frontal cortex during learning of sequential procedures. *Journal of Neurophysiology*, 80, 2671-2687.

[262] D. Navon and D. Gopher, (1979). On the economy of the human-processing system. *Psychological Review*, 86 (3), 214-255.

[263] A. Neal and B. Hesketh, (1997). Episodic knowledge and implicit learning. *Psychonomic Bulletin and Review*, 4 (1), 24-37.

[264] T. Nelson, (Ed.) (1993). *Metacognition: Core Readings*. Allyn and Bacon, Boston.

[265] A. Newell, (1990). *Unified Theories of Cognition*. Harvard University Press, Cambridge, MA.

[266] A. Newell and H. Simon, (1976). Computer science as empirical inquiry: symbols and search. *Communication of ACM*, 19, 113-126.

[267] R. Nisbett and T. Wilson, (1977). Telling more than we can know: Verbal reports on mental processes. *Psychological Review*, 84 (3), 1977.

[268] M. Nissen and P. Bullemer, (1987). Attentional requirements of learning: Evidence from performance measures. *Cognitive Psychology*, 19, 1-32. 15, 282-304.

[269] D. Norman, (1993a). Cognitive engineering—cognitive science. In: J. Carroll (ed.), *Interfacing Thought: Cognitive Aspects of Human-Computer Interaction*. MIT Press, Cambridge, MA.

[270] D. Norman, (1993b). *Things That Make Us Smart*. Addison-Wesley, Reading, MA.

[271] R. Nosofsky, T. Palmeri, and S. McKinley, (1994). Rule-plus-exception model of classification learning. *Psychological Review*, 101 (1), 53-79.

[272] M. Osborne and A. Rubinstein, (1994). *A Course on Game Theory*. MIT Press, Cambridge, MA.

[273] D. Osherson and H. Lasnik, (1990). *An Invitation to Cognitive Science*. MIT Press, Cambridge, MA.

[274] E. Owen and J. Sweller, (1985). What do students learn while solving mathematics problems? *Journal of Experimental Psychology*, 77 (3), 272-284.

[275] R. Parr and S. Russell, (1997). Reinforcement learning with hierarchies of machines. In: *Advances in Neural Information Processing Systems 9*. MIT Press, Cambridge, MA.

[276] J. Pearl, (1988). *Probabilistic Reasoning in Intelligent Systems*. Morgan Kaufmann, San Mateo, CA.

[277] C. Peirce, (1955). *The Philosophical Writings of Charles Peirce*. Dover, New York.

[278] R. Penrose, (1994). *Shadows of the Mind*. Oxford University Press, Oxford, UK.

[279] P. Perruchet and C. Pacteau, (1990). Synthetic grammar learning: Implicit rule abstraction or explicit fragmentary knowledge? *Journal of Experimental Psychology: General*, 118, 264-275.

[280] R. Pfeifer and C. Scheier, (1999). *Understanding Intelligence*. MIT Press, Cambridge, MA.

[281] K. Pfleger and B. Hayes-Roth, (1997). Plan should abstractly describe intended behavior. *Proceedings of the Joint Conference on Intelligent Systems*, 29-33. Duke University Press, Durham, NC.

[282] S. Pinker, (1994). *The Language Instinct*. W. Morrow and Co., New York.

[283] D. Plaut and T. Shallice, (1994). *Connectionist Modeling in Cognitive Neuropsychology: A Case Study*. Psychology Press, Philadelphia, PA.

[284] J. Pollack, (1989). *How to Build a Person*. MIT Press, Cambridge, MA.

[285] J. Pollack, (1991). The induction of dynamic recognizers. *Machine Learning*, 7 (2/3), 227-252.

[286] R. Port and T. van Gelder, (1995). *Mind as Motion: Dynamics, Behavior, and Cognition*. MIT Press, Cambridge, MA.

[287] M. Posner (ed.), (1989). *Foundations of Cognitive Science*. MIT Press, Cambridge, MA.

[288] M. Posner, G. DiGirolamo, and D. Fernandez-Duque, (1997). Brain mechanisms of cognitive skills. *Consciousness and Cognition*, 6, 267-290.

[289] M. Posner and S. Petersen, (1990). The attention system of the human brain. *Annual Review of Neuroscience*, 13, 25-42.

[290] M. Posner and C. Snyder, (1975). Facilitation and inhibition. In: P. Rabbitt and S. Dornick (eds.), *Attention and Performance*. Academic Press, San Diego, CA.

[291] D. Premack, (1988). Minds with and without language. In: L. Weiskrantz (ed.), *Thought without Language*. Clarendon Press, Oxford, UK.

[292] J. Proctor and A. Dutta, (1995). *Skill Acquisition and Human Performance*. Sage Publications, Thousand Oaks, CA.

[293] H. Putnum, (1975). The meaning of 'meaning'. In: K. Gunderson (ed.), *Mind and Knowledge*. University of Minnesota Press, Minneapolis, MN.

[294] Z. Pylyshyn, (1984). *Computation and Cognition*. MIT Press, Cambridge, MA.

[295] M. Quillian, (1968). Semantic networks. In: M. Minsky (ed.), *Semantic Information Processing*. MIT Press, Cambridge, MA.

[296] R. Quinlan, (1986). Inductive learning of decision trees. *Machine Learning*, 1, 81-106.

[297] R. Quinlan, (1990). Learning logical definition from relations. *Machine Learning*, 5, 239-266.

[298] M. Rabinowitz and N. Goldberg, (1995). Evaluating the structure-process hypothesis. In: F. Weinert and W. Schneider (eds.), *Memory Performance and Competencies*. Lawrence Erlbaum Associates, Hillsdale, NJ.

[299] H. Rachlin, (1994). Self control: Beyond commitment. *Brain and Behavioral Sciences*, 18 (1), 109-159.

[300] A. Reber, (1967). Implicit learning of artificial grammars. *Journal of Verbal Learning and Verbal Behavior*, 6, 855-863.

[301] A. Reber, (1976). Implicit learning of synthetic languages: The role of instructional set. *Journal of Experimental Psychology: Human Learning and Memory*, 2, 88-94.

[302] A. Reber, (1989). Implicit learning and tacit knowledge. *Journal of Experimental Psychology: General*. 118 (3), 219-235.

[303] A. Reber and R. Allen (1978). Analogy and abstraction strategies in synthetic grammar learning: a functionalist interpretation. *Cognition*, 6, 189-221.

[304] A. Reber, Allen, R., and Regan, S. (1985). Syntactical learning and judgment, still unconscious and still abstract: A comment on Dulaney, Carlson, and Dewey. *Journal of Experimental Psychology: General*, 114, 17-24.

[305] A. Reber and S. Lewis, (1977). Implicit learning: An analysis of the form and structure of a body of tacit knowledge. *Cognition*, 5, 333-361.

[306] A. Reber and R. Millward, (1971). Event of tracking in probability learning. *American Journal of Psychology*, 84, 85-99.

[307] A. Reber, S. Kassin, S. Lewis, and G. Cantor, (1980). On the relationship between implicit and explicit modes in the learning of a complex rule structure. *Journal of Experimental Psychology: Human Learning and Memory*, 6, 492-502.

[308] L. Reder (ed.), (1996). *Implicit Memory and Metacognition*. Lawrence Erlbaum Associates, Mahwah, NJ.

[309] R. Rescorla and A. Wagner, (1972). A theory of Pavlovian conditioning. In: A. Black and W. Prokasy (eds.), *Classical Conditioning II: Current Research and Theory*, 64-99. Appleton-Century-Crofts, New York.

[310] L. Resnick, J. Levine, and S. Teasley (eds.), (1991). *Perspectives on Socially Shared Cognition*. American Psychological Association, Washington, D.C.

[311] A. Revonsuo, (1993). Cognitive models of consciousness. In: M. Kamppinen (ed.), *Consciousness, Cognitive Schemata and Relativism*, 27-130. Kluwer, Dordrecht, Netherlands.

[312] L. Rips, (1989). Similarity, typicality, and categorization. In: S. Vosniadou and A. Ortony (eds.), *Similarity and Analogical Reasoning*. Cambridge University Press, New York.

[313] R. Rieber and A. Carton (eds.), (1987). *The Collected Works of L. S. Vygotsky*. Plenum Press, New York.

[314] C. Riesbeck and R. Schank, (1989). *Inside Case-based Reasoning*. Lawrence Erlbaum Associate, Hillsdale, NJ.

[315] H. Roediger, (1990). Implicit memory: Retention without remembering. *American Psychologist*, 45 (9), 1043-1056.

[316] R. Rorty, (1979). *Philosophy and the Mirror of Nature*. Princeton University Press, Princeton, New Jersey.

[317] R. Rorty, (1991). *Essays on Heidegger and Others*. Cambridge University Press, New York.

[318] E. Rosch, (1978). Principles of categorization. In: E. Rosch and B. Lloyd (eds.), *Concepts and Categorization*. Lawrence Erlbaum Associates, Hillsdale, NJ.

[319] P. Rosenbloom, J. Laird, and A. Newell, (1993). *The SOAR Papers: Research on Integrated Intelligence.* MIT Press, Cambridge, MA.

[320] S. Rosenschein and L. Kaelbling, (1986). The synthesis of digital machines with provable epistemic properties. *Proceedings of Conference on Theoretical Aspects of Reasoning about Knowledge,* 83-86. Morgan Kaufmann, San Mateo, CA.

[321] D. Rosenthal (ed.), (1991). *The Nature of Mind.* Oxford University, Oxford, UK.

[322] S. Ross, (1973). The economic theory of agency. *American Economics Review,* 63, 134-139.

[323] D. Rumelhart, J. McClelland and the PDP Research Group, (1986). *Parallel Distributed Processing: Explorations in the Microstructures of Cognition.* MIT Press, Cambridge, MA.

[324] S. Russell and P. Norvig, (1995). *Artificial Intelligence: A Modern Approach.* Prentice Hall, Englewood Cliffs, NJ.

[325] E. Sacerdoti, (1974). Planning in a hierarchy of abstraction spaces. *Artificial Intelligence,* 5, 115-135.

[326] R. Salustowicz, M. Wiering, and J. Schmidhuber, (1998). Learning team strategies: Soccer case studies. *Machine Learning,* 33 (2/3), 263-282.

[327] J. Sanders, (1996). An ecological approach to cognitive science. *Electronic Journal of Analytic Philosophy,* 4, 1-12.

[328] T. Sandholm and V. Lesser, (1997). Coalition among computationally bounded agents. *Artificial Intelligence,* 94 (1), 99-137.

[329] D. Schacter, (1987). Implicit memory: History and current status. *Journal of Experimental Psychology: Learning, Memory, and Cognition,* 13, 501-518.

[330] D. Schacter, (1990). Toward a cognitive neuropsychology of awareness: implicit knowledge and anosagnosia. *Journal of Clinical and Experimental Neuropsychology,* 12 (1), 155-178.

[331] C. Scheier and R. Pfeifer, (1998). Exploiting embodiment for category learning. *From Animals to Animats 5: Proceedings of the Fifth International Conference of Simulation of Adaptive Behavior,* 32-37. MIT Press, Cambridge, MA.

[332] W. Schneider and W. Oliver (1991), An instructable connectionist/control architecture. In: K. VanLehn (ed.), *Architectures for Intelligence.* Lawrence Erlbaum Associates, Hillsdale, NJ.

[333] J. Schooler, S. Ohlsson, and K. Brooks, (1993). Thoughts beyond words: When language overshadows insight. *Journal of Experimental Psychology: General,* 122 (2), 166-183.

[334] J. Schraagen, (1993). How experts solve a novel problem in experimental design. *Cognitive Science*, 17, 285-309.

[335] A. Schutz, (1967). *The Phenomenology of the Social World*. Northwestern University Press, Evanston, IL.

[336] W. Schultz, P. Dayan, and R. Montague, (1997). A neural substrate of prediction and reward. *Science*, 275 (14), 1593-1603.

[337] J. Searle, (1980). Minds, brains, and programs. *Brain and Behavioral Sciences*, 3, 417-457.

[338] J. Searle, (1983). *Intentionality*. Cambridge University Press, New York.

[339] J. Searle, (1992). *The Rediscovery of the Mind*. MIT Press, Cambridge, MA.

[340] C. Seger, (1994). Implicit learning. *Psychological Bulletin*, 115 (2), 163-196.

[341] M. Seidenburg, J. McClelland, (1989). A distributed, developmental model of work recognition and naming. *Psychological Review*, 96 (4), 523-568.

[342] E. Servan-Schreiber and J. Anderson, (1987). Learning artificial grammars with competitive chunking. *Journal of Experimental Psychology: Learning, Memory, and Cognition*, 16, 592-608.

[343] T. Shallice, (1972). Dual functions of consciousness. *Psychological Review*, 79 (5), 383-393.

[344] D. Shanks, (1993). Human instrumental learning: A critical review of data and theory. *British Journal of Psychology*, 84, 319-354.

[345] D. Shanks, and M. St. John, (1994). Characteristics of dissociable learning systems. *Behavioral and Brain Sciences*, 17, 367-394.

[346] L. Shastri and V. Ajjanagadde, (1993). From simple associations to systematic reasoning: A connectionist representation of rules, variables and dynamic bindings. *Behavioral and Brain Sciences*, 16 (3), 417-494.

[347] R. Shepard, (2001). Perceptual-cognitive universals as reflections of the world. *Behavioral and Brain Sciences*, 24 (2).

[348] R. Shiffrin and W. Schneider, (1977). Controlled and automatic human information processing II. *Psychological Review*, 84. 127-190.

[349] R. Shoemaker, (1982). The inverted spectrum. *Journal of Philosophy*, 79, 357-381.

[350] J. Shrager, (1990). Commonsense perception and the psychology of theory formation. In: J. Shrager and P. Langley (eds.), *Computational Models of Scientific Discovery and Theory Formation*. Morgan Kaufmann, San Mateo, CA.

[351] R. Siegler and E. Stern, (1998). Conscious and unconscious strategy discovery: A microgenetic analysis. *Journal of Experimental Psychology: General*, 127 (4), 377-397.

[352] S. Singh, (1994). *Learning to Solve Markovian Decision Processes*. Ph.D. thesis, University of Massachusetts, Amherst, MA.

[353] E. Smith, C. Langston, and R. Nisbett, (1992). The case for rules in reasoning. *Cognitive Science*, 16, 1-40.

[354] E. Smith and D. Medin, (1981). *Categories and Concepts*. Harvard University Press, Cambridge, MA.

[355] P. Smolensky. (1988). On the proper treatment of connectionism. *Behavioral and Brain Sciences*, 11, 1-43.

[356] T. Sowell, (1996). *Knowledge and Decisions*. Basic Book, New York.

[357] L. Squire and M. Frambach, (1990). Cognitive skill learning in amnesia. *Psychobiology*, 18, 109-117.

[358] L. Squire, B. Knowlton, and G. Musen, (1993). The structure and organization of memory. *Annual Review of Psychology*, 44, 453-495.

[359] M. Stadler, (1992). Statistical structure and implicit serial learning. *Journal of Experimental Psychology: Learning, Memory and Cognition*, 18, 318-327.

[360] M. Stadler, (1995). Role of attention in implicit learning. *Journal of Experimental Psychology: Learning, Memory and Cognition*, 15, 1061-1069.

[361] W. Stanley, R. Mathews, R. Buss, and S. Kotler-Cope, (1989). Insight without awareness: On the interaction of verbalization, instruction and practice in a simulated process control task. *Quarterly Journal of Experimental Psychology*, 41A (3), 553-577.

[362] L. Steels, (1998). The origins of ontologies and communication conventions in multi-agent systems. *Autonomous Agents and Multi-Agent Systems*, 1, 169-194.

[363] R. Stepp and R. Michalski, (1986). Conceptual clustering. In: R. Michalski, J. Carbonell, and T. Mitchell (eds.), *Machine Learning II*. Morgan Kaufmann, Los Altos, CA.

[364] L. Suchman, (1987). *Plans and Situated Actions: The Problem of Human Machine Communication*. Oxford University Press, Oxford, UK.

[365] R. Sun, (1992). On variable binding in connectionist networks. *Connection Science*, 4 (2), 93-124.

[366] R. Sun, (1993). The CONSPIRE architecture. Technical report, Department of Computer Science, University of Alabama, Tuscaloosa, AL.

[367] R. Sun, (1994). *Integrating Rules and Connectionism for Robust Commonsense Reasoning*. John Wiley and Sons, New York.

[368] R. Sun, (1995). Robust reasoning: Integrating rule-based and similarity-based reasoning. *Artificial Intelligence*, 75 (2), 241-296.

[369] R. Sun, (1997). Learning, action, and consciousness: A hybrid approach towards modeling consciousness. *Neural Networks*, special issue on consciousness. 10 (7), 1317-1331.

[370] R. Sun, (1999). Accounting for the computational basis of consciousness: A connectionist approach. *Consciousness and Cognition*, 8, 529-565.

[371] R. Sun, (2000). Symbol grounding: A new look at an old idea. *Philosophical Psychology*, 13 (2), 149-172.

[372] R. Sun (ed.), (2001). The special Issue on multi-disciplinary studies of multi-agent learning. *Cognitive Systems Research*, 2 (1), 1-96.

[373] R. Sun and F. Alexandre (eds.), (1997). *Connectionist Symbolic Integration*. Lawrence Erlbaum Associates, Hillsdale, NJ.

[374] R. Sun and L. Bookman (eds.), (1994). *Computational Architectures Integrating Neural and Symbolic Processes*. Kluwer Academic Publishers, Boston, MA.

[375] R. Sun, E. Merrill, and T. Peterson, (1998). A bottom-up model of skill learning. *Proceedings of the 20th Cognitive Science Society Conference*, 1037-1042. Lawrence Erlbaum Associates, Mahwah, NJ.

[376] R. Sun, E. Merrill, and T. Peterson, (2001). From implicit skill to explicit knowledge: A bottom-up model of skill learning. *Cognitive Science*, 25 (2), 203-244.

[377] R. Sun and D. Qi, (2000). Rationality assumptions and optimality of co-learning. In: C. Zhang and V. Soo (eds.), *Design and Applications of Intelligent Agents*. Lecture Notes in Artificial Intelligence, Volume 1881. Springer-Verlag, Heidelberg, Germany.

[378] R. Sun and T. Peterson, (1998a). Autonomous learning of sequential tasks: experiments and analyses. *IEEE Transactions on Neural Networks*, 9 (6), 1217-1234.

[379] R. Sun and T. Peterson, (1998b). Some experiments with a hybrid model for learning sequential decision making. *Information Sciences*, 111, 83-107.

[380] R. Sun and T. Peterson, (1999). Multi-agent reinforcement learning: Weighting and partitioning. *Neural Networks*, 12 (4-5). 127-153.

[381] R. Sun and C. Sessions, (1998). Learning to plan probabilistically from neural networks. *Proceedings of the IEEE International Joint Conference on Neural Networks*, 1-6. IEEE Press, Piscataway, NJ.

[382] R. Sun and C. Sessions, (1999a). Self segmentation of sequences. *Proceedings of the International Joint Conference on Neural Networks*. IEEE Press, Piscataway, NJ.

[383] R. Sun and C. Sessions, (1999b). Bidding in reinforcement learning: A paradigm for multi-agent systems. *Proceedings of the Third International Conference on Autonomous Agents*, 344-345. ACM Press, New York.

[384] R. Sun and C. Sessions, (2000). Self-segmentation of sequences: Automatic formation of hierarchies of sequential behaviors. *IEEE Transactions on Systems, Man, and Cybernetics, Part B: Cybernetics*, 30 (3), 403-418.

[385] R. Sun, P. Slusarz and C. Terry, (2002). The interaction between the implicit and explicit processes: A dual process approach. Submitted for publication.

[386] R. Sutton, (1988). Learning to predict by the methods of temporal difference. *Machine Learning*, 3, 9-44.

[387] R. Sutton, (1990). Integrated architectures for learning, planning, and reacting based on approximating dynamic programming. *Proceedings of the Seventh International Conference on Machine Learning*, 216-224. Morgan Kaufmann, San Mateo, CA.

[388] R. Sutton, (1996). Generalization in reinforcement learning: Successful examples using sparse coarse coding. In: *Advances in Neural Information Processing Systems 8*. MIT Press, Cambridge, MA.

[389] R. Sutton and A. Barto, (1981). Towards a modern theory of adaptive networks: expectation and prediction. *Psychological Review*, 88 (2), 135-170.

[390] K. Szymanski and C. MacLeod, (1996). Manipulation of attention at study affects an explicit but not an implicit test of memory. *Consciousness and Cognition*, 5 (1/2), 165-175.

[391] H. Tajfel, (1970). Experiments in intergroup discrimination. *Scientific American*, 223, 96-102.

[392] T. Takagi and M. Sugeno, (1985). Fuzzy identification of systems and its applications to modeling and control. *IEEE Transactions on Systems, Man and Cybernetics*, 15 (1), 116-132.

[393] J. Tani and S. Nolfi, (1998). Learning to perceive the world as articulated: An approach to hierarchical learning in sensory-motor systems. *From Animals to Animats 5: Proceedings of the Fifth International Conference of Simulation of Adaptive Behavior*, 270-279. MIT Press, Cambridge, MA.

[394] J. Taylor, (1997). The relational mind. In: A. Browne (ed.), *Neural Network Perspectives on Cognition and Adaptive Robotics*. IOP Press, Bristol, UK.

[395] T. Tesauro, (1992). Practical issues in temporal difference learning. *Machine Learning*, 8, 257-277.

[396] E. Thorndike, (1911). *Animal Intelligence*. Hafner, Darien, Connecticut.

[397] W. Timberlake and G. Lucas, (1989). Behavior systems and learning: From misbehavior to general principles. In: S. B. Klein and R. R. Mowrer (eds.), *Contemporary Learning Theories: Instrumental Conditioning Theory and the Impact of Biological Constraints on Learning*, 237-275. Lawrence Erlbaum Associates, Hillsdale, NJ.

[398] G. Towell and J. Shavlik, (1993). Extracting refined rules from knowledge-based neural networks. *Machine Learning*, 13 (1), 71-101.

[399] A. Treisman (1964). Verbal cues, language and meanings in attention. *American Journal of Psychology*, 77, 206-214.

[400] E. Tulving, (1972). Episodic and semantic memory. In: E. Tulving and W. Donaldson (eds.), *Organization of Memory*, 381-403. Academic Press, New York.

[401] A.M. Turing, (1950). Computing Machinery and Intelligence. *Mind*, Vol.LIX, No.236.

[402] J. Turner, M. Hogg, P. Oakes, S. Reicher, and M. Wetherell, (1987). *Rediscovering the Social Group: Self-Categorization Theory*. Blackwell, Oxford, UK.

[403] M. Turvey, (1992). Affordances and prospective control: An outline of an ontology. *Ecological Psychology*, 4, 173-187.

[404] A. Tversky, (1977). Features of similarity. *Psychological Review*, 84(4), 327-352.

[405] A. Tversky and D. Kahneman, (1983). Extensional versus intuitive reasoning: The conjunction fallacy in probability judgment. *Psychological Review*, 439-450.

[406] T. Tyrell, (1993). *Computational Mechanisms for Action Selection*. Ph.D. thesis, University of Edinburgh, UK.

[407] S. Ullman, (1984). Visual routines. *Cognition*, 18, 97-160.

[408] M. Usher and D. Zakay, (1993). A neural network model for attribute-based decision processes. *Cognitive Science*, 17, 349-396.

[409] A. Vandierendonck, (1995). A parallel rule activation and rule synthesis model for generalization in category learning. *Psychonomic Bulletin and Review*, 2 (4), 442-459.

[410] T. van Gelder, (1990). Compositionality: A connectionist variation on a classical theme. *Cognitive Science*, 14, 355-384.

[411] R. Van Gulick, (1993). Understanding the phenomenal mind. In: M. Davies and G. Humphreys (eds.), *Consciousness*. Blackwell, Oxford, UK.

[412] K. VanLehn, (1995). Cognitive skill acquisition. *Annual Review of Psychology*, 47.

[413] F. Varela, E. Thompson, and E. Rosch, (1993). *The Embodied Mind*. MIT Press, Cambridge, MA.

[414] M. Velmans, (1991). Is human information processing conscious? *Behavioral and Brain Sciences*, 14, 651-726.

[415] A. Vera and H. Simon, (1993). Situated action: A symbolic interpretation. *Cognitive Science*, 17, 7-48.

[416] J. Vokey and L. Brooks, (1992). Salience of item knowledge in learning artificial grammars. *Journal of Experimental Psychology: Learning, Memory, and Cognition*, 18, 328-344.

[417] B. Von Eckardt, (1992). *What is Cognitive Science?* MIT Press, Cambridge, MA.

[418] S. Vosniadou and A. Ortony (eds.), (1989). *Similarity and Analogical Reasoning.* Cambridge University Press, New York.

[419] L. Vygotsky, (1962). *Thought and Language.* MIT Press, Cambridge, MA.

[420] L. Vygotsky, (1986). *Mind in Society.* Lawrence Erlbaum Associates, Hillsdale, NJ.

[421] L. Vygotsky and A. Luria, (1993). *Studies on the History of Behavior.* Lawrence Erlbaum Associates, Hillsdale, NJ.

[422] D. Waltz, (1990). Eight principles for building an intelligent robot. In: S. Wilson and J. Meyer (eds.), *SAB-90: Simulations of Animal Behavior.* MIT Press, Cambridge, MA.

[423] E. Warrington and L. Weiskrantz, (1982). Amnesia: A disconnection syndrome? *Neuropsychologia,* 20, 233-248.

[424] E. Wasserman, S. Elek, D. Chartlosh, and A. Baker, (1993). Rating causal relations. *Journal of Experimental Psychology: Learning, Memory, and Cognition,* 19, 174-188.

[425] C. Watkins, (1989). *Learning with Delayed Rewards.* Ph.D. thesis, Cambridge University, Cambridge, UK.

[426] M. Weber, (1957). *The Theory of Social and Economic Organization.* The Free Press, Glencoe, IL.

[427] D. Wegner and J. Bargh, (1998). Control and automaticity in social life. In: D. Gilbert, S. T. Fiske, and G. Lindzey (eds.), *Handbook of Social Psychology,* 446-496. McGraw-Hill, New York.

[428] G. Weiss and S. Sen (eds.), (1996). *Adaptation and Learning in Multi-Agent Systems.* Springer-Verlag, Berlin.

[429] S. Wermter and R. Sun (eds.), (2000). *Hybrid Neural Systems.* Lecture Notes in Artificial Intelligence, Volume 1778, Springer-Verlag, Heidelberg.

[430] J. Wertsch, (1985). *Vygotsky and the Social Formation of Mind.* Harvard University Press, Cambridge, MA.

[431] J. Wertsch, (1991). *Voices of the Mind: A Sociocultural Approach to Mediated Action.* Harvard University Press, Cambridge, MA.

[432] S. Whitehead and D. Ballard, (1991). Learning to perceive and act by trial and error. *Machine Learning,* 7, 45-83.

[433] S. Whitehead and L. Lin, (1995). Reinforcement learning of non-Markov decision processes. *Artificial Intelligence,* 73 (1/2), 271-306.

[434] M. Wiering and J. Schmidhuber, (1998). HQ-learning. *Adaptive Behavior,* 6 (2), 219-246.

[435] B. Williams, (1977). Verbal operant conditioning without subjects' awareness of reinforcement contingencies. *Canadian Journal of Psychology*, 31 (2), 90-101.

[436] D. Willingham, M. Nissen, and P. Bullemer, (1989). On the development of procedural knowledge. *Journal of Experimental Psychology: Learning, Memory, and Cognition*, 15, 1047-1060.

[437] E. Wilson, (1975). *Sociobiology*. Harvard University Press, Cambridge, MA.

[438] T. Winograd and F. Flores, (1987). *Understanding Computers and Cognition*. Addison-Wesley, Reading, MA.

[439] E. Wisniewski and D. Medin, (1994). On the interaction of data and theory in concept learning. *Cognitive Science*, 18, 221-281.

[440] L. Wittgenstein, (1953). *Logical Investigation*. MacMillan, New York.

[441] D. M. Wolpert and M. Kawato, (1998). Multiple paired forward and inverse models for motor control. *Neural Networks*, 11, 1317-1329.

[442] P.L. Yu, (1991). Habitual domains. *Operations Research*, 39 (6), 869-876.

[443] J. Zhang and T. Dietterich, (1995). A reinforcement learning approach to job-shop scheduling. *Proceedings of International Joint Conference on AI*, 1114-1120. Morgan Kaufmann, San Francisco, CA.

[444] J. Zhang and D. Norman, (1994). Representations in distributed cognitive tasks. *Cognitive Science*, 18, 87-122.

Index